CLAIMING CHRIST

A Mormon-Evangelical Debate

Robert L. Millet
and Gerald R. McDermott

BrazosPress
Grand Rapids, Michigan

© 2007 by Robert L. Millet and Gerald R. McDermott

Published by Brazos Press
a division of Baker Publishing Group
P.O. Box 6287, Grand Rapids, MI 49516-6287
www.brazospress.com

Printed in the United States of America

Library of Congress Cataloging-in-Publication Data

Millet, Robert L.
    Claiming Christ : a Mormon-Evangelical debate / Robert L. Millet and Gerald R. McDermott.
        p.   cm.
    Includes bibliographical references.
    ISBN 10: 1-58743-209-9 (pbk.)
    ISBN 978-1-58743-209-5 (pbk.)
    1. Church of Jesus Christ of Latter-day Saints—Doctrines. 2. Mormon Church—Doctrines. 3. Reformed Church—Doctrines 4. Evangelicalism. I. McDermott, Gerald R. (Gerald Robert) II. Title.
BX8635.3.M55 2007
230′.9332—dc22   2007014958

This is dedicated to
Anastasia Jean McDermott
and
Brayden, Jaxon, Skler, Jordan,
Isabella Millet and Zackary Defa,
our grandchildren

We are grateful to our wives (Jean and Shauna) for their love, support, and ideas as we spent a summer writing this book. A number of colleagues gave us helpful feedback and suggestions, especially Robert Benne, John Morehead, Mark Graham, Greg Johnson, and Paul Peterson. We also want to thank Rodney Clapp, whose keen editorial insights made this a much better book, and Lew Rosenbloom, who loaned Gerry his beach house for a wonderful week of writing.

CONTENTS

Introduction: Friendship Without Compromise   7
Gerald McDermott
Robert Millet

1. How Do We Know About Jesus? Sources of Authority   15
Gerald McDermott
A Latter-day Saint Response
Robert Millet
Rebuttal and Concluding Thoughts
Gerald McDermott
2. Christ Before Bethlehem: Creator, God of the Ancients   44
Robert Millet
An Evangelical Response
Gerald McDermott
Rebuttal and Concluding Thoughts
Robert Millet
3. Jesus, God, and Us: The Trinity and God's Oneness   63
Gerald McDermott
A Latter-day Saint Response
Robert Millet
Rebuttal and Concluding Thoughts
Gerald McDermott
4. The Suffering Servant: His Passion and Atonement   92
Robert Millet
An Evangelical Response
Gerald McDermott
Rebuttal and Concluding Thoughts
Robert Millet
5. Jesus of History, Christ of Faith: The Gospels and the Book
of Mormon   111
Gerald McDermott

A Latter-day Saint Response
   Robert Millet
Rebuttal and Concluding Thoughts
   Gerald McDermott
6. The Keys of the Kingdom: The Church and the Sacraments   137
   Robert Millet
An Evangelical Response
   Gerald McDermott
Rebuttal and Concluding Thoughts
   Robert Millet
7. Salvation in Christ: Grace, Faith, and Works   163
   Gerald McDermott
A Latter-day Saint Response
   Robert Millet
Rebuttal and Concluding Thoughts
   Gerald McDermott
8. The Only Name Under Heaven? The Fate of the
   Unevangelized   192
   Robert Millet
An Evangelical Response
   Gerald McDermott
Rebuttal and Concluding Thoughts
   Robert Millet

Conclusion: Discerning the Spirits: What We Have Learned   217
   Gerald McDermott
   Robert Millet

INTRODUCTION

Friendship Without Compromise
Gerald McDermott and Robert Millet

Gerald McDermott

I am embarrassed to tell this story.

Some years ago I invited a Mormon historian to my class on New American Religions. Before class started I told him he would have 30 to 45 minutes to share about LDS beliefs and history, and after that I would open it up for Q&A. But shortly after he began, I decided to challenge something he said. Then a few minutes later I asked a question that implicitly tried to refute his second point. Before too long my students, following my lead, fired one question after another, often moving into flat-out argument. Some of them seemed happy to finally explain to this polite Mormon scholar why they believed he was not a Christian. The LDS historian was never able to finish his presentation because of all the interruptions from my students and their professor.

I had no idea I had done anything wrong until I received a letter from the speaker the following week. He said that in all his years of speaking on his faith to non-Mormon audiences, he had never been treated so rudely. He thought he would have an uninterrupted chance to present his own views, but discovered that he was barely able to finish a thought before he was interrupted by a question or assertion. The result was that instead of learning something new, the class was simply reinforced in its (and my) prejudices. We never allowed ourselves to listen. Not only were we disrespectful and insensitive, but we went away with many false impressions uncorrected.

About five years later I was invited by Fuller Seminary President Richard Mouw to a small meeting of evangelical and Mormon scholars for the purpose of learning more about each other. I remember being impressed by the erudition and piety of the Mormon scholars I met. Robert Millet, whom I now consider a close friend, was particularly articulate and open. He, Grant Underwood, and other Mormons at the conference showed what to me was remarkable familiarity with evangelical theology and history, not to mention central principles of historic Christian theology.

I invited Bob Millet to come to Roanoke College the following fall and debate me in public at the college chapel. Our subject was "Mormon and Mainstream Christian Similarities and Differences." We spoke before a packed house. Most of the traditional Christians and Mormons in attendance, who were in roughly equal numbers, said they enjoyed and profited from the exchange. In the fall of 2005 we had another debate at Roanoke College, but this time focused on the person of Jesus. We used Bob's landmark 2005 book from Eerdmans as our focal point: *A Different Jesus? The Christ of the Latter-day Saints.* Bob argued that the LDS view of Jesus was not essentially different from that of traditional Christianity. I contended that it was.

Because we received such a good response from these debates, we thought we might try to do something similar, but more extensive, in print. Thus, this book. We wanted to try to model what has been in short supply in the more than 175 years since Joseph Smith's first vision—love and respect in the midst of serious theological differences.

We wanted to try to do for evangelicals and Mormons what N. T. Wright and Marcus Borg have done for orthodox and liberal mainstream Christians in their own debates and in the book they wrote together:

> Within the bounds of friendship, and shared Christian faith and practice, we have both been puzzled, and even disturbed, by some of what the other has said. . . . Neither of us is content to let things rest with a cheap and easy suggestion that, since we are both practicing Christians, our two positions are equally valid—whatever that might mean. It might be that both of our positions are equivalent and fairly adequate expressions, from different points of view, of the same underlying reality. Neither of us quite thinks that. It might be that we are both wrong, and that some quite different position is truer. Neither of us thinks that, either. . . . Where we do agree, however, is on the following point. Debate about Jesus has recently been acrimonious, with a good deal of name-calling and angry polemic in both private and public discourse. . . . We hope, and indeed pray, that in this book we will be able to model a way of conducting public Christian disagreement over serious and central issues.[1]

1. N. T. Wright and Marcus Borg, *The Meaning of Jesus: Two Visions* (San Francisco: HarperSanFrancisco, 1999), viii, x.

We are not the first to try to forge a new way for Evangelicals and Mormons. Craig Blomberg and Stephen Robinson are to be commended for courageously opening this conversation in *How Wide the Divide? A Mormon and an Evangelical in Conversation.* But this book is different in some important respects from theirs.

First and most importantly, this book focuses on Jesus. While *How Wide the Divide?* discusses a range of issues across the evangelical-Mormon divide, this book relates most of those issues and several more besides to the person and work of the Redeemer.

Second, I write from an evangelical perspective that is somewhat broader than Professor Blomberg's. For example, while I am committed to the authority of scripture for faith and practice, I am not overly concerned with the "inerrancy" debate that raged in the 1980s, so Professor Millet and I do not discuss that particular issue. When that word is used in debates over the authority of the Bible, it is often assumed that revelation is *primarily* propositional, a presumption I do not share.[2] While Blomberg and Robinson contend that "scripture is literally true in its teachings, both historically and morally," I would say that scripture is literally true only when its authors intend it to be read literally. When Jesus says, "I am the vine" (John 15:5), he does not intend to be taken literally. I think there is a legitimate debate over the extent to which the author of Genesis 1 and 2 intended those accounts to be taken as straightforwardly historical accounts. On the other hand, when it is clear that the author intends to present straightforward history, as does Luke in the Acts of the Apostles, then I believe we are obligated to read it as such.

I do not believe, as do Blomberg and Robinson, that "supplementary material" beyond the Bible "ought not to be presented as . . . authoritative beliefs."[3] I argue in chapter 1 not only that creeds and tradition are justifiably authoritative for a religious community, but that it is impossible for them not to be. But at the same time, I insist that scripture is the touchstone for all creeds and traditions.

A third difference between this book and Blomberg and Robinson's is that this one is more theologically oriented. Both Robinson and Blomberg are scripture scholars, first and foremost. Professor Millet, on the other hand, is trained in psychology and religious studies, and has broad

---

2. "Propositional" means having to do with words and concepts used in ways that affirm or deny something. I hold that revelation is both propositional and non-propositional, both word and event. For more on the nature of revelation, see McDermott, *Can Evangelicals Learn from World Religions? Jesus, Revelation and Religious Traditions* (Downers Grove, IL: InterVarsity, 2000), ch. 2.

3. Craig Blomberg and Stephen Robinson, *How Wide the Divide? A Mormon and an Evangelical in Conversation* (Downers Grove, IL: InterVarsity, 1997), 76.

interest in Christian theology. I am trained in the history of Christianity and for years have written in historical theology and systematic theology. Both of us have primary interest in the theological meaning of this debate. The focus on Jesus Christ is a result of this theological concentration.

We need to define our terms, especially *Mormon* and *evangelical*. The most important thing I can say about "evangelical" is that it is not the same as "fundamentalist"—despite the conflation of the two by most media and academics.

Fundamentalists tend to read the Bible more literally, while evangelicals tend to look more carefully at genre and literary and historical context. Fundamentalists question the value of human culture that is not created by Christians or related to the Bible, whereas evangelicals see God's "common grace" working in and through all human culture. Fundamentalists tend to restrict their social witness to protests against homosexual practice and abortion, but evangelicals also want to fight racism, sexism, and poverty. Fundamentalists often want to separate themselves from liberal Christians (which sometimes means evangelicals), while evangelicals are more willing to work with other Christians toward common religious and social goals. While both groups preach salvation by grace, fundamentalists tend to focus so much on rules and restrictions (do's and don'ts) that their hearers can get the impression that Christianity means following behavioral rules. Evangelicals, on the other hand, focus more on the person and work of Christ, and personal relationship with him, as the heart of Christian faith.

More positively, evangelicalism has four distinctives: cross, scripture, conversion, and evangelism. Evangelicals believe that the cross is the center of the Christian life because it was at the cross that God reconciled the world to himself (2 Cor. 5:19). Hence, preaching on Christ's substitutionary atonement is a regular feature of evangelical sermons. Evangelicals also have a distinctive emphasis on the supreme authority of the Bible. They teach that God has chosen to reveal himself through scripture. Therefore, to submit to biblical authority is to receive God as God has chosen to be known, not as we would like God to be. Such submission frees us from the slavish demand that we follow every cultural trend and provides a framework from which to evaluate those trends.

Like Mormons, evangelicals are best known for their insistence on conversion and evangelism. This does not mean that evangelicals believe conversion needs to be an emotional experience. But they do assert that faith requires personal repentance and trust, not simply intellectual acceptance of Christian doctrine.

In this book I also refer to "traditional" and "orthodox" Christians and Christianity. By "traditional" I mean those within mainstream Christian traditions, such as Catholic, Eastern Orthodox, and Protestant. I consider "orthodox" to be a subset of "traditional" Christians. Orthodox Christians and movements hold to the classical, 2000-year-old teachings of the faith, such as the deity of Christ, the substitutionary atonement, the bodily resurrection of Jesus Christ, justification by grace through faith, the necessity of sanctification, and the authority of scripture for faith and practice. There are some Christians and movements within traditional Christian churches today who question one or more of these doctrines.

Robert Millet

There's a movement afloat, one that both thrills and sobers me. That movement is an effort toward better understanding on the part of two faith traditions who have a history of confrontation, two faith groups who have often been eager to point up doctrinal differences but less enthusiastic about acknowledging doctrinal similarities. I suppose that many within the counter-cult element of evangelical Christianity will always be opposed to any and all efforts at civil conversation or deeper understanding, as will Latter-day Saints who feel that serious engagement with a practicing and believing evangelical is at best a concession and at worst a compromise. During the last decade a great deal of my time has been devoted to building friendships with evangelical church leaders and academics around the country. While there have certainly been more than enough people on both sides of the religious spectrum willing to criticize and accuse us of some form of diluting ecumenism, there have also been men and women of integrity who know that what's tough is not always bad: stretching beyond our spiritual comfort zone may prove to be extremely worthwhile.

I have served on a religion faculty at a major university for a quarter of a century now, and I cannot imagine being employed in anything that would have brought greater satisfaction. I would have to admit, nonetheless, that the last ten years in which my mind has been stretched and my heart soothed in the pursuit of truth and understanding—the hundreds of hours spent in interfaith dialogue—have been the most personally and professionally rewarding hours of my life. I've come to know, in spite of what the generality of society may think, that religion is indeed an area that can be discussed seriously without dispute, name-calling, categorizing, or demonizing. Indeed, I believe Jesus meant what he said when he said that "where two or three are gathered together in my name, there am I in the midst of them" (Matt. 18:20).

It has been my pleasure and delight to become friends with Professor Gerald R. McDermott, to come to know him as an extremely bright and articulate representative of the evangelical tradition, a deeply devout follower of the Christ, and a warm human being. I have come to know him as kind, open, patient, persistent, and temperate. There's no question about where he stands on certain issues, but that dedicated dogmatism is couched carefully in a breadth of perspective that makes him an entertaining and enlightened conversationalist. It has simply been fun to get to know Gerry as a person and to better understand evangelical Christianity through his writings and our own conversations.

This book is an example of what can happen when two people first become friends, learn to trust one another, pay the price of reading and reflection and lengthy chats, go to the proper sources for information, and then engage challenging issues without rancor or defensiveness. As the reader will soon realize, there are, to be sure, doctrinal differences between the Mormon and evangelical communities, and the two of us have sought earnestly to discuss those in a climate of what our mutual friend, Richard Mouw, calls "convicted civility." But if we have done our work properly, the reader will also recognize that there are a number of areas about Jesus Christ—his person, powers, and plan—on which we agree completely and in which we both rejoice. Successful interfaith dialogue involves much more than winning an argument. It also entails building and enhancing a friendship. People across the globe may disagree in regard to many aspects of the life and mission of Jesus Christ, but no one who is slightly acquainted with the four Gospels can deny that our Savior was and is in the business of people; for him, people and people's feelings matter very much.

One of the priceless values of continuing an ongoing dialogue is that the participants are able to jettison what they thought to be true about the other person and her faith, and to learn instead what she really does believe. The last thing we need in our confused and confusing world is a collection of misinformation and a bag of misperceptions about those with whom we disagree. We can disagree without being disagreeable, but let's at least disagree about the right stuff! We could all use a dose of informed curiosity. We can be completely committed to our faith and way of life, and still be open to the possibility that interaction with this other person can result in novel thoughts, broadened perspective, and treasured new insights into the gospel.

I mentioned earlier that there is a movement afloat between evangelicals and Latter-day Saints. It is not a huge movement, certainly not anything like what has gone on between evangelicals and Roman Catholics since Vatican II. The number of people on both sides of the spectrum has, however, increased with the passing of years. To some extent, this growing interest has come about because of the awareness that both religious groups have strong and unyielding views relative to the importance of morality and decency, the institution of marriage, the importance of family, and in general, the need for a major spiritual transformation of our culture. Because God's ways are not our ways and because his thoughts and intentions are infinitely higher than our own (Isa. 55:8–9), we cannot always tell what God is bringing to pass, even through weak and simple people like ourselves. Our trust is in him—in his sovereignty, in his capacity to bring peace to troubled souls and resolution to damaged relationships, and in his ability to unite the hearts of people who profess a belief in the divinity of Jesus of Nazareth and a reliance on his atonement and resurrection.

One day each of us will stand at the bar of judgment and make our profession before the Almighty. I rather doubt that the Master will give to us a theological exam (although I certainly believe in the importance of correct doctrine). Rather, God will want to know what we have done with his Son and the extent to which we have been conformed to his image (Rom. 8:29; 2 Cor. 3:18) and have begun to embody his divine attributes and qualities. In that great day, charity will matter far more than cleverness; character will be treasured far more than charisma. Who and what we have become, how we have come to mirror our Lord and Savior in his treatment of people, and the extent to which we have become instruments and ambassadors of his peace—these are the things that will matter most.

All scripture quotations are from the King James Version, since that is the official Mormon Bible and is acceptable to most evangelicals.

1
HOW DO WE KNOW ABOUT JESUS?

Sources of Authority
Gerald McDermott

Today there are many Jesuses. Or, to put it more accurately, there are many portraits of Jesus vying for our acceptance.

There's the gay-bashing Jesus of the Rev. Fred Phelps, who claims that God loves the death of American soldiers because America is corrupted spiritually.

In April 2006 we heard about the gnostic Jesus of *The Gospel of Judas*, who asks Judas to "sacrifice the man that clothes me" so that Jesus could find his true bodiless self.[1]

There is also the Jesus of the new moral theology, which insists that Jesus would have no problem with loving and committed homosexual relationships.

The Jesus of the *DaVinci Code* has perhaps gotten the most press in recent years because this Jesus was not divine, but married Mary Magdalene and had children.

The Apostle Paul warned us that there would be "different gospel[s]" that would proclaim "another Jesus" (2 Cor. 11:4) and urged his readers not to put up with false alternatives.

So the fact that there are so many different views of Jesus is not a new problem. But the solution is rarely easy. How do we discern among competing portrayals of Jesus? How can we know which Jesus is the true one? The one whom Christians worship as their Lord?

This is especially difficult when rival portraits seem extremely similar, and in fact converge in important ways. This is the case for the subject

---

1. For the full text of the gospel, see the National Geographic translation at http://www.nationalgeographic.com/lostgospel/_pdf/GospelofJudas.pdf?fs=www7.nationalgeographic.com&fs=magma.nationalgeographic.com. The quotation is on page 7.

of this book: rival claims for Jesus between Mormons and evangelical Christians (see the Introduction for our definition of "evangelical"). Mormons and evangelicals agree that all the above portraits of Jesus are false. They agree that Jesus was fully God and that his life and death are critical to human salvation. Both groups claim that human beings must trust in Jesus and make him their Lord. Both say that we are to have a personal relationship with Jesus. They agree on these and a good number of other things about Jesus.

But there are differences. Mormons teach that Jesus visited North America after his incarnation and resurrection in Palestine in the first century. They also believe that Jesus and his Father appeared to Joseph Smith in 1820 to give him new revelation. Mainstream Christians (including evangelicals) reject these assertions about Jesus and his revelations to Joseph Smith.

This chapter is about how we go about deciding what we can believe about Jesus. The rest of the book will discuss the content of these and many other differences. But in this chapter we will look at our sources for authority—that is, where we go to gain assurance that our portrait of Jesus is the right one.

Sola Scriptura?

We evangelicals typically say we use only the Bible (*sola scriptura*) to compose our portrait of Jesus. We have criticized Mormons for going beyond the Bible to extra-biblical traditions, such as when they make assertions about Jesus based on the Book of Mormon. We pride ourselves on following Luther and Calvin in their rejection of church traditions (such as late-medieval views of purgatory and indulgences) that were not clearly rooted in scripture. When evangelicals have debated Latter-day Saints and their doctrinal differences, we have often accused Saints of following the later medieval Catholic pattern of favoring tradition over scripture. Recently, evangelical theologians have seen the importance of tradition in interpreting scripture, but generally, the evangelical approach to Jesus has been, "We teach only what the Bible teaches and refuse to accept anything outside the Bible for authority." Since evangelicals discount the authenticity of the Book of Mormon and other Mormon scriptures, they regard Mormon use of these sources as clear violations of the *sola scriptura* principle. Their conclusion is that evangelicals teach only the Word of God, while Mormons mix the words of a man (Joseph Smith) with the Word of God.

But evangelicals should reconsider this presumption. It is not at all clear that we have operated exclusively by the *sola scriptura* principle. We accept the results of the early church's Trinitarian debates (which took place *after* the closure of the canon), using, for example, the word "Trinity," which is not found in the Bible. We tacitly accept the authority of the early creeds, such as the Council of Chalcedon's model of the relationship between Jesus's human and divine natures, which we believe is based on biblical testimony but which also contains words that cannot be found in the (Greek) Bible, such as *homoousion*. Most evangelicals in the twentieth century favored a model of justification that stressed the primacy of the forensic or legal dimension of the atonement, a model that some scholars are now claiming to be based more on sixteenth-century debates than the Bible itself.[2] And many of us hold differing views about eschatology (life after death, the millennium, and the fulfillment of God's final purposes for the world), none of which has persuaded a majority that it is clearly taught by the Bible—not to mention our own differences over the proper mode of baptism, what happens in the Lord's Supper, how the local church should be governed, women's roles in ministry, and the gifts of the Spirit. Our differences on these issues owe more to interpretive traditions than to disagreement over the actual wording of the biblical text.

Even Jonathan Edwards (1703–58), often said to be evangelicalism's premier theologian, departed from strict adherence to the *sola scriptura* principle. Edwards professed repeatedly that our only authority in religion is the written text of the scriptures. But in practice he seemed to operate with the assumption that the Bible can be read only through and with tradition. For example, scholars have recently described the way, for Edwards after 1739, the real authority for theological work became, not the biblical text *per se*, but his imaginative construal of the story inscribed there, which he called the "work of redemption."[3] This was a master narrative beginning in eternity with the Trinity's plan, proceeding through the "fall of man," the history of Israel, the incarnation, and the history of the church and world, all the way until the end of the world. It was centered in the work of Christ but orchestrated by all the members of the Trinity.[4]

This plan for redemption could not be read off the face of the biblical text, for central to the plot was the assertion that Christ was the real

2. See, e.g., N. T. Wright, *What Saint Paul Really Said* (Grand Rapids: Eerdmans, 1997).

3. See, e.g., Harry S. Stout and Nathan O. Hatch, Introduction to *Sermons and Discourses 1739–1742*, vol. 22 in *The Works of Jonathan Edwards* (New Haven, CT: Yale University Press, 2003), 4–14; and Robert E. Brown, *Jonathan Edwards and the Bible* (Bloomington: Indiana University Press, 2002), 164–96. Many have remarked on Edwards's turn from a rational approach to theology to a historical one, which would require a synthetic narrative; see, e.g., Stout and Hatch, *Sermons and Discourses*, 7.

4. *A History of the Work of Redemption*, in *Works of Jonathan Edwards*, vol. 9, ed. John F. Wilson (New Haven, CT: Yale University Press, 1989), 116, 118.

actor in all of Israel's communication with God—speaking at the burning bush, for example, and camouflaged by every appearance of "the angel of the Lord" in the Old Testament.[5] Only through this story, as told by Edwards, could the true meaning of the biblical text be seen. Hence the waters of the flood were types of the blood of Christ, and the cultus of the law that included "all the precepts that relate to building the tabernacle that was set up in the wilderness and all the forms, and circumstances, and utensils of it" were directed by God "to show forth something of Christ."[6] These interpretations were just that—interpretations of the biblical story, by no means explicitly stated by the biblical text itself. Edwards was following and developing a long tradition of reading the Bible typologically.[7] Some clerical and scholarly readers of the Bible agreed with this kind of reading, but not all did, because many said they could not find this taught explicitly or clearly by the Bible.

My point is that the theologian who is routinely regarded as evangelicalism's greatest showed that he used tradition in his reading and teaching of the Bible. The text's meaning was not always obvious but often needed help from theological tradition in order to be understood better.

This was also true of the early church. The great historian Jaroslav Pelikan has observed that supporters of *sola scriptura* overlook the "function of tradition in securing what they regarded as the correct exegesis of scripture against heretical alternatives."[8] Another historian has written that "in the ante-Nicene Church . . . there was no notion of *sola scriptura*, but neither was there a doctrine of *traditio sola*."[9] Exegesis, doctrine, and liturgy were all lumped together under "tradition." Early church leaders operated without a clear demarcation between scripture and tradition: scripture was interpreted with the help of oral and written tradition (such as the *Regula Fidei* or Rule of Faith, outline statements of Christian belief that were circulated in the second century to guide biblical exegesis[10]), and the tradition of use in the churches is what determined which books were included in the biblical canon. Heiko Oberman calls

5. Ibid., 131, 196–98.

6. Ibid., 151, 182.

7. "Typology" is a way of reading the Bible that sees God-intended symbols ("types") in the Old Testament that point to Christ and his work of redemption in the New. For example, the exodus from slavery in Egypt is seen as a type of the church's liberation from slavery to sin, death, and the devil by Christ's sacrifice.

8. Jaroslav Pelikan, *The Emergence of the Catholic Tradition 100–600* (Chicago: University of Chicago Press, 1971), 115.

9. Albert Outler, "The Sense of Tradition in the Ante-Nicene Church," in *The Heritage of Christian Thought: Essays in Honor of Robert Lowry Calhoun* (New York: Harper & Row, 1965), 29, cited in Pelikan, *Emergence of the Catholic Tradition*, 115.

10. Explanations of the meaning of a text, using linguistic, literary, theological, and historical tools.

this "Tradition I," the view that tradition is simply scripture properly interpreted. Oberman argues that this was the unanimous position of the church in the first few centuries.[11]

A similar notion has become a truism today in such diverse fields as philosophy, theology, and literature—that it is impossible to read any text, much less the Bible, without tradition. To put it another way, all of our reading is done through a filter of our own cultural traditions. There is no naked text that we can access without seeing it through the screen of traditions that we have absorbed.

Stones and Creeds

We often hear it said that people who live in glass houses should not throw stones, and this applies here. If evangelicals use their own traditions to interpret the Bible, they should not criticize Mormons for reading the Bible and interpreting it according to Mormon tradition. Whether Mormon traditions and scriptures are authentic is another question. But the principle of reading the Bible with the help of a religious tradition—Latter-day Saint tradition or any other—is valid and unavoidable.

For the same reason, Mormons should not criticize evangelicals for using the early creeds to help interpret the Bible. But there is another reason: Mormons have their own creeds. This may surprise some Mormons and evangelicals because so much attention has been placed on Joseph Smith's testimony that the Father and Son told him in his First Vision (1820) that "all their creeds are an abomination in [God's] sight."[12] As a result, Mormons have distinguished themselves from most mainstream Christians by the "no-creed" principle: We read the Bible by itself and take it literally, without allowing creeds to distort our interpretation.

Yet, as Professor Millet points out in his recent important book on the identity of Jesus, "Joseph Smith was not necessarily opposed to religious creeds in general." He cites Smith's preface to the first edition of the *Doctrines and Covenants* (1835): "If men believe a system, and profess that it was given by inspiration, certainly, the more intelligibly they can present it, the better. It does not make a principle untrue to print it, neither does it make it true not to print it."[13] Bruce McConkie, Mormon elder and prolific apologist, has also stated that Smith's fifth

11. Heiko Oberman, *Forerunners of the Reformation: The Shape of Late Medieval Thought* (London: Lutterworth Press, 1967), 58.

12. Robert L. Millet, *A Different Jesus? The Christ of the Latter-Day Saints* (Grand Rapids: Eerdmans, 2005), 54.

13. Ibid., 55.

Lecture on Faith (winter 1834–35) "in effect, is a creed announcing who Deity is."[14]

It is hard not to conclude that "The Articles of Faith of the Church of Jesus Christ of Latter-Day Saints" is also a creed. These are thirteen statements that, like most other creeds, articulate the most important beliefs of a religious group. They do not merely quote the Bible word for word, but offer interpretations of the Bible that are debatable. For example, while all Catholic and many Protestant denominations have concluded there is a connection between our sins and Adam's sin, Article 2 states, "We believe that men will be punished for their own sins, and not for Adam's transgression." Article 10 predicts the "literal gathering of Israel . . . upon the American continent."[15] Most non-Mormons and perhaps not a few Mormons would agree that these statements are not straightforwardly taught by the Bible but are theological interpretations—as is the case for many propositions in most creeds.

Perhaps, then, we should call for a moratorium on evangelical-Mormon mutual criticism over whether and who has resorted to creeds and traditions in their interpretation of the Bible. We're all guilty. Or perhaps we should say that both groups have at least implicitly recognized the wisdom of George Caird's remark on the love of Christ mentioned in Ephesians 3:18: "It takes the combined experience of *all* Christians to *comprehend* it."[16]

In other words, we need the wisdom of the whole church in order to understand scripture better. This means, in turn, that not only is it impossible *not* to be influenced by some tradition in reading scripture, but it is a positive *virtue* to learn from wise and godly readers who have gone before us—which is what I would call the best of tradition. In that sense, we *should* be influenced by (good) tradition if we are to grow in our knowledge of the God who reveals himself through the scriptures.

Not Whether but Which Tradition

The real question, then, is not *whether* we will be influenced by tradition in our reading and interpreting, but *which* tradition? The one[17] that

14. Ibid.

15. The Articles are reprinted in Millet, *A Different Jesus?* 185–86.

16. George B. Caird, *Paul's Letters from Prison* (Oxford: Oxford University Press, 1976), 70 (emphasis in the original); cited in Kevin J. Vanhoozer, *The Drama of Doctrine: A Canonical Linguistic Approach to Christian Theology* (Louisville: Westminster John Knox, 2005), 30.

17. Of course, there are many traditions that have developed from those who accept the present Christian canon. But as I will argue in a future chapter, differences among the various orthodox Christian communities are not as great as their agreements, and these agreements stand at some critical points in stark opposition to Mormon tradition.

is based on the classical Christian Bible, or the one that calls both those books *and* the Mormon scriptures divine revelation?

It is easy to see that (a) the differences between evangelical and Mormon beliefs come largely from their differences over which books are inspired, and (b) this is why their traditions have evolved so differently. Mormons say God brought new revelation in the nineteenth century, thus inserting new material into an open canon. These new revelations, given to both Joseph Smith and his successors, have led to new beliefs about God and what he is doing in the world. It is no wonder that, with new sacred books containing new revelations, a new tradition—different from the one that has assumed for at least 1500 years that the canon was effectively closed—has developed.[18] As Mormon scholar Stephen Robinson has put it, "What separates Latter-day Saints from Evangelicals is less our view of the nature of scripture and more our view of the canon."[19]

Other scholars, both within and outside the Mormon communion, agree. Jan Shipps, who "has come to know the Saints better than any previous outside observer,"[20] has famously argued that Mormonism is a departure from the existing Christian tradition as much as early Christianity was a departure from Judaism, because Mormonism abandoned both Roman Catholic and Protestant beliefs about the finality of the New Testament.[21] Philip Barlow's recent study of LDS use of the Bible reinforces Shipps's contention. Like Shipps, he believes Mormonism departs from *sola scriptura*: the new tradition puts limits on biblical authority and rejects the Bible as a sufficient religious guide.[22] According to BYU historian Grant Underwood, Mormons have given Joseph Smith the same canonical status as the Apostle Paul.[23]

Therefore, the limits of the canon make up perhaps the most crucial issue for those seeking to determine how we know the true Jesus. Our answer to the question of whether the canon was closed at the end of the apostolic era may be the key factor in our deciding whether we can accept distinctively Mormon views of the person and work of Jesus.

18. I say "effectively" because I will argue shortly that in principle the canon may still be considered open.

19. Blomberg and Robinson, *How Wide the Divide?* 55.

20. Philip Barlow, "Jan Shipps and the Mainstreaming of Mormon Studies," *Church History* 73, no. 2 (June 2004), 412.

21. Jan Shipps, *Sojourner in the Promised Land: Forty Years among the Mormons* (Urbana: University of Illinois Press, 2000), 331; "Is Mormonism Christian? Reflections on a Complicated Question," in Eric A. Eliason, ed., *Mormons and Mormonism: An Introduction to an American World Religion* (Urbana: University of Illinois Press, 2001), 83.

22. Philip Barlow, *Mormons and the Bible: The Place of the Latter-day Saints in American Religion* (New York: Oxford University Press, 1991), 220.

23. Grant Underwood, "Mormons and the Millennial World-View," in Douglas J. Davies, ed., *Mormon Identities in Transition* (New York: Cassell, 1996), 141.

Is the Canon Still Open?

Is it legitimate to consider the canon still open? In principle, perhaps. Luther questioned the canon in the sixteenth century, famously calling James an "epistle of straw," and putting Hebrews, Jude, and Revelation at the back of his German Bible because he thought they did not clearly present Christ. Later he changed his mind, using all of what is now in Protestant Bibles.

Perhaps the best way to determine if the canon is or should be closed—and therefore whether we can consider its reopening in the nineteenth century—is to look briefly at how the canon came to be in the first place. Historians generally conclude that it was a "bottom-up" not a "top-down" process. In other words, it was not a matter of a small group of male bishops deciding on their own which books they would permit their flocks to read. Instead, the canon resulted from the gradual recognition of which books had "already acquired broad recognition as authoritative Christian scripture."[24]

How was the Canon Decided?

The process took several hundred years. By AD 130, a nucleus of what would later be called the New Testament was being acknowledged—consisting of the synoptic Gospels, thirteen Pauline letters, Hebrews, and perhaps Acts. The other New Testament writings were received more slowly, but by 367 Athanasius had declared the present New Testament as inspired scripture in his thirty-ninth "festal letter."[25]

The primary force driving the process was the "developing pattern of the use" of Christian writings. Essentially, Christians asked whether

24. Harry Gamble, "Canonical Formation of the New Testament," in Craig A. Evans and Stanley E. Porter, eds., *Dictionary of New Testament Background* (Downers Grove, IL: InterVarsity Press, 2000), 184.

25. Already in the NT period, Paul's writings were regarded as scripture and therefore the beginning of a canon (2 Pet. 3:16: "There are some things in [Paul's letters] that are hard to understand, which the ignorant and unstable twist to their own destruction, as they do the other scriptures" ESV). Clement of Rome (ca. AD 96) quotes the words of Jesus as on the same level as the prophets (1 Clem 13.1ff.). Ignatius of Antioch (ca. 110) refers to the Gospels as "scripture" (*To the Philadelphians* 8.2). The *Gospel of Truth*, which dates from 140–45, is a Valentinian gnostic work, probably by Valentinus himself, written in Rome. The author is familiar with the Gospels, the Pauline Epistles, Hebrews, and Revelation, and shows acquaintance with Acts, 1 John, 1 Peter, and perhaps other NT books. He also regards them as authoritative. This shows that before the middle of the second century a collection of writings was known at Rome and was accepted as authoritative. F. F. Bruce, *The Canon of Scripture* (Downers Grove, IL: InterVarsity Press, 1988), 121, 146–48; Gamble, "Canonical Formation," 183–95.

a book had been used by most or all the churches from as far back as the time of the apostles. So by the time of the Third Council of Orange, which in AD 397 endorsed the twenty-seven books of the New Testament canon, church leaders were simply endorsing what had become the general consensus in the churches of the West and the greater part of the East.[26]

F. F. Bruce calls this the principle of "antiquity": "Writings of later date [after the apostolic age], whatever their merit, could not be included among the apostolic or canonical books." This is why the writer of the Muratorian Fragment rejected the *Shepherd of Hermas*, despite having high regard for it: it did not go back far enough in time.[27] Pelikan adds that this was one reason the orthodox churches gave for rejecting the writings of the heretics: the heretics came much later, and so could not enjoy "both continuity and unity of doctrine."[28]

Yet even if a book from the first century had been read in the church for edification, it was not received as scripture unless it had been *treated as scripture* during its previous readings. *First Clement,* for example, was read in the church at Corinth for seventy years after it had been sent there, but it was never treated with the same reverence as the letters of Paul.[29] When William Whiston (1667–1752) tried to get the *Apostolic Constitutions* accepted as scripture, it was not taken seriously—not only because someone had shown it was from the fourth century, but also because no one could show that it had been treated as scripture generally before. This is the force of what Bruce calls "traditional use."

Traditional use had to be fairly "catholic" in order for it to be considered authentic. That is, it had to be found not just in a few churches, but in a wide scattering of churches. Augustine said the standard was "to prefer those that are received by all the catholic churches to those which some do not receive." If all the churches did not agree, then churches were to prefer those documents that were used by the "greater number."[30]

There was also the "apostolic test," which was somewhat elastic. There had to be some connection to the apostles, if only indirect. Mark and Luke, for example, were not among the Twelve, but Mark was thought to be Peter's translator, and Luke to be Paul's accompanist on his missionary journeys. This test was used by the early church to rule out the *Shepherd of Hermas* and the *Didache* (and was an additional factor

26. Gamble, "Canonical Formation," 192; Bruce, *Canon of Scripture,* 97.
27. Bruce, *Canon of Scripture,* 259.
28. Tertullian, *Against Marcion* 1.21.5; cited in Pelikan, *Emergence of the Catholic Tradition,* 118.
29. Bruce, *Canon of Scripture,* 268.
30. Augustine, *On Christian Doctrine,* 2.12.

in the elimination of *1 Clement* from the canon). After a time of some doubt, Hebrews was ruled back into the canon because it was believed to be Paul's composition. James and Jude seem to have been included because the authors were regarded as brothers of Jesus, and 2 and 3 John were eventually adopted because of their association with the apostolic author of the gospel.[31]

Yet in some cases even traditional use and attribution were not enough. As Augustine wrote, "If we are to look back to long custom or antiquity alone, then also murderers and adulterers, and similar persons can defend crimes in this way, because they are ancient."[32]

Besides, the early church was awash in gospels and other documents claiming apostolic authorship. There were, for example, the *Gospel of Thomas* and the *Gospel of Peter,* not to mention *The Acts of Paul* and *The Apocalypse of Peter.* How could the church decide which were authentic and which spurious? In these cases, the criterion was doctrinal. Eusebius, for instance, rejected the gospels "of Peter, Thomas and Matthias and some others as well, [and] Acts such as those of Andrew and John and other apostles" because "the stamp of their phraseology differs widely from the apostolic style, and the opinion and policy of their contents are as dissonant as possible from true orthodoxy, showing clearly that these are the figments of heretics."[33] Serapion, the bishop of Antioch, deleted the *Gospel of Peter* from church readings because he discovered it was docetic (teaching that Jesus did not really suffer).[34] The *Gospel of Thomas* was kept out of the canon because it was clearly gnostic. Similar reasons were used for the other documents cited above.

Irrelevant and Nonbiblical Criteria?

Before we consider whether this brief history helps us determine whether the canon was reopened in the nineteenth century, we should pause to respond to one Mormon scholar's charge that these early church criteria were "nonbiblical, arbitrary, self-validating and therefore irrelevant."[35]

It seems odd to call orthodox use of criteria "irrelevant" when Mormons use some of the same criteria to validate their own canon. For example, Mormons also appeal to apostolic testimony, often referring to

31. Arthur G. Patzia, *The Making of the New Testament: Origin, Collection, Text and Canon* (Downers Grove, IL: InterVarsity Press, 1995), 104.
32. Cited in Vanhoozer, *Drama of Doctrine,* 163.
33. Eusebius, *The History of the Church,* 3.25.
34. Ibid., 6.12.
35. Robinson, in Blomberg and Robinson, *How Wide the Divide?* 69.

it as coming from a "prophet,"[36] while of course expanding the circle of apostles to include Joseph Smith and his successors. They also defend their canon by saying that it contradicts nothing in the New Testament doctrinally, but instead supplements what is found there. Of course, they don't use antiquity in the same sense as do the orthodox, who accept only those books coming from the first century or before. Yet Mormons also appeal to antiquity in their arguments for the Book of Mormon when they insist that this book goes back to centuries before Christ and that they accept only what they believe to be in accord with "ancient" revelation.

Nor does it seem that the orthodox criteria are "nonbiblical." The New Testament declares that the church is "built upon the foundation of the apostles and prophets" (Eph. 2:20), thus suggesting that the final norm for all questions of revelation should be what the prophets and apostles taught about Jesus. This is why the early church used the criteria of longstanding use going back to the apostolic age, apostolicity, and (apostolic) doctrine—because, as Calvin put it, the only Jesus we know is the one the apostles have given us. If the church is built on the foundation of prophetic teaching in the Old Testament and apostolic testimony in the New Testament, then every one of these criteria seem quite fitting. Each points in its own way back to those who lived with Jesus and were trained by him. Hence, they do not seem "arbitrary."

New Revelation?

So back to the most important question: Was the canon closed with the completion of the New Testament? Not necessarily. For if we suddenly found Paul's other letter to the church at Corinth (1 Cor. 5:9), which may have been the same one he wrote "with many tears" (2 Cor. 2:4; 7:8), the Christian churches might well add it to the canon. Their reasoning, we could speculate, would be that it is apostolic and that it would have been universally circulated from its earliest reception because that is what happened to all other extant Pauline letters.

But what of a "revelation" that comes long after the apostolic generation, such as Joseph Smith's? Mormons say it is simply the re-presentation of ancient revelations. It seems to me, however, that it is like other ancient claims to revelation—like, say, the *Gospel of Thomas* or perhaps even the *Didache*. None of the three have clear historical connection to the apostles. Even if they did, the doctrinal test would rule out *Thomas* and

---

36. Robinson explains that the two offices are often used interchangeably by Mormons. Ibid., 62.

Mormon claims such as the notion that God did not create matter but has co-existed eternally with it. This claim goes beyond mere "supplementation" and appears to most non-Mormons to contradict what they take to be clearly taught in scripture.[37]

Is Ongoing Revelation Unique to Mormons?

Mormons sometimes give the impression that canonicity is finally not that important. For, as some put it, revelation is more important than a set of books, and it is ongoing revelation that most distinguishes Mormons from non-Mormon Christians. Let's look at this second idea first.

Terryl Givens has recently proposed that the most distinguishing characteristic of the LDS is that it alone, among those claiming the name "Christian," still believes in ongoing revelation.[38] Even Professor Millet has averred that "the acceptance of modern and continuing revelation, including the addition to the scriptural canon, is one of the distinctives of Mormonism."[39]

Yet Bob has also added—wisely—that things are not so simple. He points out that Roman Catholics believe God continues to reveal his will and way through popes, councils, and the Catholic tradition as it develops by the work of the Holy Spirit. Pentecostals and charismatics believe that the gift of prophecy is still being poured out on believers all over the world and particularly in their meetings. Evangelicals of all sorts believe in the "illumination" of the Spirit, whereby the third person of the Trinity gives fresh and sometimes new understanding of the written Word.[40] This idea of God still leading his church in mystical fashion goes back to the first centuries of Christianity. Post-apostolic believers did not think that inspiration had ceased with the apostles; in fact, the strong word "God-breathed" (*theopneustos*) was used of the decision of the Council of Ephesus (AD 431) to condemn Nestorius.

Therefore, the distinction between LDS and non-LDS doctrine is less over the idea of ongoing revelation from God to his people and more over (a) whether it has come to Joseph Smith and his successors, and (b) whether new revelation can supplant or change widespread Christian agreements about the teaching of scripture.

37. On "supplementation" vs. "contradiction," see Millet, *A Different Jesus?* 77. On God's creation of matter, see, e.g., not only Gen. 1:1 (which admittedly is not clear on this matter) but also Neh. 9:6; Ps. 102:25; and Heb. 11:3.

38. Terryl L. Givens, "The Book of Mormon and Religious Epistemology," *Dialogue* 34: nos. 3–4 (Fall-Winter 2001), 31–54, esp. 39–40.

39. Millet, *A Different Jesus?* 15.

40. Ibid.

Revelation versus Scripture

That brings us to the Mormon distinction between revelation and scripture, which is troubling to evangelicals like me. Professor Millet writes that "the word of God is not linked to written words . . . but rather to the spirit of prophecy and revelation that illuminated and empowered those who recorded them in the first place." He cites LDS leader Dallin Oaks: "For us, the scriptures are not the ultimate source of knowledge, but what precedes the ultimate source. The ultimate knowledge comes by revelation . . . through those we sustain as prophets, seers, and revelators."[41]

Stephen Robinson speaks in a similar vein: "The direct revelation to a prophet or an apostle is immediate and primary. . . . However, the recording, transmission and interpretation of the word depends on fallible human beings, using the fallible tools of reason and language . . . [T]he church's guarantee of doctrinal correctness lies primarily in the living prophet, and only secondarily in the preservation of the written text."[42]

These statements tend to separate the work of the Spirit in revelation from the work of the Spirit in producing a written word. The Spirit, they suggest, gave divine concepts to biblical authors, but the words those authors chose are not reliable, for they are fallible. The upshot is that we need an infallible modern interpreter to make sense of biblical words that had not been understood by the church in its first 1800 years.

This is indeed what Robinson goes on to imply: "What God has said to apostles and prophets in the past is always secondary to what God is saying directly to his apostles and prophets now."[43] This subordination of ancient to modern prophecy appears to make Joseph Smith the head, and Jesus's apostles the tail. Robinson seems not to be saying simply that Smith reiterates and confirms what was taught by the early church, but that he has given new revelation that may even be "contrary" to early teaching: "I know this makes Evangelicals wince, but the spiritual hazards are logically no greater than they were in the earliest church when Peter and Paul were still alive and interpreting previously received scripture for the church, *sometimes contrary to tradition*, even while they continued to receive more."[44]

To be fair, I should point out that Robinson probably means that Peter and Paul taught contrary to *non-biblical* tradition, such as Pharisaic traditions that could not imagine a messiah who would suffer and die. But it is

41. Ibid., 78, 16.
42. Robinson, in Blomberg and Robinson, *How Wide the Divide?* 57.
43. Ibid., 59.
44. Ibid.; my emphasis.

also clear that Peter and Paul believed they were teaching the true meaning of the Jewish tradition, which they thought pointed unambiguously to a suffering servant who would redeem. What troubles evangelicals like me is the suggestion not only that Smith was teaching things that were contrary to received interpretations of the Bible, but that his new books were also higher in hermeneutical significance than the Bible's sixty-six books. Or, just as the New Testament is the lens through which Christians are to read the Old, the new Mormon scriptures are the lens through which to read the New Testament. This means that the classical canon is not on the same par with the new Mormon canon, but on the contrary, the Mormon additions are higher and more revelatory.

Furthermore, for Robinson, the quality of the two sets of books seems different. The classical canon is composed of fallible and unreliable words, which means that there is a considerable gap between the original revelations, given by the Spirit, and the later words, composed by fallible men. But "the Joseph Smith translation (JST) [of the Bible] should be understood to contain additional revelation, alternate readings, prophetic commentary or midrash, harmonization, clarification and corrections . . . to the original."[45] While Robinson adds that the JST is not the LDS version of the Bible (the KJV is) and that variant readings in the JST do not necessarily imply that the KJV is incorrect, his words nevertheless imply that in Smith's writings we have a new super-canon that has been preserved from distortion far better than the classical canon was.

Indeed, this has been a Mormon claim since nearly the beginning—that "plain and precious truths; and also many covenants of the Lord" were removed from the Bible before its final compilation (1 Nephi 13:26; Moses 1:40–41). Evangelicals ask why, among the thousands of ancient biblical manuscripts we now possess, there is no sign that Mormon-like doctrines were erased or otherwise removed from those manuscripts. Robinson has written that this simply means that some books were excluded from the canon. But I ask, with Craig Blomberg, Why is there no historical evidence of this—even in the last forty years when new apocryphal documents have emerged from the first five Christian centuries?[46]

Important Agreement, But . . .

In a chapter on how Mormons and evangelicals differ on sources of authority, I should also mention that we agree in important ways. We agree that the Bible is God's Word, not simply human reflection on

45. Ibid., 64.
46. Blomberg, in Blomberg and Robinson, *How Wide the Divide?* 36, 63.

spiritual experience. We also agree that it has infallible authority for Christian faith and practice. But it appears that some of our important differences on Jesus go back to different canons. The Mormon canon, still open, contains the Bible, Book of Mormon, Doctrine and Covenants, and Pearl of Great Price. The classical Christian canon, theoretically open but practically closed,[47] is limited to the sixty-six books on which almost all Christians (Protestant, Catholic, and Orthodox) agree.[48] If Mormons did not regard their books as scriptural, and did not use Smith's later sermons to influence their reading of their canon,[49] it is unlikely there would be many differences between Mormons and orthodox Christians on Jesus and other doctrines. It is no wonder that different portraits of Jesus have emerged from different bodies of authoritative sources.

Has the canon been reopened with new revelation coming through Smith and his successors? If we believe that the early church had good reason to restrict the canon to sources that were at least indirectly identified with apostolic testimony, then we cannot agree. For, as I shall argue in later chapters, there are too many differences on Jesus, his earthly ministry, and his work with the Father in creation and redemption.

---

47. I say "practically"—that is, for all practical purposes—because of the canon's emphasis on apostolicity and ancient use in the earliest churches. It seems very unlikely that we will find another document, currently unknown, that was linked to the first apostles and also was widely used.

48. Catholics and some Orthodox include the Apocrypha, but the latter is not used for primary support for any major doctrine separating them from Protestants.

49. For example, later sermons by Joseph Smith refer to Jesus's having a Father and once being simply a man.

A Latter-day Saint Response
Robert Millet

Not long ago I was in conversation with an evangelical Christian friend. Our discussion turned to the place of the Bible within traditional Christianity and what I call Latter-day Saint Christianity. We went back and forth on various matters, including the concept of inerrancy, the matter of biblical infallibility, and, of course, whether and to what extent I felt that the Bible was a sufficient repository of God's word. In an effort to make his point most forcefully, my friend commented in a rather animated fashion, "But Bob, can't you see that the Bible contains the final word and is the ultimate source of truth?" I paused for a moment, took a deep breath, and said very calmly, "Bill, I don't believe that, and neither do you." He responded quickly: "What do you mean, I don't believe it? Of course I do." "No, you really don't believe that. I'm certain that you don't. As vital and important to the religious world as the Bible is, it is not God's final word, nor is it the ultimate source of truth. Jesus Christ is the source of truth! God is the source of truth!"

This conversation highlights what may well be perceived as the difference between the evangelical view of authority and the LDS view. Let me be as honest and yet straightforward as I can be: I love the Bible. I have taught the New Testament for over thirty years, and while I have not been as serious a student of the Old Testament as of the New, I treasure its truths and recognize it as foundational to an appreciation for and an understanding of the New Testament. There's no question in my mind but that the Bible is the word of God. I am not, however, a bibliolater: the Bible is precious and contains holy and sacred material, but I do not worship it. And as a Latter-day Saint, I do not consider it to be the sole repository of theological truth or the only valid compilation of revealed reality. Quite often I am asked how I can possibly accept additional books of scripture (The Book of Mormon, Doctrine & Covenants, and Pearl of Great Price) and still maintain a love and reverence for the biblical word. To me this is a bit like a young parent worrying about how he or she will love the coming second child as much as they have loved their firstborn. In the family scenario, obviously God endows moms and dads with a greater measure of love and a grander capacity to extend themselves in love to the newest member of the family without sacrificing one iota of affection for the firstborn. Gaining a love and appreciation for the second need not detract from what they feel for the first. Forgive me if I'm being juvenile, but I feel this same way when it comes to accepting all of the books within the LDS canon of scripture. That I love the Book of Mormon and sincerely believe it to be Another Testament of Jesus Christ does not mean that I do not accept what is taught about our Lord and Savior in the Gospels or in the Epistles. In some ways, interestingly enough, my love for what is contained in the Bible—namely, an account of the life and ministry of Jesus the Messiah—is enhanced and magnified by what I find taught in these other books of LDS scripture.

It's a little tough to answer the question: Which is of greater importance to you people, the living prophet or the standard works (another way of describing our scriptural canon)? I think most Latter-day Saints would be prone to answer this by pointing out the value and significance of living oracles, or continuing revelation, or ongoing divine direction through modern apostles and prophets, and thus to conclude that living prophets take precedence over canonized scripture. On the other hand, a number of LDS Church leaders have commented that while Mormons look to living prophets and modern revelation as their guide to walk and talk in modern times, they are quick to add that prophetic pronouncements will be in harmony with the standard works, the canon. From this perspective, then, it appears that the standard works trump the living prophets. And so to be honest, it's a little tough to decide which is the chicken and which is the egg. It is rather fascinating that the above does not seem to pose a particular problem for the Mormon faithful; most do not see it as an ambiguity but rather continue to study their scripture and hearken to the words of their living leaders.

Well then, to what extent does tradition serve as a source of authority within Mormonism? For us, tradition would consist of the following: (1) what apostles and prophets have said relative to scripture, that is, what might be called inspired prophetic commentary; (2) that which is recorded in official Church publications such as the general handbooks of the Church that set forth the regulations, guidelines, and acceptable/ unacceptable practices within the faith, material that is made available to general and local Church leaders; (3) a kind of "unwritten order of things," items of truth and understanding and practice that have been perpetuated through the last century and three-quarters in a more oral fashion and are not necessarily recorded in an official letter or handbook. When asked about the nature of revelation that comes to him and his associates to guide the church, President Gordon B. Hinckley responded that the LDS Church has within its possession a huge backlog of information and direction received principally by Joseph Smith. Leaders at all levels of church organization rely heavily on such direction, and when need arises in terms of a new or unusual challenge facing the church, leaders turn to God in fervent prayer and seek the mind and will of the Almighty.

There is another source of authority that Latter-day Saints take very seriously: they believe that God continues to manifest himself by personal inspiration, revelation, or illumination. Surely, no directive from Christ is more frequently given to the children of God than to ask, to knock, to seek. Mormons are quick to point to Joseph Smith's experience in the Sacred Grove in the spring of 1820 as a response to his reading and internalization of James 1:5—an invitation for those who lack wisdom to seek it from God. In short, Latter-day Saints are encouraged by their leaders to spend time on their knees, to devote themselves to serious study, meditation, and reflection, all in an effort to hear the "still small voice" of deity. Now to be sure, while all are encouraged to seek the spirit of revelation, there is order in the house of God; there is, indeed, a system of revelatory checks and balances put in place to avoid the kind of charismatic chaos that could ensue with everyone receiving revelation for everyone. Joseph Smith taught that divine direction for the entire Church comes through the First Presidency of the Church: the President of the Church (sustained as the prophet, seer, and revelator) and his two counselors. This presidency works in conjunction with the Quorum of the Twelve Apostles, men called as special witnesses of the name of Christ in all the world, men given the specific responsibility, as Peter and his apostolic colleagues were given, to bear witness of the resurrection and divinity and redemptive power of Jesus Christ.

Furthermore, an individual is entitled to revelation for persons or matters within a given stewardship or responsibility. Thus a bishop, the pastor, or the head of the local congregation could and should receive heavenly promptings relative to the welfare of his flock, while a stake president (a man called and charged to oversee the work and edification of several congregations) would be entitled to that same direction for his larger sphere. A mother and a father would likewise be entitled to heavenly illumination relative to their family and to the problems and challenges they may face in teaching and rearing their children and in dealing with household affairs. Thus, according to this system, as Joseph

Smith taught, "It is contrary to the economy of God for any member of the Church, or anyone, to receive instruction for those in authority, higher than themselves."[50]

In speaking of scripture as a major source of authority within Mormonism, we need to understand that Latter-day Saints are encouraged by their leaders to be involved in a daily program of scripture study and devotion. Such study is to serve several functions. First of all, there is the simple matter of scriptural literacy: people who claim to be followers of the Lord Jesus Christ ought to know what God has revealed concerning Jesus Christ and ought to strive to become competent witnesses of the Master. In other words, there is much to be gained from scripture study by simply reading, understanding, and committing to memory passages or sections of scripture in order to be more conversant with both the history and implications of God's dealings with his people through the millennia.

Second, Latter-day Saints are encouraged to study scripture to better understand the doctrines of salvation, those principles and precepts that provide answers to so many of life's questions. It is perhaps in this light that the Apostle Peter encouraged his readers to be ready at all times to provide answers, to provide reasons for the hope within them (1 Pet. 3:15). That is to say, Christians are charged to know the scriptures well enough to provide a rational explanation for the personal spiritual witness residing within their souls. It's a marvelous thing to be able to declare that Jesus is the Christ, our Savior and Redeemer, and that salvation comes in and through his name and in no other. It is far more effective, however, to be able to bear such a witness and at the same time be in a position to explain such matters as why we are in need of redemption (the nature of fallen humanity); our absolute and utter dependence on One greater and grander than ourselves for salvation (humility); and the means and manner by which Jesus of Nazareth is able to forgive our sins, cleanse our hearts, raise us from the dead, and glorify us hereafter (redemption in Christ).

Third, Latter-day Saints are encouraged to search the scriptures and the revelations with great earnestness in an effort to "liken the scriptures" unto themselves—to be familiar enough with the context and the text to place one's self in the narrative, to feel and sense the personal relevance of scriptural principles, and to incorporate and inculcate such ideas and ideals into daily living. A passage in the Doctrine and Covenants declares: "These words [the words of the revelations in the Doctrine and Covenants] are not of men nor or man, but of me; wherefore, you shall testify they

---

50. Smith, *Teachings of the Prophet Joseph Smith*, comp. Joseph Fielding Smith (Salt Lake City: Deseret Book, 1976), 21. Hereafter cited as *TPJS*.

are of me and not of man; for it is my voice that speaketh them unto you; for they are given by my spirit unto you, and by my power you can read them one to another; and save it were by my power you could not have them; wherefore, you can testify that you have heard my voice, and know my words" (D&C 18:34–36). In his last general conference address, given only days before his death, LDS apostle and theologian Bruce R. McConkie made the following observation, just as he began a major sermon on the atonement of Jesus Christ: "In speaking of these wondrous things I shall use my own words, though you may think they are the words of scriptures, words spoken by other apostles and prophets. True it is they were first proclaimed by others, but they are now mine, for the Holy Spirit of God has borne witness to me that they are true, and it is now as though the Lord had revealed them to me in the first instance. I have thereby heard his voice and know his word."[51]

There is another matter that needs clarification. People often ask me, "So do you place the Book of Mormon on a higher spiritual standing than the Bible?" Well, while Mormons love the Book of Mormon and appreciate the ministry of the Prophet Joseph, and to be sure, certain Mormons may have preferences regarding certain collections of scripture, to me (and I speak only as one person) the Bible falls within the family of scripture, and I do not love one member of the family any more than I love another. Each has its message. Each makes its distinctive contribution. Each bears witness of the Lord in a unique way. Thus it would not be unusual for me to deliver a sermon or a lecture on a religious topic in which I had quoted or paraphrased passages from Romans, from Alma (in the Book of Mormon), from Doctrine and Covenants, and from the Book of Moses (the Pearl of Great Price). I do not pause and say, for example, "Now, Brothers and Sisters, I'm going to move into the Book of Mormon," or "If you feel okay about this, I'd like to turn now to the New Testament." No, Latter-day Saints study and use and teach from and draw upon all members of the family of scripture.

Latter-day Saints do not believe in the concept of scriptural inerrancy, first of all because we believe that indeed there have been plain and precious truths lost through the centuries through scribal error.[52] Now such a statement does not in any way invalidate the Bible or negate the influence it has had upon civilization for thousands of years. But to us it does suggest the need for confirmatory and, yes, even supplementary

51. Conference Report, April 1985, 9.

52. Professor McDermott indicates that there is little evidence to suggest that "Mormon-like doctrines were erased or otherwise removed from those manuscripts." For an interesting study of this question, see David L. Paulsen "Are Christians Mormon? Reassessing Joseph Smith's Theology in the Bicentennial," *Brigham Young University Studies* 45, no. 1 (2006), 35–128.

scriptural works. Second, we do not believe in the inerrancy of scripture because we do not find the concept especially useful. The man or woman in the pew who is concerned with whether or to what extent they are justified in believing in the reliability of the text of their King James Version or their New International Version is not particularly benefited or edified by the notion that the original autographs, the first manuscripts produced by the apostles themselves, were without flaw. This is a lovely idea, one that I probably would not object to rigorously, but we come face to face very quickly with a challenge—we do not possess the original manuscripts! If by biblical infallibility one means that the hand of God has been over the preservation of the holy word, I suppose I would accept such a proposition. Let me say this another way: Mormons do not believe that the present Bible has to be flawless and identical to the original manuscripts in order for its central messages to be true and normative and binding on our lives. How David met Saul matters precious little to me. Whether there were one or two angels at the tomb when Jesus rose from the dead does not bother me a great deal. Whether those traveling with Saul of Tarsus on the road to Damascus heard the voice or just saw the light is for me irrelevant. Essence, not infinite detail is what matters.

I appreciate very much Professor McDermott's discussion of the Reformation concept of *sola scriptura*. I believe he is absolutely right: both Mormons and evangelicals need to get off their high horse in pointing the finger of scorn at one another about sticking with scripture alone; both faith groups rely heavily on tradition and subsequent scriptural interpretation through the years. I for one believe we ought to be especially careful about claiming for scripture what it does not claim for itself. For example, there is the matter of biblical sufficiency—whether the Bible is the final and complete word of God, the "seal of the prophets" to borrow a phrase from our Muslim friends. Do we really know that God has chosen not to reveal himself beyond the Bible? Is it necessary, in order to maintain one's love for and devotion to the Bible, to deny any and all scripture beyond the first century AD?

A slightly different question is this: How is it that such doctrines as the Trinitarian formulations and the concept of creation *ex nihilo* could have gained such canonical status as they now enjoy? On many occasions I have been told that I am not a Christian because I do not subscribe to basic biblical truth such as the doctrine of the Trinity and the concept that all things were created by God out of nothing. The fact is, these ideas are definitely post-biblical, post-New Testament concepts that present-day Christians seek to prove from the Bible. I have great difficulty imagining, however, that a naïve reader of the Old or New Testament—one uninfluenced by the historic Christian tradition or by

LDS beliefs—would come up with these notions on their own through a simple reading of the text. They are post-biblical, not biblical.

So often I encounter religious persons who state emphatically that their position is based entirely upon "the authority of scripture." The fact is, God is the source of any reputable religious authority. In the words of N. T. Wright, "The risen Jesus, at the end of Matthew's gospel, does not say, 'All authority in heaven and on earth is given to the books you are all going to write,' but 'All authority in heaven and on earth is given to me.'" In other words, "scripture itself points—authoritatively, if it does indeed possess authority!—away from itself and to the fact that final and true authority belongs to God himself, now delegated to Jesus Christ."[53] Barbara Brown Taylor expressed her own feelings toward scripture: "I will keep the Bible, which remains the Word of God for me, but always the Word as heard by generations of human beings as flawed as I. As beautifully as these witnesses write, their divine inspiration can never be separated from their ardent desires; their genuine wish to serve God cannot be divorced from their self-interest. *That God should use such blemished creatures to communicate God's reality so well makes the Bible its own kind of miracle, but I hope never to put the book ahead of the people whom the book calls me to love and serve.* I will keep the Bible as a field guide, which was never intended to be a substitute for the field."[54]

Lee M. McDonald, a Baptist pastor who has taught at Fuller Theological Seminary, has posed some probing questions relative to the present closed Christian canon of scripture. "The first question," he writes, "and the most important one, is whether the church was right in perceiving the need for a closed canon of scriptures." McDonald also asks: "Did such a move toward a closed canon of scriptures ultimately (and unconsciously) limit the presence and power of the Holy Spirit in the church? More precisely, does the recognition of absoluteness of the biblical canon minimize the presence and activity of God in the church today? . . . On what biblical or historical grounds has the inspiration of God been limited to the written documents that the church now calls its Bible?" While McDonald poses other issues, let me refer to his final question: "If the Spirit inspired only the written documents of the first century, does that mean that the same Spirit does not speak today in the church about matters that are of significant concern?"[55]

I remember very well sitting in a doctoral course entitled "Seminar on Biblical Studies" in the late 1970s. There were eight of us in the course,

53. N. T. Wright, *The Last Word* (San Francisco: HarperSanFrancisco, 2005), xi, 24.
54. Barbara Brown Taylor, *Leaving Church: A Memoir of Faith* (San Francisco: HarperSanFrancisco, 2006), 216, emphasis added.
55. Lee M. McDonald, *The Formation of the Christian Biblical Canon* (Peabody, MA: Hendrickson Publishers, 1995), 254–56.

as I recall, from various religious backgrounds—two Southern Baptists, a couple of Methodists, a Reform Jew, a Roman Catholic, a Nazarene, and a Latter-day Saint. It was an excellent class and helped introduce me to the vocabulary of the academic study of religion as well as to some of the problems and challenges of biblical scholarship. The professor, a former Methodist minister, was a superb instructor. He was organized, well-prepared, and considerate of students. He responded well to questions and was always available for consultation. We studied various topics, including the nature of scripture, covenant, prophecy, interpretation, authorship, and the dating of scriptural records. One of the things that stands out in my mind is our discussion of the canon of scripture. We had covered in some detail the historical roots of the Old and New Testament canons and the relationship between canonicity and authority of scripture; that is, we had debated whether a document belonged in the canon because it was considered authoritative, or whether it was considered authoritative because it was included in the canon.

For two periods the instructor had emphasized that the word *canon*—referring, of course, to the biblical books that are generally included in the Judeo-Christian collection—implied the rule of faith, the standard against which we measure what is acceptable. Furthermore, he stated that the canon, if the word meant anything at all, was *closed*, *fixed*, *set*, and *established*. I look back at my notes more than three decades later and realize that he must have stressed those four words at least ten times. I noticed in the next session that the instructor seemed a bit uneasy. I remember thinking that something must be wrong. Without warning, he stopped what he was doing, banged his fist on the table, turned to me and said: "Mr. Millet, will you please explain to this group the Latter-day Saint concept of canon, especially given your acceptance of the Book of Mormon and other books of scripture beyond the Bible?" I was startled. Certainly surprised. I paused for several seconds, looked up at the board, saw the now very familiar four words written under the word canon, and said somewhat shyly: "Well, I suppose you could say that the Mormons believe the canon of scripture is *open*, *flexible*, and *expanding*!" We spent much of the rest of the period trying to make sense out of what I had just said.

Professor McDermott is a bit more optimistic about what the Christian world would accept and add to the canon than I am. My experience in speaking with Christians across the denominational spectrum suggests to me that addition to the canon is not only something not to be taken lightly but something that is highly unlikely to ever occur. The Bible has a spirit and a power all its own, and few reasonable people would feel competent or qualified to decide what should or should not be added to the holy collection. It is fairly clear to me why such documents as the

Gospel of Thomas or the more recent *Gospel of Judas* would never be added to the canon, for they clearly demonstrate their gnostic character. It is a little tougher, however, to understand why *1 Clement* or the *Didache* or *The Shepherd of Hermas* would not now be given serious consideration. Mormons simply believe that God loves his children in all times and in all ages. Traditional Christians agree. Mormons believe God wants his children to know his mind and will and not to be required to wander aimlessly in the dark. Traditional Christians agree. Mormons believe that God continues to speak to his people through personal revelation and divine illumination. Traditional Christians agree. But Mormons believe that God continues to speak in modern times through living apostles and prophets and that the canon of scripture is not now and will never be complete. Traditional Christians vehemently disagree.

A friend of mine became closely acquainted with a high Catholic prelate (a cardinal) many years ago. They spent scores of hours together in theological discussions, comparing and contrasting Mormonism and Catholicism, pointing up differences and yet acknowledging similarities. Over the years their respect for one another grew, and they were able to discuss almost any issue without fear or reservation. My friend indicated to me that in his last trip to Rome to visit the cardinal he noticed right away that the church official was unusually distant; he was quieter, more reserved, more hesitant to speak the feelings of his heart. After a few moments of this tense and uncomfortable environment, my friend turned to his Catholic associate: "What's wrong? You seem to be treating me differently today than before. What's bothering you?" The cardinal responded: "Well, I've concluded, with the evangelicals, that Latter-day Saints are not Christian." My friend was stunned and retorted: "Not Christian? How can you say such a thing? You and I have talked and listened and felt many things together. You know what is deep within my heart and how I feel about the Lord Jesus Christ. You know what my religion teaches about Jesus Christ. How can you say such a thing?"

Softly but sternly, the cardinal replied: "You're not Christian because you believe in additional books of scripture. You believe in continuing revelation." The Latter-day Saint then responded: "Wait a minute! You believe in revelation, don't you? Don't you profess that the pope is entitled to revelation in his role as head of the Roman Catholic Church?" The cardinal sat up in his chair and his countenance changed dramatically as the volume of his voice rose and as he began to shake his finger in my friend's face. He said simply: "I can assure you that no pope has ever received revelation!" My friend was mystified. Stunned. Speechless. He said they spoke together for awhile longer, and then the meeting ended. They have not met together again.

"What in the world was he talking about?" my friend asked me on a subsequent occasion. "Do they really not believe in revelation?" At first my reaction to the cardinal's comments were similar to my friend's, but I soon began to realize what he meant. "What he means," I said, in essence, "is that no pope has ever received a revelation of the magnitude of the revelations given to the apostles of old and that now constitute holy scripture. Of course our cardinal friend believes that the pope is entitled to divine direction for the welfare and oversight of the Church, but he does not believe that any pope has ever dared go beyond holy scripture; indeed, they claim that all declarations and encyclicals are couched within and framed by the word of God as given in the Bible."

Personally, one of the saddest things for me in associating with my many friends of other faiths, particularly evangelicals, is their refusal to even consider the additional books of scripture we have in light of their content. By that I mean that so much effort is put forward to seal the canon against all potential intruders and to question the historicity and origins of the Book of Mormon and Book of Abraham, that little if any interest is expressed in what the books actually teach.

Some years ago historian Nathan Hatch observed: "For all the recent attention given to the study of Mormonism, surprisingly little has been devoted to the Book of Mormon itself. What are the patterns deep in the grain of this extraordinary work and what do they reveal about the perceptions and intentions of the prophet Joseph Smith? Mormon historians, of course, have been more interested in pointing out the ways in which the book transcends the provincial opinions of the man Joseph Smith, thus establishing its uniquely biblical and revelatory character. Mormon detractors, on the other hand, have attempted to reduce the book to an inert mirror of the popular culture of New York during the 1820s, thus overlooking elements that are unique and original. . . . Scholars have not taken seriously Joseph Smith's original rationale about the nature of his prophetic mission. The pivotal document of the Mormon church . . . still receives scant attention from cultural historians, while scholars rush to explore more exotic themes, such as the influence upon Joseph Smith of magic, alchemy, and the occult."[56]

I would like to make one final comment about the Bible and what it stands for. It is not just a collection of doctrinal answers to people's favorite questions. It is not a catechism. "At some level," LDS historian Richard Bushman observed, "Joseph's revelations indicate a loss of trust in the Christian ministry. For all their learning and their eloquence, the clergy could not be trusted with the Bible. They did not understand what the

56. Nathan Hatch, *The Democratization of American Christianity* (New Haven, CT: Yale University Press, 1989), 115.

book meant. It was a record of revelations, and the ministry had turned it into a handbook. The Bible had become a text to be interpreted rather than an experience to be lived. In the process, the power of the book was lost." Bushman continues, "To me that is Joseph Smith's significance for our time. He stood on the contested ground where the enlightenment and Christianity confronted one another, and his life posed the question, Do you believe God speaks? Joseph was swept aside, of course, in the rush of ensuing intellectual battles and was disregarded by the champions of both great systems, but his mission was to hold out for the reality of divine revelation and establish one small outpost where that principle survived. Joseph's revelatory principle is not a single revelation serving for all time, as the Christians of his day believed regarding the incarnation of Christ, nor a mild sort of inspiration seeping into the minds of all good people, but specific, ongoing directions from God to his people. At a time when the origins of Christianity were under assault by the forces of enlightenment rationality, Joseph Smith returned modern Christianity to its origins in revelation."[57]

57. Richard Bushman, "A Joseph Smith for the Twentieth-first Century," *Believing History: Latter-day Saint Essays*, ed. Reid L. Neilson and Jed Woodworth (New York: Columbia University Press, 2004), 274.

Rebuttal and Concluding Thoughts
Gerald McDermott

In his response, Professor Millet makes five assertions that I would like to address a bit further. First, he maintains that God, not scripture, is our final authority and truth. Formally, I would agree. But the way that is stated suggests a false dichotomy—either God *or* scripture. If scripture is God's Word, we don't have to make that choice, for he will never contradict what he has already said in scripture. If we set God over and against his Word, how do we decide truth when a human voice claims to be speaking for him things that are contradicted by the Word?

Second, Bob asserts that just because they accept new revelation, this does not mean that Mormons don't love the revelation in the Bible. I don't doubt that. What I do see, despite some claims to the contrary, is a higher status for the Mormon additions to the canon because they are said to be better preserved than the classical canon, and they seem to serve as the lens through which the classical canon is read. For example, because of Mormon revelation, LDS readers see the Bible teaching the eternality of matter, whereas almost all Christians who have ever read the Bible have seen instead creation from nothing.

Third, Bob suggests that Mormons alone preserve the concept of revelation for modern Christianity. He says that traditional Christians "vehemently disagree" that God continues to speak, cites Lee McDonald's statement that a closed canon means the Spirit no longer speaks, and implies that the Bible had stopped being a book to be experienced by Joseph Smith's time or perhaps is still that way in traditional churches today. This would be a surprise to millions of traditional Christians today, especially evangelicals, who sense they are "led by the Spirit" (Rom. 8:14) regularly and who repeatedly feel they are being given "a spirit of wisdom and revelation in the knowledge of him" (Eph. 1:17) as they read scripture, listen to sermons, pray, and meditate. Philip Jenkins, in his award-winning *The Next Christendom*,[58] has documented the legions of Pentecostal believers in the Southern Hemisphere for whom the leading of the Spirit and fresh illuminations from God are a daily experience. In addition, America in the 1830s was still being washed with waves from the Second Great Awakening, which produced tens of thousands of believers who said the Bible spoke to them as a voice from heaven. In short, huge numbers of non-LDS Christians would insist God is still speaking, but not in ways that add to the biblical canon.

Fourth, Professor Millet is disappointed that non-LDS seem not to even consider the contents of the Book of Mormon. This is probably true for most Christians. But some of us have considered it and concluded that we have sufficient reasons for rejecting its claim to be new revelation. I spell out my reasons in chapter 5. I think Bob is right to doubt the orthodox churches will ever expand the canon, but I think there is good reason for this: it is highly unlikely we will ever find some new document clearly linked to the apostles (which seems a wise criterion, given Paul's definition of the church's foundation in Eph. 2:20). This is why *1 Clement*, the *Didache*, and *The Shepherd of Hermas* were not included in the canon. *First Clement* never carried the authority that Paul's letters did even among its original recipients at Corinth; the *Didache* had no link to the apostles; and *Shepherd of Hermas* contained questionable teaching (only one sin after baptism could be forgiven).[59]

Fifth and last, Bob says that the doctrines of the Trinity and *creatio ex nihilo* are post-biblical and not biblical. My rejoinder is that of course their precise formulations waited for the post-biblical period, but the basic outline of each is in the Bible. Mormons do not reject God's threeness, but his oneness. Yet the latter is repeatedly proclaimed in scripture: "The Lord your God is one Lord" (Deut. 6:4); "I am the first and the last; and besides me there is no God" (Isa. 44:6); "Thou believest that there is one God; thou doest well" (Jas. 2:19).

Creatio ex nihilo is implied by Colossians 1:16–17: "For by him were *all things* created, that are in heaven, and that are in earth, *visible* and invisible, whether they be thrones, or dominions, or principalities, or powers: all things were created by him, and for him: And he is before all things, and by him all things consist" (my emphasis). If God created "all things," which clearly includes all things that are "visible," that must include matter, so matter cannot be eternal. No mention is ever

58. Philip Jenkins, *The Next Christendom: The Coming of Global Christianity* (New York: Oxford University Press, 2002).
59. Bruce, *Canon of Scripture*, 268; *Shepherd*, vision 2.2.

made in the Bible of any preexisting matter out of which the world was made.[60] The original creation is never represented as reshaping matter into definite forms, as LDS teaching puts it. Instead, "Things which are seen were not made of things which do appear" (Heb. 11:3).

Those differences aside, we can say that Bob and I agree on a number of things:

1. We all read scripture though some tradition or other. Therefore, we should stop accusing each other of bringing meaning to the biblical text from a tradition that has reflected on scripture, as if that were a problem in principle. It is impossible not to read a text through the lens of our whole life experience, which includes religious tradition.
2. We all have our own creeds. That is, each community of believers has come to its own understandings of God and life under him and expresses those understandings in formal ways (such as the LDS "Articles of Faith" and the myriad of evangelical churches' statements of faith).
3. What separates evangelicals and Mormons is less our view of scriptural authority and more our different views of the canon.
4. We both believe the Bible is God's Word, not merely human reflection on human religious experience. It is authoritative for Christian belief and practice.
5. We both believe in the Spirit's continuing work to lead believers into greater knowledge of God in Christ, and we believe that this happens principally through the Bible.

---

60. There is legitimate debate over the meaning of the opening words of Genesis 1, some preferring, "When God began to create the heavens and the earth—the earth being without form and void—God said . . ." But in the absence of explicit mention of eternal matter, and in light of the biblical assertions of God's creation of everything, such as the Colossians passage above, it seems tendentious to claim otherwise.

2

CHRIST
BEFORE BETHLEHEM

Creator, God of the Ancients
Robert Millet

I want to wax a bit personal for a few moments and then dive into the question of the LDS view of Christ's life before life, the concept of his pre-mortal existence. I think this brief autobiographical detour will assist the reader to better appreciate why it matters so much to me to be understood and why it troubles me when Mormons are misunderstood, especially in their beliefs concerning the person and powers of Jesus Christ.

Backgrounds

I was born and reared in Baton Rouge, Louisiana. My paternal grandfather had joined the Church of Jesus Christ of Latter-day Saints in the 1930s and, with his wife, had raised their four sons in the LDS faith. I was raised as a Latter-day Saint in the Baton Rouge area, and in every way one might choose to measure it, we were in the minority. Most of my friends were Southern Baptist or Roman Catholic, though religion seldom came up in play or conversation. I honestly don't ever remember having to defend my faith with any of my friends, nor do I recall them making light of the fact that I was a religious "outsider."

My first serious religious encounter came as a freshman in college between my two roommates and me. One of them was a very brilliant math major, a Roman Catholic. The other young man was Pentecostal. We had long hours of conversation and debate, and for the first time I was asked to prove my points from the Bible; I was not allowed to draw upon Mormon doctrine or any other sources extraneous to the Christian canon. As I look back on those months in the dorm, it was an important formative season for me, one that opened my eyes to the fact that not everyone saw things exactly as I did and that in fact my position was a minority position.

My initial contact with anti-Mormon materials came when I was on a full-time mission in the late 1960s. I first became aware of Walter Martin's book *Kingdom of the Cults* in 1967 and realized there were people who considered Latter-day Saints to be members of a cult. Whatever that meant, it didn't seem complimentary. I also encountered anti-Mormon brochures that had been given to the parishioners by local clergy. At almost every door we approached, the adult at home would smile, open the door, and say: "Oh, you must be the Mormons. This is for you." They would then hand over the tract. But to be totally frank, I cannot remember ever being told or ever reading anywhere that Mormons are not Christian until the 1970s, although I now realize that Walter Martin was making just such a claim earlier in his masterwork.

For well over twenty years I dismissed the cry that Mormons aren't Christian with a wave of the hand and a smirk, concluding that the people who said this were uninformed, perhaps even downright ignorant. I mean, Jesus Christ is in the very title of our church. We read the New Testament, just like our Baptist and Methodist and Catholic friends. We believe Jesus is our Savior and Redeemer and that his suffering and death, his atoning sacrifice and his resurrection, cleanse our souls and raise us from the dead.

As time has passed, however, I find myself more and more concerned about what I consider to be the major problem with the claim that Latter-day Saints are not Christian. I do understand that we are not a part of the historic Christian tradition—we are not Roman Catholic, Eastern Orthodox, or Protestant. People are simply not sure where to place us on the religious spectrum. I understand that our non-acceptance of the post–New Testament creeds, particularly the Trinitarian formulations, also makes us suspect.

My concern is not really why the pastors or theologians do not feel comfortable identifying us as Christians, for I think I understand where they are coming from. My worry is that the woman in the pew and the man on the street will hear the idea that Latter-day Saints are not Christian and ask themselves: Do these people not believe in Jesus? Do they not believe in his virgin birth? Do they not accept the fact that he performed miracles? Do they not receive him as Lord and Savior and accept his substitutionary atonement? Do they deny the literal bodily resurrection of the Master? Few Catholics or Protestants in the congregations have the theological acumen to actually know or explain why Mormons aren't Christian. It's just what they've heard and been taught.

By the way, I have witnessed with much interest how evangelical Christians (and I have many wonderful evangelical friends throughout the world) have, to a large extent, appropriated the word "Christian" to themselves, thus causing its meaning and perception to be changed quite drastically in everyday life. I have noticed this, for instance, on more than one occasion while speaking to a person about religious matters. I ask: "Are you a Christian?" only to be told: "No, I'm a Catholic." What a fascinating development! In the minds of these folks, clearly evangelicals or fundamentalists are Christian, while Catholics (from whom the Protestants broke away) are simply Catholics. In other words, to say "I'm not a Christian; I'm a Catholic" is to say "I'm not an evangelical or a fundamentalist."

Pre-Mortal Existence

One of the reasons I've been told that I am not a Christian is because of the unusual LDS view of Christ as God—our teachings (or lack of clarity in our teachings) concerning his eternal Godhood. Let's first turn our attention to the LDS view of the doctrine of pre-mortal existence. When Latter-day Saints read John 1:1–2, they understand it to mean the following: In the beginning, meaning in a pre-mortal existence, was the Word, that is, Jesus Christ. And the Word (Christ) was with God (the Father). And the Word was God; that is to say, Jesus Christ was God in the pre-mortal world, before he was born in Bethlehem of Judea. For Latter-day Saints, Jesus Christ is truly from everlasting to everlasting. He is, as stated on the title page of the Book of Mormon, "The Eternal God." He existed from eternity past, and he will exist into eternity future. His birth in Bethlehem was in actuality the beginning of phase two of his eternal ministry.

Mormons believe that that pre-mortal existence was not only a life before life for God and Christ and the Holy Spirit, but also a sphere of existence, a "first estate" (Jude 1:6) for each one of us. Joseph Smith taught that each man and woman born into this world was a spirit son or daughter of God in the pre-mortal existence; Jesus Christ was the firstborn spirit child of God. This is why you will occasionally hear Mormons refer to Jesus as our "Elder Brother," although the phrase and concept refer strictly to pre-existence and not to any other phase of God's plan. In that first estate, and as spirits with consciousness, identity, and moral agency (including the freedom to choose), we knew God, had association with him, and were taught of his plan of salvation and how we were to prepare for mortality.

To be sure, the idea of a pre-mortal existence of all men and women was not completely foreign to the early Christian church. Justin Martyr observed that "if the world is begotten, souls also are necessarily begotten; and perhaps at one time they were not in existence, for they were made on account of men and other living creatures, if you will say that they have been begotten wholly apart, and not along with their respective bodies."[1] Teachings attributed to the Apostle Peter include the following: "But after all these things [the creation of the earth] He made man, on whose account he had prepared all things, *whose internal species is older*, and for whose sake all things that are were made."[2] It was, of course, Origen who spoke most clearly and boldly about this concept. He taught that our spiritual receptivity in this life (or our lack of the same) is directly tied to our faithfulness in the world before.[3] God is just, Origen explained, and a person comes to earth "according to his merits; nor will the happiness or unhappiness of each one's birth, or whatever be the condition that falls to his lot, be deemed accidental." For example, Jacob, or Israel, became the holder of the birthright as a result of "the deserts of his previous life."[4] Though Origen was an important early teacher of Christian doctrine, the concept of the pre-mortal existence of souls and other teachings were condemned as "Anathemas Against Origen" in the mid-sixth century.

I have frequently spoken with extremely bright Christians about the doctrine of the Trinity in an earnest effort to better understand how three separate persons may be construed to be ontologically one, how three personalities can constitute one divine Being. Because I teach courses in Christian History occasionally, it is important to me that I represent properly the traditional Christian view of the doctrine of the Trinity. After long discussions on this topic, however, inevitably my interlocutor appeals to the doctrine of the Trinity as a "blessed mystery," something that finite mortals simply cannot fathom. I'm not turned off by this explanation, for I am the first to admit that there are many sacred things, many deep and penetrating topics that are of tremendous significance to those who believe in God and confess Jesus as Lord that cannot be properly articulated. Even efforts to create metaphors either fall short or pervert the intended meaning.

I say all of this to suggest that for me there is no inconsistency between Latter-day Saints believing Jesus Christ was the firstborn spirit child of God and yet that he is also the Eternal God. A commonly asked question by critics of the Latter-day Saints is: "Is it true that you believe that Jesus and Lucifer are brothers?" Well, we do believe in a pre-mortal existence

---

1. "Dialogue with Trypho," in *The Ante-Nicene Fathers*, ed. Alexander Roberts and James Donaldson (Grand Rapids: Eerdmans, 1951), 1:197.
2. From the "Clementine Recognitions," in *Ante-Nicene Fathers* 8:85, emphasis added.
3. See *Ante-Nicene Fathers* 4:336–37.
4. *Ante-Nicene Fathers* 4:292.

for all; that Lucifer was a spirit child of God just as Jesus was; and that they did, in fact, live in that same pre-mortal existence. But Jesus Christ was God, and there was never a time when Jesus and Lucifer were on the same plane. In a sense, I suppose, this would represent a kind of "blessed mystery" put forward by the Latter-day Saints, namely, that while Jesus was, in that first estate, our elder brother, he was also God and is certainly God today.

War in Heaven

The great plan of happiness, what the early apostles called the gospel of God (Rom. 1:1; 15:16; 1 Pet. 4:17), was the plan we were to follow in our efforts on earth to discover God, encounter his blessed Son, and engage the gospel of Jesus Christ with all our hearts. Bruce R. McConkie has written: "After this plan had been taught to all the hosts of heaven; after it was known and understood by all; after all its facets had been debated and evaluated—then the Father asked for a volunteer to put the full terms and all of the conditions of his plan into force."[5] The great question posed to the assembled spirits in the Grand Council in heaven was not, therefore, "What shall we do?" or "Does anyone here have any suggestions?" Rather, the question was simply, "Whom shall I send?"

Lucifer, one of the spirit sons of God, a "son of the morning," one who was "in authority in the presence of God" (D&C 76:25–26), said, "Behold, here am I, send me, I will be thy son, and I will redeem all mankind, that one soul shall not be lost, and surely I will do it; wherefore give me thine honor" (Moses 4:1). In contrast, the Firstborn replied: "Father, thy will be done, and the glory be thine forever" (Moses 4:2). These words, though brief, are poignant and all-sufficient: They are the words and the wisdom by which Jesus governed his life in both the pre-mortal and mortal realms. In the Garden of Gethsemane, Jesus pleaded: "O my Father, if it be possible let this cup pass from me: nevertheless not as I will, but as thou wilt" (Matt. 26:39). And as he breathed his last mortal breath, having descended below all things and trodden the winepress alone, "when he had cried again with a loud voice, [he said], Father, it is finished, thy will is done, [and he] yielded up the ghost" (Matt. 27:54, Joseph Smith's Translation [JST]).

Just how long the discussions and controversy raged in the pre-mortal realm between those who sustained the plan of the Father and those who accepted Lucifer's amendatory offer is not known. Surely, it must have been the topic of conversation and the subject of much teaching over an

5. McConkie, *The Promised Messiah* (Salt Lake City: Deseret Book, 1978), 49.

extended period. What was it that made Lucifer's words so appealing to so many, especially given how fundamental to the plan of salvation moral agency is? Knowing how competent and conniving Lucifer is today, we suppose he must have been extremely persuasive then. Joseph Smith explained: "The contention in heaven was—Jesus said there would be certain souls that would not be saved; and the devil said he could save them all, and laid his plans before the Grand Council, who gave their vote in favor of Jesus Christ. So the devil rose up in rebellion against God, and was cast down, with all who put up their heads for him."[6]

"And there was war in heaven: Michael and his angels fought against the dragon; and the dragon fought and his angels, and prevailed not; neither was their place found anymore in heaven" (Rev. 12:7–8). Lucifer and those we know today as demons were cast down to earth. These were the fallen angels, the ones who would tempt and taunt the sons and daughters of God and seek to thwart the plan of salvation. Then, as now, "the accuser of our brethren" was cast down and overcome by the blood of the Lamb and the testimony of Jesus (Rev. 12:10–11). Thereafter, the Firstborn was proclaimed as the Mediator for man and the Way to the Father; Christ was foreordained to be Lord and Savior of all humankind (1 Pet. 1:18–20), became "the Lamb slain from the foundation of the world" (Rev. 13:8; see also Moses 7:47), and the infinite atonement went into effect, even in that early day (see D&C 93:38).

Under the direction of the Father, who is designated by Joseph Smith as "God the First, the Creator,"[7] Christ created this world and all things on the face of it. In addition, Mormons believe, he became the creator of worlds without number (Moses 1:33; D&C 76:24). The people of the Book of Mormon were told that Jesus Christ is "the Lord Omnipotent," the "Father of heaven and earth, the Creator of all things from the beginning" (Mosiah 3:5, 8). To the people of the Book of Mormon called the Nephites, he declared: "Behold, I am Jesus Christ the Son of God. I created the heavens and the earth, and all things that in them are. I was with the Father from the beginning" (3 Nephi 9:15). As the Bible teaches, God the Father "created all things by Jesus Christ" (Eph. 3:9). He who was "appointed heir of all things" became the One "by whom also [God] made the worlds" (Heb. 1:2).

The God of Both Testaments

More than once I've been accused, as a Latter-day Saint, of being an Arian. This is silly. Arius taught that Jesus Christ was of a lesser

6. *TPJS*, 357.
7. *TPJS*, 190.

divinity than the Father, and Mormons believe no such thing. The man Jesus was and is he who was, he who is, he who will forevermore be. He is the self-existing One, he who causes to be, he who brings into existence. He manifested himself to Adam and Eve after the fall, revealed himself to Enoch (Moses 7:53) and to Noah (Moses 8:19), and he made known the plan of life and salvation to Abraham (see Gal. 3:8), Isaac, Jacob, and all of the other faithful souls in the Old Testament (see 1 Nephi 19:10). It was this Lord God Omnipotent who gave the Law of Moses to ancient Israel (3 Nephi 15:5) and who manifested himself to the people from the days of Samuel to the closing of the Old Testament with Malachi.

While it seems easy for some to see a difference between the God of the Old Testament (who is stern, inflexible, and vengeful) and the God of the New Testament (who is warm, loving, and inclusive), Latter-day Saints believe that Jehovah and Jesus are one and the same. One modern LDS apostle has taught:

> I make my own heartfelt declaration of God our Eternal Father this morning because some in the contemporary world suffer from a distressing misconception of Him. Among these there is a tendency to feel distant from the Father, even estranged from Him, if they believe in Him at all. And if they do believe, many moderns say they might feel comfortable in the arms of Jesus, but they are uneasy contemplating the stern encounter of God. . . .
>
> In reflecting on these misconceptions we realize that one of the remarkable contributions of the Book of Mormon is its seamless, perfectly consistent view of divinity throughout that majestic book. Here there is no Malachi-to-Matthew gap, no pause while we shift theological gears, no misreading the God who is urgently, lovingly, faithfully at work on every page of that record from its Old Testament beginning to its New Testament end. Yes, in an effort to give the world back its Bible and a correct view of Deity with it, what we have in the Book of Mormon is a uniform view of God in all His glory and goodness, all His richness and complexity—including and especially as again demonstrated through a personal appearance of His Only Begotten Son, Jesus Christ. . . .
>
> Jesus did not come to improve God's view of man nearly so much as He came to improve man's view of God and to plead with them to love their Heavenly Father as He has always and will always love them. The plan of God, the power of God, the holiness of God, yes, even the anger and the judgment of God they had occasion to understand. But the love of God, the profound depth of His devotion to His children, they still did not fully know—until Christ came.[8]

8. Jeffrey R. Holland, Conference Report, October 2003, 73–75.

Latter-day Saint Dispensationalism

One of the earliest distinctive doctrines Joseph Smith proclaimed was a rather unusual view of dispensationalism. He taught that a dispensation was a period of time in which the fullness of the plan of salvation and divine authority were dispensed by God to earth for the blessing of humanity. Mormons often speak, for example, of seven major dispensation heads: Adam, Enoch, Noah, Abraham, Moses, Jesus Christ, and Joseph Smith. The dispensation head is called to be the preeminent prophetic revealer of God and the plan of salvation. His voice becomes the mind and will and voice of the Almighty, and he stands as a prophet's prophet to the people. The prophets who follow the dispensation head bear a like witness and teach the same doctrine, their witness and doctrine being largely an echo of that of the dispensation head. In a modern revelation dictated to Joseph Smith are found these simple words: "This generation shall have my word through you" (D&C 5:10). Mormons believe that similar words could have, and perhaps were, spoken to each of the other dispensation heads. Now to be sure, while Christ is viewed as a prophet, he is, of course, the Great High Priest of our profession, the Son of the Living God, Emmanuel, God with us.

LDS doctrine thus asserts that Christian prophets have declared Christian doctrine and administered Christian ordinances or sacraments since the beginning of time. Consequently, Peter could say to Cornelius of Christ, "To him give all the prophets witness" (Acts 10:43). Likewise, Jesus could boldly proclaim to the leaders of the Jews that "Before Abraham was, I AM" (John 8:58). One Book of Mormon prophet put it this way: "Behold, I say unto you that none of the prophets have written, nor prophesied, save they have spoken concerning this Christ" (Jacob 7:11). Or to put this another way, bearing witness of Christ is the chief responsibility of a prophet, for as the Revelator explained, "the testimony of Jesus is the spirit of prophecy" (Rev. 19:10).

Three Brigham Young University religion professors and I sat with representatives of the Southern Baptist Convention in 1998 and had a fairly pleasant conversation for about two hours. Then one of our guests proceeded to criticize the Book of Mormon—questioning its origins, stressing how little archeological evidence there was for its peoples, and so forth. Then he said, "Besides, I have read through the Book of Mormon and cannot understand how Joseph Smith could be so ignorant as to have people centuries before the birth of Jesus speaking of and believing in Jesus. In other words," he said, "there's too much Christ in the Book of Mormon." I looked at my faculty colleagues, smiled, and remarked: "Now there's a fascinating indictment. I don't think I've heard that one before."

Of course, I understood what he meant—Mormons believe in Jesus before the coming of Jesus. In actuality, what we believe in is an everlasting gospel, an infinite and eternal atonement, one that is timeless. Thus, ancient prophets could preach concerning the coming of one Jesus the Christ long before he came into the flesh. They could call on people to exercise faith in the coming atonement, repent through the sacrificial offering and blood that would be shed in the meridian of time, and be baptized into the Church of Jesus Christ—all by virtue of the fact that his coming and atonement were foreknown, certain, and fixed in the mind of God and of God's people.

The story in the Book of Mormon begins in approximately 600 BC (in the first year of the reign of King Zedekiah) with the call of a man named Lehi to serve as a prophet. His son Nephi taught: "Six hundred years from the time that my father left Jerusalem, a prophet would the Lord God raise up among the Jews—even a Messiah, or in other words, a Savior of the world. And he also spake concerning the prophets, how great a number had testified of these things, concerning this Messiah, of whom he had spoken, or this Redeemer of the world, wherefore, all mankind were in a lost and in a fallen state, and ever would be save they should rely on this Redeemer" (1 Nephi 10:4–6). Similarly, another of Lehi's sons, Jacob, testified: "And he [Christ] cometh into the world that he may save all men if they will hearken unto his voice; for behold, he suffereth the pains of all men, yea, the pains of every living creature, both men, women, and children, who belong to the family of Adam" (2 Nephi 9:21).

This colony of people claimed to possess a fullness of the gospel of Jesus Christ but, inasmuch as they had come from Jerusalem to America and had lived under the law of Moses before their departure, they kept the law and at the same time looked forward to its fulfillment in Christ. "Wherefore, the prophets, and the priests, and the teachers, did labor diligently, exhorting with all long-suffering the people to diligence; teaching the law of Moses, and the intent for which it was given; persuading them to look forward unto the Messiah, and believe in him to come as though he already was. And after this manner did they teach them" (Jarom 1:11).

One or two other examples of Book of Mormon statements about Christ will indicate just how central to the record the name and work of Jesus are. Approximately 125 years before the birth of Jesus, one prophet-king named Benjamin explained that "the natural man is an enemy to God, and has been from the fall of Adam, and will be, forever and ever, unless he yields to the enticings of the Holy Spirit, and putteth off the natural man and becometh a saint through the atonement of Christ the Lord" (Mosiah 3:19). As an earlier prophet declared, "My soul delighteth in proving unto my people the truth of the coming of Christ; for, for this end hath the law of Moses been given; and all things which have been given of God from the beginning of the world, unto man, are the typifying of him. . . . And my soul delighteth in proving unto my people that save Christ should come all men must perish. For if there be no Christ, there be no God; and if there be no God we are not, for there could have been no creation. But there is a God, and he is Christ, and he cometh in the fulness of his own time" (2 Nephi 11:4, 6–7). In short, "we talk of Christ, we rejoice in Christ, we preach of Christ, we prophesy of Christ, and we write according to our prophecies, that our children may know to what source they may look for a remission of their sins" (2 Nephi 25:26).

Even if one cannot accept Joseph Smith's explanation for the coming forth of the Book of Mormon or cannot accept the book as holy scripture, a casual perusal of the text will reveal just how Christocentric it is. One of my colleagues, Susan Easton Black, conducted a statistical analysis of the Book of Mormon to determine how often the name or work of Jesus Christ was mentioned. Even she was surprised to learn that Christ or his ministry is mentioned approximately every 1.7 verses. He is called by many titles, including Almighty, Almighty God, Alpha and Omega, Beloved Son, Christ, Christ Jesus, Christ the Son, Creator, Eternal Father, Eternal God, Eternal Head, Eternal Judge, Everlasting Father, Everlasting God, Father of Heaven and of Earth, Founder of Peace, and many others.

The majority of the Book of Mormon story takes place before Jesus's mortal birth (400+ pages out of 531 speak of him who is to come). In addition, and Latter-day Saints believe as a fulfillment of his promise in Jerusalem to visit his "other sheep which are not of this fold" (John 10:16) that the Book of Mormon speaks of the coming of Jesus to this branch of American Hebrews—of his appearing to some 2,500 people; of their being allowed to feel the nail marks in his hands and in his feet; of his delivering a sermon very similar to the Sermon on the Mount; of his healing the sick and blessing a multitude of children; of his institution of the sacrament of the Lord's Supper; of his teachings concerning the destiny of the House of Israel; of his quotation of Isaiah, Micah, and Malachi; of the establishment of the Church of Jesus Christ and the ordination of his servants; and of his ascension into heaven in approximately AD 34.

Conclusion

From an LDS perspective, the story of Jesus Christ does not begin in the manger, with the shepherds, or later with the coming of the wise men.

Rather, the story of Jesus has no beginning, for he has no beginning. He is the Eternal God. Moreover, and we will speak of this at greater length later, Latter-day Saints take seriously the idea that the blessings of the atonement of Jesus Christ are available to all. As one Nephite prophet asked his son: "Is not a soul at this time [about 73 BC] as precious unto God as a soul will be at the time of his coming? Is it not as necessary that the plan of redemption should be made known unto this people as well as unto their children [i.e., when the Savior comes in the flesh]? Is it not as easy at this time for the Lord to send his angel to declare these glad tidings unto us as unto our children, or as after the time of his coming? (Alma 39:17–19). In short, God does not do "anything save it be for the benefit of the world; for he loveth the world, even that he layeth down his own life that he may draw all men unto him. Wherefore, he commandeth none that they shall not partake of his salvation. . . . He saith: Come unto me all ye ends of the earth, buy milk and honey, without money and without price" (2 Nephi 26:24–25).

I have taken the time to quote specific passages from the Book of Mormon for at least two reasons: (1) because the Book of Mormon story purports to take place, as I mentioned earlier, before the first advent of the Savior in the flesh; and (2) to give some slight indication of why it is painfully incongruous for a typical Latter-day Saint to be told that he or she is not a Christian. People may disagree with what the Book of Mormon is, but they can hardly claim that its content does not proclaim the centrality of Christian redemption through the Father's plan of salvation. As is true with any religious organization, there is much about the faith that is rumor, urban legend, or apocrypha. The reader may disagree here and there, but that's part of the learning process. We can disagree, but let's at least disagree on the right stuff. Archbishop Fulton Sheen once wrote: "There are not over a hundred people in the United States who hate the Roman Catholic Church; there are millions, however, who hate what they wrongly believe to be the Catholic Church."[9]

And so it is with the Mormon faith. My purpose in this chapter, as well as in the entire book, is not to convince the readers that they should walk where I walk; it is to invite them to stand in my shoes for a season at least, and then to be in a position to make a meaningful and informed assessment of LDS Christianity.

9. Cited in Scott and Kimberly Hahn, *Rome Sweet Home* (San Francisco: Ignatius Press, 1993), xi.

An Evangelical Response

Gerald McDermott

I'm afraid I am one of those who has misunderstood and misrepresented Mormons. I told the story in the Introduction of how I mistreated a distinguished Mormon historian when he came to speak to my class more than a decade ago. Besides treating him rudely, I did not understand how central Jesus Christ was to his faith and to the LDS Church generally. As I remember it, I suspected he wasn't telling me the whole truth when he insisted he was trusting in Jesus for his salvation, and I suggested as much to my class by my repeated counter-assertions and questions.

I have since learned that, as Professor Millet demonstrates in the preceding essay, Jesus Christ is indeed at the center of Mormon faith. As I have learned from my own reading of the Book of Mormon, Jesus Christ is central to the story, and this centrality is epitomized by 2 Nephi 25:26: "We talk of Christ, we rejoice in Christ, we preach of Christ, we prophesy of Christ, and we write according to our prophecies, that our children may know to what source they may look for a remission of their sins" (2 Nephi 25:26). That verse alone says a lot—that Christ is at the center of Nephi's consciousness, and it is through Christ that he seeks forgiveness of his sons. I will suggest in chapter 3 that the Mormon view of Jesus Christ is different from that of evangelicals and other orthodox Christians, but the fact remains that Christ is central to LDS consciousness. I am struck by Susan Black's calculation that Christ or his ministry is mentioned on the average of every 1.7 verses in the Book of Mormon.

Two more verses that would surprise evangelicals who have been led to believe that all Mormon doctrine is totally wrong on Jesus are 2 Nephi 11:4 and 7. These passages assert plainly that there is no salvation apart from Jesus Christ: "And my soul delighteth in proving unto my people that save Christ should come all men must perish." They also proclaim that Christ is God: "But there is *a God*, and he is Christ."[10] This and many other passages in the Book of Mormon prove clearly that the Mormon Jesus is not Arian (less than fully God), despite the belief of many evangelicals and other Christians.

Evangelicals should be thankful for a host of other Mormon declarations about Jesus that Professor Millet detailed—that his suffering and death save us, that we are cleansed of our sins by his atonement and resurrection, and that his sufferings were endured for the sake of all human beings (2 Nephi 9:21). In good evangelical fashion, the Book of Mormon proclaims that "the natural man is an enemy to God, and has been from the fall of Adam" and that that will never end until he "putteth off the natural man and becometh a saint through the atonement of Christ the Lord" (Mosiah 3:19). It declares that "all mankind were in a lost and in a fallen state, and ever would be save they should rely on this Redeemer" (1 Nephi 10:4–6). In other words, every human being must trust personally in the Redeemer for salvation.

Some Mormon emphases are, in fact, theological improvements to some contemporary evangelical beliefs. Many evangelicals, for example, see little connection between the Old and New Testaments, or at best see the Old as a lower-level launching pad for, or prelude to, the higher revelation of the New. Part of the reason for this often at best benign view of the Old Testament is the assumption that while the Old Testament is about the wrathful Father who gives us his cold law, the New Testament is about meek Jesus who offers us warm love.

The reality is far different. The Father is also warm and tender in the Old Testament (think of Psalm 23), and Jesus can be wrathful and forbidding in the New (he wields a two-edged sword in Revelation 1). But more importantly, Jesus told his disciples on the road to Emmaus that he was in "all the scriptures" of the Old Testament (Luke 24:27). Paul implied the same, suggesting at one point that the rock that followed the Israelites wandering in the wilderness was really Christ (1 Cor. 10:4).

The *prisca theologia* tradition, found especially in the Reformed tradition from the seventeenth through the early nineteenth centuries, taught something very similar: that God told Adam and Eve about the coming Messiah and salvation through his death, and that these and other "Christian" truths were passed down by tradition to the patriarchs and Noah's sons, and then, through the latter, to the fathers of all the nations.

10. Emphasis added. This also suggests that Joseph Smith at the time of the Book of Mormon believed there was only one God, and that the three persons were not three separate Gods—which suggests he changed his mind later. More on that in chapter 3.

One upshot of this was that after the fall, the Father delegated all direct contact with sinful humanity to the Son, since he was the Mediator. Hence, every communication from God to humans, such as the voice at the burning bush, was coming from the Son.[11] The Son therefore is the major character of the Old Testament.

This tradition is largely lost today and nearly absent among evangelicals except among some Reformed evangelical groups. But in LDS literature it is alive and well. Professor Millet points out a running theme in the Book of Mormon, that the prophets of old, before the incarnation, taught "Christian truths." Not only is Christ the central subject of the Book of Mormon, most of whose events precede the incarnation, but the Mormons also believe Jesus is the central subject of, and actor in, the Old Testament. I think Mormons misstep when they say he is Jehovah, for it seems to me and most other scholars that the Hebrew word "YHWH" that is translated as "Jehovah" is the same person in the Godhead whom Jesus called "Father." But the fact that they see the Son on nearly every page of the Old Testament is theologically refreshing. For it sees the Old Testament the way Jesus and his apostles saw it—full of the Christ, not only prefigured but also speaking and acting. "All things . . . are the typifying of him" (2 Nephi 11:4).

A second point of theological truth that we see in the Book of Mormon is the repeated attribution of creation to Jesus Christ, which Professor Millet has shown. Of course, we differ in what we mean by creation. Historic Christianity has held to *creatio ex nihilo* (creation from nothing), whereas Mormons believe God reshaped matter that always existed. But many evangelicals believe creation was exclusively the work of the Father, despite the fact that scripture clearly states that the Father worked through the Son (John 1:3; Col. 1:16) and suggests the involvement of the Spirit (e.g., Gen. 1:2). Mormons are more emphatic about the former and thus closer to the Bible on the instrumentality—if not the nature—of creation.

Finally, Mormons are not afraid to say politically incorrect things in theology. In an era when even evangelicals, who should know better, shy away from talking about hell and the devil, Mormons talk openly about both. I commend them because these are biblically important realities that the spirit of the age does not like to hear. Yet, as Professor Millet relates, in the King Follett Discourse, Joseph Smith taught that the devil promised salvation for everyone, but Jesus warned that some would not be saved. Universal salvation is a doctrine particularly popular today

11. For more on the *prisca theologia*, see McDermott, *Jonathan Edwards Confronts the Gods* (New York: Oxford University Press, 2000), ch. 5; McDermott, *God's Rivals: Why God Allows Different Religions* (Downers Grove, IL: InterVarsity Press, 2007), chs. 5 and 7.

but hard to reconcile with dominical teachings about the reality of a populated hell (Matt. 8:12; 13:42; 22:13; 24:51; 25:30, 46). Although some popular evangelical writers are leery of talking about hell,[12] Professor Millet and other Mormons are not so shy. At the same time, I don't think my Mormon friends go far enough, as I will explain further in chapter 8. That is, I am glad that, unlike liberal Christians today, they are willing to recognize the reality of the devil and say that not everyone is saved or receives full salvation. But by the time they explain all the ways in which unbelievers in this life can have other chances in the next to enter one of their three spheres, it comes close to universalism.

All this being said *for* what Professor Millet has said, I must also say that there are points at which I disagree. First, while Bob tells us more than once that Jesus Christ is God, he does not make clear whether Jesus in the Mormon view was *always* God. As I argue in the next chapter, there is plenty in the Mormon canon and other LDS literature to suggest that Jesus grew into his Godhood. In his King Follett Discourse, Joseph Smith famously said that "God himself was once as we are now." This discourse is not in the LDS canon, but there are similar statements in the canon: Jesus is portrayed as maturing until he became "like unto God" (Abraham 3.24). Bob himself has written recently that "as a premortal spirit, Jehovah [Jesus] grew in knowledge and power to the point where he became 'like unto God.'"[13] So while evangelicals and Mormons see eye to eye on many things about Jesus, they see very differently on the origins of Jesus: Latter-day Saints believe Jesus once was not God and then became God, while evangelicals see the scriptures teaching that he was always God. As Athanasius taught during the Arian controversy, there never was a time when Jesus as God was not.

For this reason, it is not clear to me what Professor Millet means when he concludes that Jesus "is the Eternal God." According to the *Random House College Dictionary*, "eternal" means "lasting forever; without beginning or end." Even Joseph Smith seemed to suggest that anything that is eternal had no beginning.[14] Thus my question: If Jesus was the eternal God, wouldn't that mean he was just that from before the beginning of time? Yet all the Mormon literature I have seen points in the opposite direction—that Jesus became God at some point in time. This seems

12. In *The Last Word and the Word After That* (San Francisco: Jossey-Bass, 2005), Brian McLaren's fictional pastor makes a more convincing argument for universalism (the idea that all people are saved) than for any orthodox alternative.

13. Millet, *A Different Jesus?* 20.

14. *TPJS*, 181.

to be the answer to my question, but would seem to limit the adjective "eternal" to the meaning "with no end."[15]

There are other assertions in Professor Millet's essay that I find both unbiblical and unpersuasive. First is the idea of pre-existence for human souls. Origen did indeed teach this, but, as Professor Millet concedes, the universal church has denounced it, and not just once but in three ecumenical councils (Council of Alexandria in 400; Council of Constantinople 543; Second Council of Constantinople 553). Almost all Christians have found it to be lacking either biblical or philosophical support. It seems to be based on an unbiblical dualism of body and spirit, thus implicitly rejecting the Hebraic emphasis on the unity of body and soul. I imagine this is disconcerting for some Mormons who reflect on the LDS attempt to be faithful to the Bible and reject post-biblical creeds.

None of the citations adduced in support of this is convincing. The quotation from Justin Martyr does not clearly teach this, and it is found in the midst of a discourse by Justin in which he repeatedly takes issue with Platonic philosophy, which made this doctrine one of its staples. Neither does the excerpt from the *Clementine Recognitions* manifestly teach pre-mortal existence. Besides, this document is now known to have come from an Arian splinter group, and so cannot be said to represent "the early Christian church."[16]

I have already mentioned Mormon rejection of *creatio ex nihilo*. Doctrines and Covenants teaches that "the elements are eternal" (93.33). According to *The Encyclopedia of Mormonism*, Joseph Smith said that "the spirit of man is not a created being; it existed from eternity" (2:867). For Mormons, therefore, Jesus was Creator, but not as historic Christianity has imagined it. Our human spirits were never created out of nothing, but instead always existed. Smith explained that the word "create" has been misunderstood by traditional Christianity:

> The word create . . . does not mean to create out of nothing; it means to organize; the same as a man would organize materials and build a ship. Hence we infer that God had materials to organize the world out of chaos—chaotic matter, which is element. (EOM 2:868)

I mention this Mormon understanding of creation in order to clarify what Mormons mean when they say that Jesus was Creator, along with the Father. They did not create out of nothing, as historically understood

---

15. Some have thought this means Mormons believe in an Arian view of Christ (a being less than God but more than human). But this is clearly not the case. The Mormon Christ is fully God. What I am questioning is their view of whether Christ ever became God.

16. See "Clementines," *Catholic Encyclopedia*, at http://www.newadvent.org/cathen/04039b.htm.

by the Christian church and, I would add, as suggested by the Bible (e.g., Heb. 11:3; Rom. 4:7).

Lastly, I have a little quibble about my friend's characterization of evangelicals. But first let me say that I appreciate the effort he shows here and elsewhere to be fair to evangelical beliefs. For example, I appreciate his intellectual honesty in saying in this chapter, in effect, "Yes, my evangelical friends are right to say that some things are mysteries that cannot be rationally codified. So their defense of the Trinity as mysterious should not be dismissed out of hand by Mormons." In this respect he works harder to be fair than many of us evangelicals have done in our treatment of Mormons.

But then, toward the beginning of his essay in this chapter, Professor Millet describes evangelicals as representing "the far right of the theological spectrum." I have always regarded fundamentalists in that position rather than evangelicals, as I explained in the Introduction. I won't rehearse all those points again, but suffice it to say that evangelicals engage secular culture and their theological opponents more than fundamentalists do, and see several different layers to scripture. For example, evangelicals, far more than do fundamentalists, read Genesis 1–2 more as a theological document than a scientific one. Also, evangelicals are far less separatist than fundamentalists, who tend to separate themselves from liberal Christians (which sometimes means evangelicals) and even from conservatives who associate with liberals. Besides, fundamentalists would never join a dialogue like this with Mormons.

On balance, however, I want to conclude with my happy agreement with Professor Millet that Jesus is God and is the only way to salvation (although evangelicals and Mormons disagree on what these things mean). These two points alone are extremely significant, and in themselves they make a promising starting point for a discussion of Jesus.

Rebuttal and Concluding Thoughts

Robert Millet

Clearly, both Latter-day Saints and evangelicals believe that Jesus Christ existed before the world and that he was a member of the Godhead before this world was created. He was God for centuries and millennia prior to his birth in Bethlehem, and, as LDS teachings and the *prisca theologia* tradition suggest, God has been at work informing and inspiring his children through the generations, leading them toward faith, all before the coming of Jesus in the flesh.

While we will discuss the nature of the Godhead or Trinity in more detail in the next chapter, it might be worthwhile to make a few observations here. Yes, Latter-day Saints do believe that Jesus was the firstborn spirit Son of God and that over time in a pre-mortal existence he grew to become "like unto God." And yes, this does bring into question the extent to which Latter-day Saints believe that he was always God. But I would ask a rather simple question: To what extent does it truly matter whether Jesus was always God or at a certain point in the pre-mortal realm he became God? If in fact he was God and could be known and worshipped by the prophets, could reveal the mind of heaven to the ancient house of Israel, and could lead his covenant spokesmen and his covenant people, what difference does it really make whether he was not always God? This is not an effort to resort to Arianism or to adopt the position held by Jehovah's Witnesses—Jesus was never a lesser divinity or a secondary form of God; when he was God, he was God. If we know that he is now one with the Father in all things—in mind, in thought, in purpose, indeed, in all things—why should it matter to us that he is in fact as the scriptures refer to him scores of times, the Son of God?

Then how do we reconcile this with the New Testament teaching
that Christ is the same yesterday, today, and forever, and with the Book
of Mormon itself that teaches that he is the Eternal God? Professor
McDermott points out from one dictionary that *eternal* means "lasting
forever; without beginning or end." In fact, this is but one of the defini-
tions of eternal. What is also true is that the Hebrew word *olam* and the
Greek word *aeon* may represent an era, a long period of time, a lengthy
season. For Latter-day Saints, the word *eternal* may be used in more
than an adjectival sense. The words *endless* and *eternal* are also nouns,
synonyms for God himself. Notice, for example, the following from the
Doctrine and Covenants:

> And surely every man must repent or suffer, for I, God, am endless. . . .
> Nevertheless, it is not written that there shall be no end to this torment,
> but it is written *endless torment*. Again, it is written *eternal damnation*;
> wherefore it is more express than other scriptures, that it might work
> upon the hearts of the children of men, altogether for my name's glory.
> For, behold, the mystery of godliness, how great is it! For, behold, I am
> endless, and the punishment which is given from my hand is endless
> punishment, for Endless is my name. Wherefore—Eternal punishment is
> God's punishment. Endless punishment is God's punishment. (D&C 19:6–7,
> 11–12; compare Moses 1:3; 7:35).

As Stephen Robinson pointed out some years ago, "In both Hebrew
and Greek the words for 'eternity' . . . denote neither an endless linear
time nor a state outside of time, but rather 'an age,' an 'epic,' 'a long
time,' . . . even 'a lifetime,' or 'a generation'—always a measurable period
of time rather than endless time or timelessness. . . . It was only in post-
Biblical times and mainly under the influence of Greek philosophy that
the concept of eternity (or forever) as endless time, or timelessness, or
as a state outside of time replaced the original meaning of a period, or
of an age."[17]

All I can do is speak personally, but I affirm that my witness of Christ,
as well as my ready acknowledgement of his majesty, magnificence, and
infinity is no less than if I believed he had been so forevermore. For both
of our faith traditions, Christ-Messiah is God. That is the message of
messages, the doctrine of doctrines. My adoration or worship of him is
not dependent on when or how or under what circumstances he became
God. All that matters to me is that he is the Anointed One, the Promised
Messiah, the Captain of my Salvation, my Lord and God.

17. Robinson, "Eternities That Come and Go," *BYU Religious Studies Center Newsletter*
8, no. 3 (May 1994), 1.

3

JESUS, GOD, AND US

The Trinity and God's Oneness

Gerald McDermott

Evangelicals and Mormons agree on lots of things about Jesus. Many evangelicals are surprised to learn, for example, that Mormons believe not only that Jesus is the Son of God but also that he is God the Son. I find that many evangelicals have somewhere picked up the idea that Mormons deny the deity of Jesus Christ. They are often amazed to learn that, unlike Jehovah's Witnesses and other groups they typically classify as "cults," which do indeed deny the deity of Christ, Mormons declare emphatically that Jesus was and is incarnate God. As Professor Millet puts it, Jesus is "the Only Begotten Son in the Flesh."[1]

Professor Millet goes on to say that Jesus didn't just teach the truth but *is* the truth. He didn't just *bring* resurrection; He *is* the resurrection and life.[2]

In 2001, pollster George Barna told us that only 33 percent of American Catholics, Lutherans, and Methodists, and 28 percent of Episcopalians agreed with the statement that Christ was without sin. Mormons, on the other hand, teach straightforwardly that while Jesus was fully human, he never sinned, and, according to Barna, they were among the "most likely" to say that Jesus was sinless.[3] Liberal Christians have been denying the virgin birth of Jesus and his bodily resurrection for more than

---

1. Millet, *A Different Jesus?* 66.
2. Ibid., 69.
3. Ibid., 74; see also Robert L. Millet, "Overview," in "Jesus Christ," *Encyclopedia of Mormonism: The History, Scripture, Doctrine, and Procedure of The Church of Jesus Christ of Latter-day Saints,* ed. Daniel H. Ludlow (New York: Macmillan, 1992), 2:724. This 4-volume encyclopedia will subsequently be cited as *EOM.* For Barna's statistics, see "The Barna Update: Religious Beliefs Vary Widely By Denomination," June 25, 2001, http://www.barna.org/FlexPage.aspx?Page=BarnaUpdate&BarnaUpdateID=92.

a century, but Mormons emphatically affirm both. Other commonalities, such as our common agreement that Jesus's passion is what saves us, that we don't save ourselves by our works, and that the Gospels are reliable sources for Jesus's life and teaching, will become clear in later chapters. Thus, I have to say that evangelical agreement with Professor Millet on Jesus is significant and, when compared to a history of evangelical denunciations of Mormonism, remarkable.

But does Stephen Robinson's declaration of evangelicalism's and Mormonism's "common devotion to the Christ of the New Testament"[4] go too far?

I think it may.

I will argue in this chapter that while there is considerable (and important) overlap in evangelical and Mormon views of Jesus, there is also considerable difference. The result of the difference, as I see it, is that I cannot say with complete confidence that the Jesus whom Mormons worship is "the Christ of the New Testament." To be more precise, Mormons accept the Jesus of the New Testament as a religious and historical figure, the same one evangelicals worship, but their understanding of Jesus differs because of revelations they believe to have come in the last two centuries.

Now don't get me wrong. *Much* of the LDS Christ is the same as the Christ of the New Testament. But it is precisely where Mormons follow Joseph Smith, especially in his later sermons and writings, that they picture a Jesus who diverges from the Christ of the New Testament.

In short, each of the following Mormon beliefs about Jesus differs from evangelical (and generally orthodox) doctrine: the Mormon Jesus is a different God from the Father; he is one of (at least) three Gods; he was a man who once was not God; his nature is the same as ours; he is one whose nature and fullness we ourselves can attain; and he does not transcend the cosmos.

In all of these respects, this view of Jesus is different from that seen by evangelicals and other orthodox when they worship the Christ of the New Testament.

A Different God

Mormons deny that Jesus is a member of the Trinity. They insist that they still believe that God is both three and one, but simply disagree with the early creeds that rendered that three-in-oneness as "Trinity." They say they believe every word of the New Testament but do not find

4. Robinson, in Blomberg and Robinson, *How Wide the Divide?* 141.

those words suggesting what the orthodox church has conceived in its classic Trinitarian formulas.

The basic difference lies in the relationship between Jesus and the Father. Mormons say Jesus is a different *being* from the Father, and in fact a different God (we will treat that in just a bit). The orthodox say Jesus is of the *same* being with the Father, and so is the same God but a different person within the Godhead.

We evangelicals, along with all other Christians of the orthodox persuasion, believe this difference is very important. Among our reasons for saying this is the observation that, as Sinclair Ferguson has put it, Jesus spent his last hours with his disciples, as the world was about to collapse upon them all, talking about Father, Son, and Holy Spirit, and how they relate to one another.[5]

But we also recognize that talking about the Trinity is risky. According to Augustine, in no other subject is error more dangerous. That may be why Calvin said it is more important for us to adore the Trinity than to investigate it. Or why Bernard Lonergan quipped, "The Trinity is a matter of five notions, four relations, three persons, two processions, one substance or nature, and no understanding."[6]

Of course Lonergan was speaking hyperbolically, for he himself wrote all sorts of things about what the Trinity does and does not mean. The orthodox church has never claimed to have comprehensive understanding of the Trinity, but has insisted that we can have limited understanding of what is finally a mystery. From its early days, the church has rejected tritheism ("three gods," which is one way of describing the Mormon view), and for two reasons. First, both the Old and New Testaments insist repeatedly that there is only one God. Second, Jesus makes statements that suggest he is the same being or God as the Father—"Don't you believe that I am in the Father, and the Father is in me?" and "He who has seen me, has seen the Father" (John 14:10, 9).

The historic Christian churches also say that the Trinity is at the very center of their faith and has important implications for ethics and for interreligious dialogue.

For theologians such as Jonathan Edwards, the moral life is not something we try hard to do "down here" in order to be worthy of our calling. No, it is different by a quantum-leap: it is actually participation in the mystical communion among the three persons of the Trinity. This means that all human love is a refraction of the love among the three divine persons. When a Christian loves her neighbor, she not only imi-

---

5. Ferguson, email to Robert Letham, quoted in Letham, *The Holy Trinity: In Scripture, History, Theology, and Worship* (Phillipsburg: P&R Publishing, 2004), 1.

6. Augustine, *De Trinitate* 1.3.5; Lonergan quoted in Letham, 1.

tates God's love in Christ but participates in the mutual love between the Father and the Son. To love the neighbor, then, is not simply to be like God but to *have* God.

This conception of love cannot work on the Mormon model, in which there are three different Gods. The New Testament tells us that Christians participate in the divine nature (2 Pet. 1:4). If that is the case, and love is an instance of that participation, but there are three different Gods, which God's nature do we participate in? Not only does this puzzle show why this participation model will not work in the Mormon view of the Godhead, but to my knowledge no Mormon theologian makes a claim similar to Edwards's. Please don't misunderstand me: I am not saying Mormons cannot love with God's love. Mormons are some of the most loving people I know. What I *am* saying is that they cannot *conceive* of love as participation in the very life of the Godhead, as those can who see God as one but also as a society of three persons.

The Trinity also has implications for inter-religious dialogue. This is because the most compelling religious alternatives to Christian faith today are deism,[7] Islam, and Eastern monisms, which are variations of Hinduism, Buddhism, and Daoism that teach the ultimate *oneness* of all things (this is not monotheism, which says there is only one God). Both LDS and orthodox Christian churches can point to their Godheads as able to make sense of multiplicity. Monism, on the other hand, cannot explain coherently why there seems to be more than one thing—in fact, many things—in the cosmos. Nor can the undifferentiated unity in Muslims' Allah and the deist God explain why we humans sense an underlying unity in the cosmos at the same time that we are convinced of multiplicity. They can show us why there is unity, since there is one God, but they can say very little about how the many relate to the one. Nor can philosophical postmodernism, which is the West's most attractive secular rival to religion today—or, for that matter, spiritual postmodernism, which is a compelling rival to "organized religion" today. Postmodernism as a worldview celebrates diversity but has a very difficult time telling us if and why there could be an underlying one among the many. In fact, postmoderns are fond of saying there is no "metanarrative" (overarching story) that can connect all the many things of the cosmos.

Mormons can point to unity of purpose among their three Gods (Father, Son, and Holy Spirit) as a way to help explain unity in diversity. But

7. This is the idea, first made popular in the eighteenth century, that God and heaven are a long way off and have very little to do with us day to day. This is why, as Tom Wright points out, many say they believe in God but don't go to church or pray or think much about God. N. T. Wright, *Simply Christian: Why Christianity Makes Sense* (San Francisco: HarperSanFrancisco, 2006), 62–63.

the Christian Trinity does a better job. It says that unity is far deeper than simply having a common purpose. The Father, Son, and Spirit are actually one in being; they are together, mysteriously, only one God. Yet amidst that one God are three persons. Real difference in profound unity.

I must concede that this is a weak argument for the reality of the Trinity. But its purpose is not to prove the Trinity. Instead, I am merely highlighting why the orthodox church says the Trinity is significant. Among other things, it describes reality more fittingly than tritheism or henotheism.[8] The truth is that reality *is* both one and many, and the Trinity does a better job of making sense of both than any of its religious or secular alternatives.

But it is not just for these reasons that I favor the Trinity over the Mormon understanding of the three persons. With other evangelicals and orthodox Christians, I think the Trinity, which involves only one God, makes better sense of the biblical story than does the Mormon testimony to three different deities.

It also seems to me that the Mormon account itself contains problems. For example, Stephen Robinson and other Mormon theologians say that almost all references to "God" and "Father" in the Old Testament refer, in fact, to Jesus. So too for "Yahweh" and "Jehovah."[9] They are two more names for Jesus Christ. Do not these assertions point to a unity among the three that is deeper than merely "oneness of mind, purpose and intent"?[10] If the Father and Jesus are really different Gods, why would the Bible (which the Holy Ghost inspired) use the same name for two different beings? Why would Jesus be called "Father" if they are two distinct Gods? Doesn't it make more sense to think of them as being the same God if they are both called "Father"? It is for this reason that I say the names used by Mormon theologians and the Book of Mormon point to a Trinity rather than the Mormon notion of three Gods.

The other internal problem is in the Book of Mormon, where a surprising number of passages contain language that boldly asserts God's oneness. 2 Nephi 31:21, for example, speaks of "the only and true doctrine of the Father, and of the Son, and of the Holy Ghost, which is *one* God, without end." So too do Alma 11.44 and Mormon 7.7. We will see later in this chapter that near the end of his life, in writings that are not part of the official LDS canon but are often cited by Mormon writers, Joseph Smith declared that the three persons in the Godhead are three distinct Gods. Yet in the Book of Mormon we see these and other assertions that there is only one God.

8. Henotheism is the notion that there is more than one God, but that one is chief over all others.
9. Robinson, in Blomberg and Robinson, *How Wide the Divide?* 134; *EOM* 2:741.
10. Robinson, in Blomberg and Robinson, *How Wide the Divide?* 125, 129.

Strangely, it is at this very point of what evangelicals call doctrinal error that Mormons might be of service to the orthodox tradition. For their over-emphasis on divine plurality might help correct our own (i.e., the entire Western orthodox tradition's) over-emphasis on divine simplicity. By the latter I mean that the West has been so eager to emphasize the oneness of God that God's threeness has sometimes nearly been lost.

This may have been the way Augustine and his successors guarded the faith against recurring Arianism. By insisting that all the divine attributes were common to each of the three, they protected the notion that the second of the three was fully equal to the first. But the unfortunate result was a recurring risk of modalism—the heresy that God is only one person, and the three are simply different forms the one person took at different points in history. Augustine, for example, in his aversion to both Arianism and tritheism, doubted whether it is "possible for us, who are compelled to explain and to reason about the Trinity, to say three persons."[11] In Augustine's Trinity, there are distinctions, "but in the end they do not constitute a community."[12] Calvin and many other Reformed theologians were also reluctant to use the word "persons" for the three, resorting instead, like Thomas, to "modes" of "subsistence" to explain the relation between one essence and three *hypostases* (a Greek word for "person"). Even Rahner and Barth, who helped resurrect Trinitarianism in Christian theology, tend to suggest that there is finally only one person in God. The implication of all these ways of describing the three is that they are merely varying modes of one divine person.

The problem with starting with God's essence, as did Augustine and much of the West, is that it suggests that there is something impersonal in God before the three persons. Moreover, following exclusive use of the psychological model (which uses the threefold structure of the human mind as an analogy for the Trinity), the Holy Spirit becomes simply the bond of love between the first two persons, which tends to reduce the Spirit to something less than a person.

If Mormons go too far by teaching a full-blooded tritheism, they nevertheless remind us that we will never be true to the biblical testimony unless we make plurality within the Godhead central to our theology.

Which gets us back to the point of this first section—that the Mormon view of Jesus is different because it rejects the Jesus of the Trinity, who is not a separate God but the second person within the one God.

11. *De Trinitate* 7.3.
12. Krister Sairsingh, "Jonathan Edwards and the Idea of Divine Glory: His Foundational Trinitarianism and its Ecclesial Import," Ph.D. diss. (Harvard University, 1986), 72.

One of (at Least) Several Gods

Not only is Jesus the second person of the Trinity, but he is also the only God there is. The Mormon perspective, in contrast, is that Jesus is one of several (or more) Gods.

Robinson denies that Mormonism is polytheistic,[13] and strictly speaking he is right. Polytheism portrays a world in which competing gods either vie for ultimate authority or have delimited provinces over which they rule. The Mormon picture is closer to henotheism, which posits a supreme God over other lesser, subordinate gods. The Latter-day Saints say that the Father is at least functionally over the Son and the Holy Ghost, and that they are the only Gods with which we have to do.

Contemporary LDS authorities speak of God in the plural. Professor Millet says our goal is to strive to be "one with the Gods."[14] The *Encyclopedia of Mormonism* proclaims that there is a Mother in Heaven, who is like the Heavenly Father "in glory, perfection, compassion, wisdom and holiness." God "is plural," it declares.[15]

Mormon belief in the "plurality of the Gods" goes back to Joseph Smith's later sermons, especially his sermon at King Follett's funeral in 1844. This sermon is not part of the official Mormon scriptures, but, as Robinson put it, its views have by now become semi-official and are regarded as normative in the LDS Church.[16]

In this sermon Smith made some remarkable statements that seem to affirm henotheism without using the word: "The head God called together the Gods and sat in grand council to bring forth the world. . . . In the beginning, the head of the Gods called a council of the Gods. . . . The doctrine of a plurality of Gods is as prominent in the Bible as any other doctrine. . . . In the beginning the heads of the Gods organized the heavens and the earth."[17]

Not only did Smith teach a plurality of Gods, but he also pronounced that the plurality extends before the Father of Jesus Christ: "If Jesus Christ was the Son of God, and John discovered that God the Father of Jesus Christ had a Father, you may suppose that He had a Father also. Where was there ever a son without a father? And where was there ever a father without first being a son? Whenever did a tree or anything spring into existence without a progenitor? . . . hence if Jesus had a Father, can we not believe that *He* had a Father also?"[18]

13. Robinson, in Blomberg and Robinson, *How Wide the Divide?* 132.
14. Millet, *A Different Jesus?* 68.
15. *EOM*, 2:961.
16. Robinson, in Blomberg and Robinson, *How Wide the Divide?* 87.
17. Joseph Smith, "The King Follett Discourse," in *TPJS*, 349, 370, 372.
18. Ibid., 373.

Early LDS apostle Orson Pratt extended Smith's logic to what appears to be an infinite regression of gods: "The person of our Father in Heaven was begotten on a previous heavenly world by His Father; and again, He was begotten by a still more ancient Father; and so on, from generation to generation, from one heavenly world to another still more ancient, until our minds are wearied and lost in the multiplicity of generations and successive worlds."[19] The implication is that, since Smith's cosmos did not have a beginning, there may have been an infinite number of gods going back into the mists of eternity.

We must hasten to add that the best LDS authorities do not teach this infinite regression of gods, and insist rightly that this is not taught in the LDS canon. Even in his controversial King Follett Sermon, Smith said that "to us there is but one God—that is *pertaining to us*."[20] He seems to have meant that if other gods (besides Father, Jesus, and Holy Ghost) inhabit other worlds, they have nothing to do with this one or us, and are the only ones to whom we will ever relate.

The existence of other gods beyond the Father, Son, and Holy Ghost is not taught as official LDS doctrine, and it is absent from the LDS canon. Yet it is taught by LDS authorities that Jesus is one of three Gods. For Christian orthodoxy, on the other hand, Jesus is one person of only one God. He has a Father and is in communion with the Father and the Spirit, but the three constitute only one being and therefore one God.

Jesus Grew into God

But for Mormons, Jesus was not always God. He was once as we are now, but he eventually grew in his attributes until he became "like unto God" (Abraham 3:24). This is another belief about Jesus that seems to have been inspired by Smith's King Follett Discourse. There the prophet said, "God himself was once as we are now. . . . We have imagined and supposed that God was God from all eternity. I will refute that idea, and take away the veil, so that you may see."[21]

Smith continued in this vein, assuring his audience that God "was once a man like us; yea, that God himself, the Father of us all, dwelt on an earth, the same as Jesus Christ himself did."[22]

Lest there be any confusion that this was true of God and not also Jesus, we have Professor Millet's statement that "as a premortal spirit,

19. Orson Pratt, *The Seer* 1 (Sept. 1853), 132.
20. "The King Follett Discourse," 370; original emphasis.
21. Ibid., 345.
22. Ibid., 345–46.

Jehovah [Jesus] grew in knowledge and power to the point where he became 'like unto God.'"[23]

The contrast with Christian orthodoxy is considerable: the Jesus of the historic church was always the second person of the Trinity, fully divine and fully equal to the Father, who in turn was always God. There never was a time when the Trinity was not fully God, each of the three persons co-equal and co-divine. Jesus never grew in his powers. There were times in his incarnation when he voluntarily "emptied himself" of some of his divine prerogatives, such as knowing the day and the hour of the end of all things (Phil. 2:7; Matt. 24:36). But these were powers that he had possessed until the incarnation and that he chose not to use while on earth in bodily form.

So for orthodoxy, the movement of divine attributes in Jesus is the reverse of that for the LDS view: instead of gradually accumulating the divine nature, he always was divine. Only at a point long after the creation did he appear to have relinquished his divinity. But this was merely an appearance, camouflaging the "fullness" of deity (Col. 1:19) by a divine humility willing to forego certain privileges.

Jesus No Different From Us

Because, for Mormons, Jesus was once as we are now, he is no different in kind from what we are. He shares our species. Like Jesus, we never had a beginning but are co-eternal with God. "[Our intelligence] always existed and never was created or made (D&C 93:29). In due time that intelligence was given a spirit body, becoming the spirit child of God the Eternal Father, and his beloved companion, the Mother in Heaven."[24]

Another way of seeing this essential sameness of Jesus's nature with ours is to hear Smith describe our ability to become a God just as he became a God: "You have got to learn to be Gods yourselves . . . the same as all Gods have done before you." We too must strive until we also "arrive at the station of a God, and ascend the throne of eternal power." Then we will have "advance[d] like himself," assisted by "laws" which our God "institute[d]" in order to give us the same "privilege" he enjoys.[25] Because we are all of the same species and nature, potentially divine and realized divinities, we are all on the same path of progression—if we take advantage of it. "Then they shall be gods, because they have all power, and the angels are subject unto them."[26]

---

23. Millet, *A Different Jesus?* 20.
24. *EOM*, 1123–24.
25. "The King Follett Discourse," 346, 347, 354.
26. D&C 132:20.

This is why Mormon scholar Terryl Givens says Mormonism rejects what Kierkegaard called the "infinite qualitative difference" between the human and the divine: "The [Mormon sense of the] divine, in other words, was not characterized by the radical otherness that [mainstream Christian] religious tradition equated with the sacred. For this reason, [Smith's] religious innovation was more the naturalizing of the super-natural than the other way around."[27] For Givens, the Mormon sacred is not, after all, the traditional understanding of *mysterium tremendum et fascinosum*. Religion is not mystery; God, in a sense, has been reduced (at least in difference from humanity) and humanity exalted. As one scholar (whom Givens cites) puts it, Mormons teach an "anthropomorphic God and theomorphic man."[28]

The upshot is that for Latter-day Saints, Jesus is ontologically (at the level of *being*) no different from human beings. He fully realized his potential, but we have the same potential. He is simply at the end of the progression along which we too can proceed.

For the orthodox tradition, in contrast, God is *qadosh*, Hebrew for "wholly other," even from the supernatural beings of the divine council implied in Psalm 89:6: "Who among the clouds is equal to Yahweh? Who is like Yahweh among the sons of God?" Psalm 86:8 is similar: "There is no one like you among the gods."

If Yahweh, according to the orthodox tradition, is wholly different from other supernatural beings, he is all the more different from human beings. Evangelicals and other orthodox believers point to stories like the story of Balaam, where even the pagan prophet avers, "*God is not a man*, that he should lie; neither the son of man, that he should repent" (Num. 23:19; emphasis added). They also highlight Samuel's recognition that God and man are ontologically removed from one another: "The Strength of Israel will not lie nor repent: for he is not a man [*adam*], that he should repent" (1 Sam. 15:29). In order to underline the one God's absolute uniqueness, the orthodox have often used Isaiah 44:6: "I am the first, and I am the last; and beside me there is no God."

Once more, then, we find that Mormons and evangelicals (along with the entire orthodox tradition) differ on Jesus. Whereas Mormons believe we are the same species as Jesus, evangelicals say Jesus is ontologically as different from human beings as the infinite is different from the finite.

27. Terryl L. Givens, "'This Great Modern Abomination,' Orthodoxy and Heresy in American Religion," in *Mormons and Mormonism: An Introduction to an American World Religion*, ed. Eric A. Eliason (Urbana: University of Illinois Press, 2001), 116.

28. Terryl L. Givens, "The Book of Mormon and Religious Epistemology," *Dialogue* 34: 3–4 (Fall-Winter 2001), 53 n.65.

A Different Deification

Professor Givens has argued recently that the Mormon view of deifi-cation is no different from that of the early church, particularly that of the Greek fathers of the church.[29] Deification means the participation of humans in divinity or God. Givens insists that, like Smith and the LDS Church, the church fathers never broke down the wall of ontologi-cal separation between creature and Creator. They too, like Mormons, believed that Jesus and human beings are really the same kind of being, only Jesus has moved perfectly and further along. Is Givens right about this?

Not really. Norman Russell's new authoritative study of deification among the Greek fathers shows that deification language was used "in one of three ways, nominally, analogically, or metaphorically." The first used the word "gods" for human beings simply as a term of honor. The second stretched the nominal by saying that humans can become "sons of gods 'by grace' in relation to Christ who is Son and God 'by nature.'" The metaphorical use takes two approaches, the ethical and realistic. In the ethical, humans attempt "likeness" to God by moral imitation. In the realistic, humans participate in God's being. But the relationship even here is "asymmetrical," bringing together beings of "diverse ontological type"—the opposite of Mormon claims that God and humanity share the same ontology.[30]

Justin Martyr used Psalm 82:6 ("Ye are gods; and all of you are chil-dren of the most High.") to argue that "all human beings are deemed worthy of becoming gods and of having power to become sons of the Most High" (*Dialogue with Trypho* 124). But he relates deification only to John's statement that "to all who received [Christ], who believed in his name, he gave power to become children of God" (John 1:12). He never developed this statement into a doctrine resembling Mormon deification.[31]

Irenaeus linked Psalm 82:6, not to Johannine "children of God," but to Pauline adoption. His doctrine of deification ("Because of his infinite love he became what we are in order to make us what he is in himself" [*Against Heresies* 5, Preface]) therefore "involves an exchange of proper-ties, not the establishment of an identity of essence. He who was Son of God by nature became a man in order to make us sons by adoption (*Against Heresies* 3.19.1)."[32]

29. Givens, "This Great Modern Abomination," 101–2.
30. Norman Russell, *The Doctrine of Deification in the Greek Patristic Tradition* (Oxford: Oxford University Press, 2004), 1–2.
31. Ibid., 96–101.
32. Ibid., 106, 108.

Clement's view of deification is similar. It is "not ontological—human nature per se is not transformed by the Logos—but exemplary. . . . Christians who have attained perfection will be enthroned in glory with the highest grade of the saved, but still on a lower level than Christ." Clement is careful to distinguish between the most exalted men or angels and Christ: *The divinity of the perfect is a divinity by title or analogy.*"[33]

Even Origen, who is widely considered to have been more deeply influenced by Hellenistic notions of divinization, maintains this ontological distinction. According to Origen, a "fundamental distinction should be made between that which is immortal, rational, good, etc. of itself and that which merely participates in these attributes, although the term 'god' may be predicated equally of both. . . . Although like the Logos they are recipients of divinity, [those made in the image of God] are much further removed from God. The Logos alone abides intimately with God in ceaseless contemplation of the Fatherly depths. . . . Origin maintains that men are virtuous in a contingent sense by participation in a goodness which is self-subsistent."[34]

Athanasius, whose exchange formula is most often quoted ("He became human that we might become divine" [*On the Incarnation* 54]), shows most emphatically that Mormon deification is qualitatively different from patristic deification. Athanasius argued that "recipients of adoption and deification have simply received the name of sons and gods; Christ, however, is Son and God 'by nature and according to essence.'" Athanasius insisted on a "radical division" between the "agenetic" Godhead and the "genetic" created order, the *agenētos* and the *genēta*. "If to be deified by participation must be contrasted with true divinity, then the Logos is certainly not deified." The Christ is the Father's "only own and true Son deriving from his essential being." Hence, the participant (an ordinary believer) is essentially different from the participated (Christ). In Athanasius' determination to defeat Arianism, he denied any similarity at all between Christ and those who are participate in him. In those discussions, he "played down the designation of men as gods." Hence, for Athanasius, there was no question of humans ever becoming the same as God. "They are sons and gods only in name."[35]

Augustine is little different. In the *City of God* he writes, "It is one thing to be God, another thing to be a partaker of God" (22.30). In *On Nature and Grace* we find the following: "The creature will never become equal with God even if perfect holiness were to be achieved in us. Some think that in the next life we shall be changed into what he is; I am not

33. Ibid., 137, 133–34; emphasis added.
34. Ibid., 145; ibid., 147.
35. Ibid., 171, 170, 182, 181, 185, 186.

convinced" (33.37).[36] Of course, the fact that Augustine needed to make this clarification suggests that the ontological line between humanity and deity was not clear for some in the church of his day.

The upshot, for our purposes, is that the early orthodox view of Jesus and deification is substantially different from the LDS view. For the orthodox, we will never be able to attain his nature and powers. But according to LDS teaching, deification means we can one day possess even what orthodox theologians have called Jesus's "incommunicable" attributes such as omniscience and omnipotence.

A Physical Jesus Limited by the Cosmos

The Mormon view of Jesus pictures a deity who is limited in significant ways. Doctrine and Covenants (88.12) tells us that his spirit fills the immensity of space, but there is nothing beyond the material cosmos, even for the Father and his Son. This means that Jesus does not transcend the universe, as the orthodox tradition has always believed, citing such biblical passages as Psalm 90:2: "Before the mountains were born, and before you gave birth to the earth and the world, even from everlasting to everlasting, you are God!" God was there before the creation of the world and so stands apart from it. But according to Mormon teaching, matter always existed, co-eternally with both the Father and the Son, so the Son is within but not outside the cosmos. To put it crudely, Jesus is not bigger than the universe.

He can't be, because he is a physical being who occupies a limited amount of space. So is the Father, who "has a body of Flesh and bones as tangible as man's" (D&C 130.22). For that matter, the Holy Ghost is in a similar position—physical and therefore no larger than the physical cosmos. Doctrine and Covenants (131.7) informs readers that all spirit is matter. Spiritual matter is simply "more fine or pure, and can only be discerned by purer eyes."

Jesus's body is limited in another way—to one spatial location. While the Holy Ghost can be omnipresent throughout the cosmos—but without going outside it—Jesus's body cannot do the same. This is different from some major Christian traditional views, such as Catholic and Lutheran, both of which hold to the Real Presence of Jesus's body in the Eucharist—no matter where in the world it is celebrated and all at the same time. If Mass is celebrated in Beijing at the same moment Catholics are celebrating it in New York City, the body of Jesus Christ is present in both places at the same time. Mormon believers would say

36. Ibid., 332.

this is impossible, because Jesus's body can be in only one place at a time. Not surprisingly, Mormons don't believe in a Real Presence in the Lord's Supper. As we shall see in a later chapter, they hold to a memorial view, that the Supper is simply a "remembrance" of what happened two thousand years ago.

If the Godhead, and therefore Jesus, is limited in the sense that he is not outside the cosmos but is constrained by the limits of the physical cosmos, there are other elements within the cosmos that also limit Jesus, such as law. The *Encyclopedia of Mormonism* teaches that eternal law is independent and co-eternal with God, just as matter is. In fact, not only is law independent of God, but God is governed by it. Mormon apologist Bruce McConkie has written that "God himself governs and is governed by law." Philosopher David Paulsen states, "God does not have absolute power . . . but rather the power to maximally utilize natural laws to being about His purposes."[37]

There's an old question from Greek philosophy that goes something like this: Is something "good" because God wills it, or because it is good apart from God? Another way of putting this is to ask if God created good, or if good is an eternal principle apart from God. The evangelical (and orthodox Christian) response is that the good is rooted in God's nature, while the Mormon tradition opts for the latter. Moral goodness comes, not directly from God, but from principles that are just as ancient and eternal as God himself. Therefore, God himself must submit, as it were, to these principles. Even if he delights to be "governed" by these principles and chooses to be governed by them, nevertheless he is limited by them. They are outside of himself and control the ways in which he acts. He is not the ultimate cause of all things, but there are other things just as ultimate as he. And if this is so for the Father, it is also the case for Jesus. Goodness fills Jesus, but it is also outside of him, informing and guiding all of his words and deeds. Ethical values are derived ultimately not from Jesus himself but from principles that stand outside him.

We have to conclude, therefore, that the Mormon tradition speaks of a Jesus who is limited. He occupies a limited space (even if immense), and things outside of him (law and matter) limit his power and acts.

These are the reasons why I take the position I did at the beginning of this chapter—that while Mormons and evangelicals agree on much about Jesus, and in significant ways, there are also significant differences.

37. Bruce McConkie, *Mormon Doctrine*, 2nd ed. (Salt Lake City: Bookcraft, 1966), 432; David Paulsen, "Comparative Coherency of Mormon (Finitistic) and Classical Theism," Ph.D. diss. (University of Michigan, 1975), 74.

Jesus is a different God insofar as the orthodox Jesus is the second person of the Triune God, while the Mormon Jesus is a God distinct from God the Father. The Mormon Jesus is one of at least several Gods. He was once merely a man who over the course of time grew into being a God. His nature is the same as ours to the extent that he is on the same level of being as we are; we are of the same species. We can become the same as he not only in his communicable attributes but also in his "incommunicable"ones, such as omniscience and omnipotence. And he is limited—his body is limited to one location, and his being and acts are limited by co-eternal law.

Because of these differences, I cannot agree with Professor Robinson that evangelicals and other orthodox share a common devotion to the New Testament Jesus. In my view, we share a common devotion to both Jesus and the New Testament, but the two communities' portraits of Jesus are different in some important ways.

A Latter-day Saint Response
Robert Millet

The first article of faith, written by Joseph Smith in 1842, is as follows: "We believe in God, the Eternal Father, and in His Son, Jesus Christ, and in the Holy Ghost" (Articles of Faith 1:1). There has never been any question in LDS history among those who are at least slightly informed of our theology but that Latter-day Saints believe in the Godhead or, as it was often referred to by earlier LDS Church leaders, in the Trinity. In this article I will most often speak of the Godhead, but I may slip occasionally and use the word Trinity. Before doing so, let me distinguish between the Trinity as that divine community made up of three holy persons and of the *doctrine* of the Trinity as set forth more specifically in the teachings of traditional Christianity since the time of Nicaea in AD 325. To be clear from the start, Latter-day Saints believe in the Trinity; they do not accept the doctrine of the Trinity, meaning the various Trinitarian formulations that we believe were conceived three to four centuries following the time of Jesus.

My reading and extended conversations with evangelical friends persuade me that Latter-day Saints would not disagree with evangelicals on a number of things about God and the Godhead. For example, I believe God is, as set forth by Joseph Smith in the Lectures on Faith, "the only supreme governor and independent being in whom all fullness and perfection dwell; who is omnipotent, omnipresent, omniscient; without beginning of days or end of life; and that in him every good gift and every good principle dwell; and that he is the Father of lights; in him the principle of faith dwells independently, and he is the object in whom the faith of all other rational and accountable beings center for life and salvation."[38]

38. Joseph Smith, *Lectures on Faith* (Salt Lake City: Deseret Book, 1985), 2:2.

I believe in Jesus Christ. I believe he is the Son of God, the Only Begotten in the flesh, the one sent of the Father to bind up the broken-hearted and set at liberty the captive, to forgive sins and renew human souls, to reconcile fallen men and women with an infinite and immortal deity. He is our Savior, our Redeemer, our Mediator with the Father, our Lord, and our God. He is not only the Son of God but also God the Son. He possesses a fullness of the glory and power of the Father, a portion of which glory and power he set aside through his incarnation. In Paul's words, he "emptied himself" of his Godhood that he might live and minister among mortals.

I believe in the Holy Ghost, the Holy Spirit. Like the Son, he possesses all of the attributes of God in their fullness. His roles are numerous: Comforter, Teacher, Revelator, Sanctifier, Sealer, and Messenger of the word of truth. It is the work of the Spirit not only to plant truth within the human mind and soul but also to purge dross and iniquity from the heart, doing so by virtue of the precious blood of Christ.

Latter-day Saints believe that while the members of the Godhead are totally and completely one—infinitely more one than they are separate—there exists an ordinal relationship among them; that is, the order of Father, Son, and Holy Spirit is not arbitrary. As Professor McDermott appropriately points out, Latter-day Saints do not believe in an ontological oneness within the Trinity, that is, that our Heavenly Father, our divine Redeemer, and the Holy Spirit are in fact the same being. Joseph Smith went so far in Lecture 5 of the Lectures on Faith to suggest a kind of mental and spiritual unity of the Father and Son, accomplished through the medium of the Spirit, that I find especially attractive. Joseph taught that Jesus,

> having overcome, received a fullness of the glory of the Father, possessing the same mind with the Father, which mind is the Holy Spirit, that bears record of the Father and the Son, and these three are one; or, in other words, these three constitute the great, matchless, governing and supreme, power over all things . . . and these three constitute the Godhead, and are one; the Father and the Son possessing the same mind, the same wisdom, glory, power, and fullness—filling all in all; the Son being filled with the fullness of the mind, glory, and power; or, in other words, the spirit, glory, and power, of the Father . . . which Spirit is shed forth upon all who believe on his name and keep his commandments.[39]

I personally have great difficulty imagining that a person who is absolutely ignorant of traditional Christian views on the Trinity or completely oblivious to LDS teachings on the same, would read the Gospels or the Epistles and come away believing that Father, Son, and Holy Spirit

39. Ibid., 5:2.

are somehow three persons but one Being. I know that there are many more books or articles that I could read on the doctrine of the Trinity, but I have read all that my time and energy will allow and all that my mind can handle. No matter how hard I try, I cannot find either insight or comfort in accepting a concept that is at odds with human reason and in many cases downright confusing or even misleading. Please do not misunderstand what I mean: I certainly mean no disrespect to my Catholic, Protestant, or Orthodox friends who hold tenaciously to the doctrine of the Trinity; I love and respect them and am pleased to allow them to believe as they choose. I just happen to be one who feels that coming to know God—and I have reference here not only to knowing *about* him but to experience him and acknowledge him for who he is—does not require the intricate orchestration of a mystery that few men and women in the pews can comprehend and even fewer, including pastors and theologians, can articulate. Because most Christians, when pressed to fully explain the concept of the Trinity, quite naturally resort to the fact that it is a blessed mystery, I also have difficulty fathoming how those same people could feel comfortable excluding from the category of Christian someone who doesn't accept the incomprehensible nature of such a doctrine. To act completely ignorant, I simply ask: How can 1 + 1 + 1 = 1? Again, meaning no irreverence, I ask: If we were to invite the Trinity to dinner, how many place settings would I need to set? Three persons are three persons. Three persons cannot be one person, nor can I conceive how three persons can be one being.

I have another question to ask: Why is it that the Christian Church should fight and struggle for centuries and even millennia to maintain Jewish monotheism? The Jews, according to the Shema, believed in one God. But we know there is a Father, a Son, and a Holy Spirit, namely, three persons who constitute, as Joseph Smith said, the great governing and supreme power over all things. The Jews seemed to have no concept of a Savior/Redeemer who was a separate person from God, nor did they believe that the Holy Spirit was a separate person from God or Christ. Jesus came into the world to do many things, but one thing he came to do for sure is to reveal the Father and teach of the Holy Spirit; that is, he came to teach the Godhead. Obviously, I do not consider Latter-day Saints to be polytheistic, and I appreciate Professor McDermott's description of what constitutes polytheism. But Latter-day Saints do not believe that an ontological merger was necessary in order to truly understand the magnificent and infinite oneness of the three persons within the Trinity.

It was my colleague David Paulsen from the Philosophy Department at Brigham Young University who stated that the LDS concept of the Godhead is a kind of variation on what some have called "social trinitarianism." Our belief might be stated as follows: We believe in three persons in the Godhead—the Father, the Son, and the Holy Spirit. We believe the Father is the Fount of all power and knowledge and goodness, the Father of Lights. We believe that each of the members of the Godhead possesses all of the attributes and qualities of godliness in perfection. We believe that the love and unity that exist among the three persons in the Godhead constitute a divine community that is occasionally referred to simply as *God* (see 2 Nephi 31:21; Alma 11:44; Mormon 7:7). In other words, we have no problem speaking of a Mormon monotheism in the sense that we believe in one God, one Godhead, one Trinity, one collection of divine persons who oversee and bless and save the human family.

Let me now respond to some specific issues raised by Professor Mc-Dermott. Gerry suggests that specific statements in the New Testament point to the fact that Jesus is the same being as God the Father. He alludes specifically to John 14:10 in which Jesus instructs the apostles at the Last Supper that he is "in the Father, and the Father is in me." The problem I have with this particular scriptural passage is not that it does not describe the divine indwelling relationship between the Father and Son but that the concept of being "in the Father" is not unlike the concept used by the Apostle Paul almost 160 times when he speaks of those who have been born again as being "in Christ." To be "in Christ" is to be in harmony with him, to have given one's life to him, to have surrendered one's will to him, to be in union with him, to have joined with him by covenant. It is to have, as Paul stated, "the mind of Christ" (1 Cor. 2:16). So Christ could be "in the Father" and yet be an entirely separate being in the sense that he enjoyed that indwelling spirit and unity—what Joseph Smith called the mind or Spirit of God.

Professor McDermott also suggests that unless one accepts the doctrine of the Trinity, he or she cannot enjoy "participation in the mystical communion among the three persons of the Trinity." All I have, of course, is my own personal experience to respond to this, but I would disagree as a result of my own communion with the Infinite. Must one really accept the ontological oneness of the members of the Godhead in order to be close to them, to be at peace with them, to feel their power and presence in his or her life? I think not. Wise Latter-day Saints do not worry about which aspect of God's nature we participate in when we worship; that is, when I say I feel the Spirit of the Lord in my life, I do not stop and ask, Is this the Spirit of the Father or the Son or the Holy Spirit? Frankly, to me it doesn't matter: it is God's Spirit. Nor do I feel that my capacity to love others—more specifically to enjoy the love of God in my own personal life and then to be empowered and enabled to extend that love to my brothers and sisters about me—is in any way hindered or misdirected because I do not believe in an ontological oneness. In other words, my theological posture does not determine my capacity to love and be loved, my motivation to devote myself to the Lord Jesus Christ and to go in search of his wandering sheep. My ability to give to my wife, children, and grandchildren from deep resources within me is not a product of my intellectual conceptualization of the divine. Rather, it is a product of personal devotion, communion, and divine grace.

It is inevitable that Joseph Smith's teachings in the King Follett Sermon would surface in any serious discussion of the matter of the Godhead. It seems to me that there are three major issues that make traditional Christians extremely uncomfortable with the King Follett Discourse: a denial of the *ex nihilo* creation, the suggestion that men and women may become as God is, and the introduction of the idea that the Almighty was once a mortal man who lived on an earth. For now I will choose to put the issue of the *ex nihilo* creation aside, perhaps for another occasion or another book. As to the matter of our becoming like God, the New Testament itself contains Jesus's directive for us to "be perfect, even as the Father is perfect" (Matt. 5:48); Paul's allusion to people becoming "joint heirs with Christ" (Rom. 8:17); Peter's lofty counsel for us to become "partakers of the divine nature" (2 Pet. 1:4); and John's poignant and penetrating insight that those who become the children of God may not now understand what they will be like in their glorified, resurrected condition, but they do know this: "When he shall appear, we shall be like him; for we shall see him as he is" (1 John 3:2).

Professor McDermott goes to some length to demonstrate that the early church fathers spoke of human deification but definitely did not mean the same thing Mormons mean today when they speak of the subject. The fact of the matter is, Latter-day Saints simply do not know which of God's attributes are or will be communicable and which are incommunicable. There is no question in my mind but that God is God, and there is now and will forevermore be a chasm between the two of us. I am not aware of any authoritative statements in our literature that suggest that men and women will ever worship any beings other than the three persons within the Godhead. Parley P. Pratt, one of the early LDS leaders and a close associate of Joseph Smith wrote in one of the LDS Church's first major theological treatises: "The difference between Jesus Christ and his Father is this—one is subordinate to the other, does nothing of Himself, independently of the Father, but does all things in the name and by the authority of the Father, being of the same mind in all things. The difference between Jesus Christ and another immortal and celestial man is this—the man is subordinate to Jesus Christ, does nothing in and of himself, but does all things in the name of Christ, and by his authority, being of the same mind and ascribing all the glory to him and his Father."[40]

Again, as pertaining to the matter of deification, one Orthodox scholar has written: "There's hardly a person alive who has not asked himself, 'Why do we live upon this earth?' In the last analysis there is only one answer. We live on earth in order to live in heaven, in order to be 'divinized,' in order to become one with God. This is the end and the fulfillment of our earthly destiny." After citing Psalm 82:6 and John 10:34 ("You are gods, sons of the Most High—all of you"), he continued:

> Do we hear that voice? Do we understand the meaning of this calling? Do we accept that we should in fact be on a journey, a road which leads to Theosis? As human beings we each have this one, unique calling, to achieve Theosis. In other words, we are each destined to become a god, to be like God Himself, to be united with Him. . . . This is the purpose of your life; that you be a participant, a sharer in the nature of God and in the life of Christ, a communicant of divine grace and energy—to become just like God, a true god. . . . Theosis! What does this deep and profound word mean? It means the elevation of the human being to the divine sphere, to the atmosphere of God. It means the union of the human with the divine. That, in its essence, is the meaning of Theosis.[41]

"In the Orthodox understanding," another Orthodox thinker observed, "Christianity signifies not merely an adherence to certain dogmas, not merely an exterior imitation of Christ through moral effort, but direct union with the living God, the total transformation of the human person by divine grace and glory—what the Greek Fathers termed 'deification' or 'divinization' (*theosis theopoiesis*). In the words of St. Basil the Great, man is nothing less than a creature that has received the order to *become God*."[42]

Professor Veli-Matti Kärkkäinen similarly taught that "According to Eastern theology, Latin traditions have been dominated by legal, juridical, and forensic categories. Eastern theology, on the contrary, understands the need of salvation in terms of deliverance from mortality and corruption for life everlasting. Union with God is the goal of the Christian life,

---

40. Parley P. Pratt, *Key to the Science of Theology* (Salt Lake City: Deseret Book, 1978), 20–21.

41. Archimandrite Christoforos Stavropoulos, *Partakers of Divine Nature*, trans. The Rev. Dr. Stanley Harakas (Minneapolis: Light and Life Publishing Company, 1976), prologue, 17–18; see also Panayiotis Nellas, *Deification in Christ: Orthodox Perspectives on the Nature of the Human Person*, trans. Norman Russell (Crestwood, NY: Saint Vladimir's Seminary Press, 1997).

42. Bishop Kallistos of Diokleia, Foreword to Georgios I. Mantzaridis, *The Deification of Man* (Crestwood, NY: Saint Vladimir's Seminary Press, 1984), 7, emphasis in original.

even becoming single 'in-godded.' The idea of divine-human cooperation in salvation is not only accepted but is enthusiastically championed, although it is not understood as nullifying the role of grace."[43] He also added that "Eastern theology even speaks about Christians as 'christs,' anointed ones: The Spirit who rests like a royal unction upon the humanity of the Son communicates himself to each member of Christ's body."[44]

C. S. Lewis pointed out that "the whole offer which Christianity makes is this: that we can, if we let God have His way, come to share in the life of Christ. . . . Christ is the Son of God. If we share in this kind of life we also shall be sons of God. We shall love the Father as He does and the Holy Ghost will arise in us. He came to this world and became a man in order to spread to other men the kind of life He has—by what I call 'good infection.' Every Christian is to become a little Christ. The whole purpose of becoming a Christian is simply nothing else."[45] Or, as John MacArthur has written: "The first characteristic of a genuine disciple is that he is like his Lord. He bears the character of Christ. That's why in Acts 11:26 people called the believers Christians: *Christiani*—'iani' means 'belonging to the party of.' They were little christs; they manifested His character and bore the marks of His life in them."[46]

As to the matter of Joseph Smith's statement that God was once a man, I will simply ask a couple of questions: First, are Christians bothered by the fact that Jesus was embodied through the incarnation, that he had a physical body? When our Master stated before his ascent into heaven that all power in heaven and on earth had been given to him (Matt. 28:18), does it sound like he was in some way limited? In other words, why does the concept of divine embodiment trouble traditional Christians? My understanding is that evangelicals believe that Jesus experienced an actual, literal, physical, bodily resurrection from the dead and that he took that body with him into heaven, where he now resides as the one embodied member of the Godhead or Trinity. So when it comes to the matter of divine embodiment, I suppose I am troubled about why Christians are troubled.

It is worth noting that a recent LDS Church president, Gordon B. Hinckley, when asked about the distinctive LDS belief that God was once a man responded in the following way: "I don't know that we teach it. I don't know that we emphasize it. I haven't heard it discussed

43. Veli-Matti Kärkkäinen, *One With God: Salvation as Deification and Justification* (Collegeville, MN: Liturgical Press, 2004), 29–30.

44. Ibid., 34.

45. C. S. Lewis, *Mere Christianity* (New York: Touchstone, 1996), 153–54.

46. John MacArthur, *Hard to Believe: The High Cost and Infinite Value of Following Jesus* (Nashville: Nelson, 2003), 125.

for a long time in public discourse. I don't know all the circumstances under which that statement was made. I understand the philosophical background behind it, but I don't know a lot about it, and I don't think others know a lot about it."[47] In other words, Latter-day Saints really do not know much about this concept. To be honest with you, I hear far more about it on a regular basis from evangelicals than I ever do from Latter-day Saints! While Latter-day Saints certainly believe that God our Heavenly Father has a body of flesh and bones as tangible as man's (D&C 130:22), we really do not know anything about God before he was God, except for Joseph's words in the King Follett Sermon and a couplet by later LDS Church president, Lorenzo Snow. To suggest to the reader that this is a shelf doctrine, something that is not a central saving teaching would be an understatement. I would further ask how Christian readers would respond if Joseph Smith's ideas, as expressed in Lorenzo Snow's couplet, were restated somewhat:

> As man is, Christ once was;
> As Christ is, man may become.

As Professor McDermott ably points out, one of the other more troubling LDS teachings for many is the notion that Jesus was a spirit child of God, just as every other man or women once was. In other words, there is a good deal of discomfort among those who study our theology that we do not believe in the eternality of Jesus Christ. I will simply respond this way: I do in fact believe, and modern revelation attests, that Jesus was the firstborn spirit child of our eternal Heavenly Father, but those same scriptures teach that he became "like unto God." Indeed, he was God (John 1:1–2), the Creator of worlds and the God of Abraham, Isaac, and Jacob. I suppose the only thing I can say at this point is that it is not inconsistent for Latter-day Saints to believe that Jesus became God and that he is also, as the title page of the Book of Mormon affirms "the Eternal God." He is from everlasting to everlasting. Perhaps my evangelical friends will cut me a bit of slack here and allow Mormons to identify a blessed mystery of their own.

I would disagree with Professor McDermott's characterization of Mormonism as reducing God in an effort to exalt humanity. We simply do not have the space in this work for me to detail the scriptural passages that point to God's majesty, magnificence, and infinity. I may believe that God and man are not of a different species, but the last thing in the world I want to be accused of is shortening the distance between a

47. Cited in Richard N. Ostling and Joan K. Ostling, *Mormon America* (San Francisco: HarperSanFrancisco, 1999), 296.

frail, weak, and imperfect mortal and an omnipotent, omniscient, and perfected God. If Latter-day Saints become too chummy with the divine or speak of God or Christ as if they were next-door neighbors, they do so without doctrinal support and to their own spiritual detriment. God is God, and I am a mere mortal. I agree with Professor McDermott that God is *qadosh*, that he is "holy other," meaning that he is separate and apart from unholiness and profanity. Latter-day Saints do not believe, however, that he is wholly other in the sense of being aloof, passionless, and set free from his children; we do not see him through the eyes of Neoplatonism.

Finally, let me make a comment about God, law, and virtue. It would not be hard to find Latter-day Saints who would take a different stand than I am about to take regarding God and virtue. I do not believe, and I do not believe that Joseph Smith taught, that justice or mercy or good or evil are independent entities in the universe. As an illustration, when a man or woman sins, I cannot conceive of him or her being bombarded and punished by some universal eternal law that we know as justice. No, the only justice I'm aware of is the justice of God. Joseph Smith taught repeatedly that God is the author of law and in that sense is the author of virtue. In the long run, we cannot, simply cannot define good or evil by consensus, nor can we speak of divine ethics independent of Divinity. Jesus was the embodiment of every godly attribute. In the ultimate sense, for example, when he teaches us that we will know the truth and the truth will make us free (John 8:32), it is nice to know that a knowledge of certain things will keep us from ignorance and bondage. It is critical to know that Jesus is the Truth, and it is only in and through him that an individual is made free.

In conclusion, I still find myself asking whether the Christ of the creeds of Nicaea or Chalcedon or Constantinople or Ephesus is the Christ described in the Gospels. It is hard for me to imagine explaining to the group of people converted through the preaching of Peter on the day of Pentecost (Acts 2) or the Philippian jailor (Acts 16) that they cannot really enjoy intimate communion with deity or an adequate immersion into Christian thinking or piety unless they first understand the ontological oneness of the members of the Trinity. For me, one of the most moving moments in all the four Gospels is to be found in Christ's Great Intercessory Prayer before leaving the upper room (John 17). His plea for unity, his plea for those whom the Father had called out of the world, his plea for his chosen disciples, and, more directly, his plea for the unity of the body of believers—that they would be one as he and the Father were one—for me has little to do with any kind of ontological oneness and much to do with having their minds transformed, their hearts sanctified, and their vision fixed upon the same distant scene of salvation.

"Despite their orthodox confession of the Trinity," Roman Catholic Karl Rahner observed, "Christians are, in their practical life, almost mere 'monotheists.' We must be willing to admit that, should the doctrine of the Trinity have to be dropped as false, the major part of religious literature could well remain virtually unchanged." Rahner continued: "The theological and religious emphasis lies only in the fact that 'God' became man, that 'one' of the divine persons (of the Trinity) took on the flesh, and not on the fact that this person is precisely the person of the Logos. One has the feeling that, for the catechism of head and heart (as contrasted with the printed catechism), the Christian's idea of the incarnation would not have to change at all if there were no Trinity. For God would still, as (the one) person, have become man, which is in fact about all the average Christian explicitly grasps when he confesses the incarnation."[48]

And just perhaps, that is what is needed, in terms of theological understanding: to grasp, to some extent at least, what it cost the Father and the Son to purchase our salvation; what fruits follow on the heels of a genuine expression of faith; and simply what it means to be a Christian. "As the Son partakes of the fullness of the Father through the Spirit," Joseph Smith taught, "so the saints are, by the same Spirit, to be partakers of the same fullness, to enjoy the same glory; for as the Father and the Son are one, so, in like manner, the saints are to be one in them. Through the love of the Father, the mediation of Jesus Christ, and the gift of the Holy Spirit, they are to be heirs of God, and joint-heirs with Jesus Christ."[49]

48. Karl Rahner, *The Trinity* (New York: Crossroad, 1998), 10–11.
49. Smith, *Lectures on Faith*, 5:3.

Rebuttal and Concluding Thoughts
Gerald McDermott

I am very sorry that Professor Millet got the impression I said that unless he agrees with me on the Trinity, he cannot participate in the mystical communion among the three persons of the Trinity.

That's not what I said. I wrote that Mormons cannot "*conceive* of love as participation in the very life of the Godhead" where the believer "participates in the mutual love between the Father and the Son."

I was not as precise as I should have been. I should have made it clear that this mutual love is within one being of God. So I would still say that unless you believe in the orthodox Trinity, you cannot *think* of love as participation in the love between the Father and the Son as one God—simply because you don't believe in one God among three persons. *That* kind of love is impossible to conceive if you think of the Father and Son as two distinct Gods.

In actuality, Bob is one of the most loving persons I know. I think he does indeed participate in orthodox Trinitarian love of the one God among the three persons, but that is not the way he would think of it. This is what I was trying to say.

I must confess I am surprised that Bob says he rejects the Trinity because it is "against reason" and is "confusing." Can reason clearly demonstrate all Mormon beliefs, such as the idea that Jesus was both a man and God at the same time? Or that God is all-powerful and all-loving and yet rules over a world infested with horrible evil? Or even the simple philosophical notion that our souls are united with our bodies in such manner that the immaterial acts on the material? So matter has a kind of immaterial perception? Aren't all these notions confusing at some level? Don't they all conflict with at least one kind of reason? Later in his response, Professor Millet himself asks evangelicals for slack when he says he considers the LDS idea that "God was once a man" a mystery.

As I said in my rebuttal at the end of chapter 1, Mormons and evangelicals agree that God is three, but differ over whether God is also one. Yet there are plenty of scriptures attesting to the unity of God.[50] The Bible says over

---

50. That is, one Creator and Redeemer. While both the OT (e.g., Ps. 86:8; 96:4; 135:5, et al) and NT (1 Cor. 8:5; Eph. 6:12) speak of other gods, they are created spirits who

and over that there is only one God. It calls both the Father and the Son "God," but never refers to them as two Gods. It says "God" is the Savior of all men (1 Tim. 4:10–11) and teaches that the Son saves by the grace of the Spirit, but the three are never called three Saviors. Scripture *never* refers to God in the plural, although it does use the plural for men, women, angels, devils, demons, principalities, and powers.[51] This is true in both Testaments. God asks, "Is there a God beside me?" (Isa. 44:8), and declares, "I am God, and there is none else" (Isa. 45:22). The psalmist cries, "Thou art God alone" (86:10). Jesus himself quotes Torah, "The Lord our God is one Lord" (Matt. 12:29), thus affirming Torah's insistence on monotheism. (This makes me wonder why Bob criticizes Christians for retaining "Jewish monotheism." Was it wrong in its emphasis on God's oneness? If it was, how can we then regard Old Testament scripture as authoritative?)

Bob quotes several Eastern Orthodox theologians, trying to show they agree with Mormon deification. I think it unlikely that when St. Basil the Great said we are to "become God," he meant anything different from what his predecessors emphasized—that we are not the same species as Jesus, and that while he was divine by nature, we can become divine only by grace and in limited, participatory fashion. Timothy Ware, whose *The Orthodox Church* has become the standard introduction to Eastern Orthodoxy, writes, "Union with God means union with the divine energies, not the divine essence. . . .The human being does not become God *by nature*, but is merely 'a created god,' a god *by grace* or *by status*."[52]

Nor was C. S. Lewis's notion of deification quite like the LDS view. In a recent issue of the LDS journal *Dialogue*, Evan Stephenson shows

---

have turned against their Creator and disguise the fact that they are neither creators nor omnipotent. Isa. 40:25–26 is typical of a profusion of biblical texts that speak of other *elohim* (gods) but clearly distinguish between the one Creator-Redeemer and different kinds of inferior, created spirits, also called *elohim* (demons, spirits from Sheol, the Angel of Yahweh, other angels): Deut. 32:17; 1 Sam. 28:13; Hos. 12:4–5 [Hebrew text]; Gen. 48:15–16; Gen. 28:12, 32:1–2, 35:1–7. See my *God's Rivals* (Downers Grove: InterVarsity, 2007), chapters 1 and 2.

51. Some Mormons make much of the fact that *elohim* is a plural form, pointing to its use in Genesis 1with language such as "Let *us* make man in our image . . ." (Gen. 1:26). But while the word is plural in form, it is regularly used as a singular when referring to Israel's God, typically used with singular verbs and adjectives. For example, in Gen. 1:1, the text says, "*Elohim* [plural form] created [singular verb] the heavens and the earth." Since in the OT even a singular pagan god is designated with the plural (e.g., Judges 11:24; 1 Kgs. 11:5; 2 Kgs. 1:2), the use of the plural form is taken by most scholars to represent either plural of majesty, species uniqueness (God is the only god who is Creator and Re-deeemer), or the divine council (the Creator with his lesser, created angels and spirits, as in Ps. 89:5–8). On the divine council, see *God's Rivals*, 53–58.

52. Timothy Ware, *The Orthodox Church* (London: Penguin, 1993), 232; emphasis added.

that C. S. Lewis believed "the gulf between . . . creator and creature can never be bridged." According to Stephenson, Lewis would "protest . . . [the] nonsense" that God is an exalted man."[53]

It seems, then, that the LDS attempt to identify Mormon deification with the early church fathers, Eastern Orthodoxy, and C. S. Lewis cannot be sustained.

Professor Millet objects to my characterization of Mormonism as "reducing God in an effort to exalt humanity." Paraphrasing Mormon scholar Terryl Givens, who had said Mormonism dispenses with mystery, I wrote, "God in a sense has been reduced (*at least in difference from humanity*) and humanity exalted. As one scholar (whom Givens cites) puts it, Mormons teach an 'anthropomorphic God and theomorphic man.'" This still seems to me to be on target: since we are of the same species as Jesus, he has come closer down to us, as it were, and we have ascended closer to him.

Bob says that he knows of no statement by Joseph Smith in which he holds to the independence of moral law from God. But what about Smith's statement that "the first step in salvation of man is the laws of eternal and self-existent principles"[54]? One would guess these self-existent principles to have something to do with morality. Mormon theologian B. H. Roberts, a member of the First Council of Seventy, has written,

> What then, is meant by the ascription of the attribute of Omnipotence to God? Simply that all that may or can be done by power conditioned by other eternal existences—duration, space, matter, *truth, justice*—God can do. *But even he may not act out of harmony with the other eternal existences which condition or limit him.*[55]

These two quotations suggest that Smith might have had in mind moral laws that are self-existent, apart from God.

Bob accurately quotes Karl Rahner to the effect that the Trinity is not central to Christian faith. Yet ever since Karl Barth's cries of protest in the early and mid-twentieth century, Christian theologians have said quite the contrary. So did Augustine, the greatest of all theologians. I would add my two cents here: If the Father and the Son are two distinct Gods, then I cannot know with assurance that the Father really understands my suffering—for he did not come to earth to suffer and die, but remained in heaven above watching the travails of earth. That would also mean

53. Evan Stephenson, "The Last Battle: C. S. Lewis and Mormonism," in *Dialogue* (Winter 1997): 51, 66.

54. *TPJS*, 181.

55. B. H. Roberts, *Seventy's Course in Theology: Third Year and Fourth Year* (Salt Lake City: Caxton Press, 1910), 4:70; cited in Beckwith, Mosser, and Owen, eds., *The New Mormon Challenge*, 225; emphasis added.

that God did not save us (contrary to the declarations of scripture), but that he sent his Son to do his dirty work for him. This is why I consider the ontological oneness of the Father and the Son to be essential to our sense that God saved us and knows what it is like when we suffer.

Lest I close on this point of difference, I want to reiterate where we Mormons and evangelicals find our own kind of oneness—in convictions about Jesus and God, to wit: We agree that Jesus is not only the Son of God but also God the Son. We affirm that Jesus was and is incarnate God, "the Only Begotten Son in the Flesh." I heartily concur with Professor Millet's bold proclamation that Jesus didn't just teach the truth but *is* the truth. He didn't just *bring* resurrection; he *is* the resurrection and life. And we also concur with the classical understanding that Jesus was tempted as we are but never sinned.

4

THE SUFFERING SERVANT

His Passion and Atonement
Robert Millet

If I retire to bed at the right time, my eyes usually begin to focus once again at about 5:30 the next morning. I roll out of bed onto my knees for prayer, do a series of stretching exercises for an aging back, and then make my way into the bathroom. I flip on the light, stare into the mirror, and become a part of a doctrinal epiphany: I have affirmed in my mind and heart that the doctrine of the fall is true! Most of my hair is gone, my narrow waist and broad chest have changed places, and my feet do not yet have any feeling in them; I need to be patient as the blood gradually makes its way into my extremities. Yes, I am indeed closer to the casket than the cradle.

An Unusual View of the Fall

There is, however, more to it than that. Although I plead and pray for kindness and patience and meekness—the "fruit of the Spirit" (Gal. 5:22)—and struggle to bite my tongue and stifle my sarcasms, yet I still find myself, in unexpected moments, saying what I ought not say, feeling what I ought not feel, acting in ways that remind me that in the spiritual realm the Lord has a great deal of work to do on my soul, that I have miles and miles to go before I rest. The effects of the fall are a stark and sobering reality to me.

On the one hand, Latter-day Saints are in complete agreement with most of their Christian brothers and sisters when it comes to understanding the effects of the fall of Adam and Eve. Because of that fall, death of two kinds have become a part of our world: physical death and spiritual death. Physical death takes place when my heart stops beating and I stop breathing, when my spirit leaves my body. Spiritual death takes place as I am cut off or separated from God or from things of righteousness. This comes as a result of the fall and as I choose to sin and thereby separate myself from Deity. Now while the words "total depravity" will generally cause a Mormon to cringe because of what they can connote, Latter-day Saints do believe that the fall is real and that it takes a toll on our physical body as well as on our thoughts, our emotions, and, of course, our actions. If by total depravity one means that men and women are so corrupt, so worm-like, that they cannot even do a good deed, then we reject the idea. But if total depravity means that every aspect of my life is affected adversely by the fall and that I am totally incapable of extricating myself from the effects of the fall (on my own), then we are agreed. Humanity cannot forgive its own sins, renew its own nature, raise itself from the dead, or save itself here and hereafter. These things require the mediation of one who is greater than death; they require the intervention of God.

On the other hand, Joseph Smith and his successors have repeatedly taught that the fall of Adam and Eve does not represent, as most all Christians have concluded, a great act of rebellion on the part of our first parents in Eden. The LDS view is far more optimistic—that Adam and Eve's choice to partake of the forbidden fruit was neither selfish nor self-serving; it was neither meddlesome nor megalomaniacal. It was not man's first effort to lust after power or usurp God's place on the throne. Barbara Brown Taylor recently asked some interesting questions about Adam and Eve: "If God did not want them to eat from the tree, then why did God put it there in the first place? . . . If it was all a test of the first couple's obedience, then why didn't God let them work up to it a little?" Taylor went on to observe:

> Some lovers of this story say that Adam and Eve were destined to do what they did—not because of original sin but because of God. God knew that they had to eat the fruit. It was the only way for them to wake up, so that they could make real choices from then on. . . . But nowhere in this story is the word "sin" mentioned, much less the phrase "original sin." That tagline was assigned to the story much later—in the fourth century CE—by Augustine of Hippo, who turned the tale of Adam and Eve into an explanation for the human tendency to choose evil instead of good.[1]

Mormons teach that Adam and Eve were placed in the Garden of Eden in a paradisiacal, immortal condition, a state in which there was no opposition, no death, no procreation, and thus no progression. One

1. Barbara Brown Taylor, *Speaking of Sin: The Lost Language of Salvation* (Cambridge, MA: Cowley, 2000), 46–47.

passage in the Book of Mormon describes it like this: "And now, behold, if Adam had not transgressed he would not have fallen, but he would have remained in the garden of Eden. And all things which were created must have remained in the same state in which they were after they were created; and they must have remained forever, and had no end. And they would have had no children; wherefore they would have remained in a state of innocence, having no joy, for they knew no misery; doing no good, for they knew no sin." Now note this summary statement, a distillation expression that Latter-day Saints quote regularly: "Adam fell that men might be; and men are, that they might have joy." Then follows the connection between the fall and the atonement, a vital link in God's plan of salvation: "And the Messiah cometh in the fulness of time, that he may redeem the children of men from the fall" (2 Nephi 2:22–26).

In other words, the fall and the atonement are a package deal. They are companion doctrines. Think on this: if there had been no fall, there would have been no atonement. Perhaps the reader is prone to wonder: Well, wouldn't it have been better if there had been no fall and thus no need for an atonement? Our answer is absolutely not. In the words of an early LDS apostle, Orson F. Whitney, "The fall had a two-fold direction—downward, yet forward. It brought man into the world and set his feet upon progression's highway."[2] That is to say, the fall brought cataclysmic changes to the earth and all forms of life on it, including sweat and toil and sickness and pain and suffering and sorrow. But from our perspective, it also brought about mortality and children and families and challenges to engage—and the joy and happiness that come as a result of overcoming obstacles. Furthermore, and much more significant, it placed men and women in a position of need, of total dependence on a source of cleansing and strength beyond their own; it pointed out, in short, the need for a Savior.

C. S. Lewis observed that the fall offered "a deeper happiness and a fuller splendour" than if there had been no fall. Because man has fallen, he pointed out, "for him God does the great deed." For man, the prodigal, "the eternal Lamb is killed." Thus "if ninety and nine righteous races inhabiting distant planets that circle distant suns, and needing no redemption on their own account, were made and glorified by the glory which had descended into our race"—namely Jesus Christ, the Lamb of God—then "redeemed humanity" would become "something more glorious than any unfallen race." "The greater the sin," he continued, "the greater the mercy: the deeper the death the brighter the rebirth. And this super-added glory will, with true vicari-

---

2. *Cowley and Whitney on Doctrine*, comp. Forace Green (Salt Lake City: Bookcraft, 1963), 287.

ousness, exalt all creatures and those who have never fallen will thus bless Adam's fall."[3]

John Wesley acknowledged that men and women are fallen and in a desperate condition without divine assistance. But because the fall impels men and women to seek after such assistance, in the long run, it was a good thing. "May the Lover of men," Wesley yearned, "open the eyes of our understanding to perceive clearly that by the fall of Adam mankind in general have gained a capacity, first, for being more holy and happy on earth; and secondly, of being more happy in heaven, than otherwise they might have been." Quoting from the Apostle John, Wesley stated that "'We love him, because he first loved us' [1 John 4:19], but this greatest instance of his love had never been given if Adam had not fallen." In other words, "God permitted [the fall] in order to a fuller manifestation of his wisdom, justice and mercy, by bestowing on all who would receive it an infinitely greater happiness than they possibly have attained if Adam had not fallen."[4]

To put this another way, Latter-day Saints believe in the creation, and we believe in the fall. In the creation, God placed his image and likeness upon humanity. Through the fall that image is marred. Through the divine work we know as the atonement of Jesus Christ, wrongs are righted, the unfixable is fixed, and people may be delivered from the tyranny of sin and the inevitability of death. Through accepting the substitutionary atonement of Jesus, they make a divine connection that purifies and empowers, a connection that opens them to an entirely new view of reality, to a new way of life. To choose Christ is to choose to be changed.

Christ's Atonement

For Latter-day Saints, God loves his children, all of them, and desires to do all he can to save them. The greatest evidence of God's infinite and perfect love is the gift of his Son, Jesus Christ, as our Savior, Redeemer, Lord, and God. Jesus was both fully human and fully God. From his mother, Mary, a mortal woman, he inherited mortality, the capacity to experience completely all the aspects of this life, including hunger, thirst, fatigue, pain, alienation, and, of course, physical death. Jesus also had within him the powers of divinity, which enabled him to do what no other man or woman in human history had ever done—to look upon every soul with a Godlike empathy and compassion, to lift souls and

3. C. S. Lewis, *Miracles* (New York: Touchstone, 1996), 162.
4. In Albert C. Outler and Richard P. Heitzenrater, eds., *John Wesley's Sermons: An Anthology* (Nashville: Abingdon, 1991), 477, 479, 483–84.

liberate captive human hearts, to resist temptation and remain sinless, to forgive sins, and to rise from the dead. "Therefore doth my Father love me," Jesus said, "because I lay down my life, that I might take it again. No man taketh it from me," he continued, "but I lay it down of myself. *I have power to lay it down, and I have power to take it again.* This commandment have I received of my Father." (John 10:17–18; emphasis added.) Similarly, a Book of Mormon teacher stated that "there is no flesh that can dwell in the presence of God, save it be through the merits, and mercy, and grace of the Holy Messiah, who layeth down his life according to the flesh [his humanity], and taketh it again by the power of the Spirit [his divinity]" (2 Nephi 2:8).

Jesus came to earth to *atone* for fallen men and women. What does that mean? The Hebrew word for atone is *kafar*, which means to cover or to forgive, while the Aramaic and Arabic word *kafat* means to embrace. Our Lord covers our sins as a beautiful white sheet might cover a scarred and dusty table. Furthermore, he covers our sins in the same sense that we might speak of one party at lunch grabbing the check and saying, "I'll cover it" or "I'll pay the bill." The unfathomable irony of the whole matter is that Jesus not only forgives those who sin against him ("Father, forgive them, for they know not what they do"), but he also forgives their misdeeds against other persons (as though the sins were against him), a gesture and a labor that no one but a God could bring to pass.

There is a sense in which Jesus's whole life was central to his atoning mission. Every pain he suffered, every ingratitude he endured, every time he was the butt of someone's joke—these and ten thousand other moments of his matchless life ministered to him, shaped his character, and perfected his empathy, all of which was vital in order for him to perform the atonement. Truly, he was sent to "bind up the brokenhearted, to proclaim liberty to the captives," to substitute oil for mourning, beauty for ashes (see Isa. 61:1, 3). Alma, a Book of Mormon prophet, described, more than eighty years before Jesus's birth, the breadth and depth of Christ's suffering: He "shall go forth, suffering *pains* and *afflictions* and *temptations* of every kind; and this that the word might be fulfilled which saith he will take upon him the pains and the *sicknesses* of his people. And he will take upon him *death*, that he may loose the bands of death which bind his people; and he will take upon him their *infirmities, that his bowels may be filled with mercy, according to the flesh, that he may know according to the flesh how to succor his people* according to their infirmities" (Alma 7:11–12; emphasis added).

As someone has wisely remarked, the atonement is not just for big bad sinners.[5] It is available to encourage and encompass us in the arms

5. See Bruce C. Hafen, *The Broken Heart* (Salt Lake City: Deseret Book, 1989), 1–23.

of his love, to lift and liberate us, to refresh and renew us. Jeffrey R. Holland has pointed out:

> This reliance upon the merciful nature of God is at the very center of the gospel Christ taught. I testify that the Savior's Atonement lifts from us not only the burden of our sins but also the burden of our disappointments and sorrows, our heartaches and our despair. From the beginning, trust in such help was to give us both a reason and a way to improve, an incentive to lay down our burdens and take up our salvation. . . . Considering the incomprehensible cost of the Crucifixion and Atonement, I promise you He is not going to turn His back on us now. When He says to the poor in spirit, 'Come unto me,' He means He knows the way out and He knows the way up. He knows it because He has walked it. He knows the way because He *is* the way.[6]

Jesus Christ, our Advocate with the Father, thereby knows "the weakness of man and how to succor them who are tempted" (D&C 62:1).

Mark records that following the Last Supper Jesus and his disciples "came to a place which was named Gethsemane [literally, the garden of the oil press]: and he saith to his disciples, Sit ye here, while I shall pray. And he taketh with him Peter and James and John, and began to be sore amazed, and to be very heavy; and saith unto them, My soul is exceeding sorrowful unto death: tarry ye here, and watch" (Mark 14:32–34). Other translations indicate that Jesus began to be awestruck, astonished, then depressed, dejected, even suffering anguish of soul. Why? For what reason? What would cause the Son of God to feel such agony? It is inconceivable to me that the Messiah's suffering came out of fear of what lay ahead, namely, the crucifixion the next day. Now to be sure, crucifixion was a hideous form of torture and death, one the Romans had perfected. No one would want to go through such agony—at least not if it could be avoided. As Jesus had remarked after the raising of Lazarus, "Now is my soul troubled; [but] what shall I say? Father, save me from this hour: but *for this cause came I unto this hour*" (John 12:27; emphasis added). This is why Christ came to earth. This is why the Father sent him. This is that toward which all other things in his ministry pointed, the moment in history that would prove to be the hinge on which the door of eternity would swing.

Gethsemane and Golgotha

In speaking of the "awful arithmetic" of the atonement, Elder Neal A. Maxwell said: "Imagine, Jehovah, the Creator of this and other worlds,

6. Jeffrey R. Holland, Conference Report, April 2006, 71–72.

'astonished!' Jesus knew cognitively what He must do, but not experientially. He had never personally known the exquisite and exacting process of an atonement before. Thus, when the agony came in its fulness, it was so much, much worse than even He with His unique intellect had ever imagined!"[7] John MacArthur stated that it was not the fear of death that horrified our Master, but rather the awful anticipation of facing head-on the "bitter cup." "What is the cup?" he asked. "It is not merely death. It is not the physical pain of the cross. It was not the scourging or the humiliation. It was not the horrible thirst, the torture of having nails driven through His body, or the disgrace of being spat upon or beaten. It was not even all those things combined. . . . Clearly what Christ dreaded most . . . was the outpouring of divine wrath He would have to endure from His holy Father." That is, "God the Father would turn his face from Christ the Son, and Christ would bear the full brunt of the divine fury against sin."[8]

Mormons believe and teach that one of the consequences of sin is the withdrawal of a portion of God's Spirit (see Alma 34:35; D&C 19:20), and that what we feel as emptiness, alienation, disappointment, disapproval—these are but manifestations of the loss of the Spirit. It is very important to remember that Jesus Christ had never known such feelings, had never experienced such separation, simply because he had never yielded to temptation; he was completely free of sin and its effects (2 Cor. 5:21; Heb. 4:14–15). As he explained, "The Father hath not left me alone; for I do always those things that please him" (John 8:29; see also verse 16). But through the atonement during those hours of infinite irony, Christ became "sin for us" (2 Cor. 5:21); he was made a curse for us (Gal. 3:13); he tasted death for every person (Heb. 2:9). In other words, while Jesus himself had never done anything to merit God's displeasure, in the atonement there was imputed to him the effects of our sins; he became, as it were, the great sinner. Consequently, as Brigham Young pointed out, it was the withdrawal of the Father's Spirit that caused him to suffer, to agonize, to feel an awful and unusual (for him) alienation, and, as set forth in the Bible (Luke 22:44), Book of Mormon (Mosiah 3:7), and Doctrine and Covenants (D&C 19:18), to bleed from every pore.[9]

And so it is that Latter-day Saints believe that what the lowly Nazarene was undergoing in Gethsemane was not only anticipatory but actual, that the Lord's anguish in the garden was the beginning of his passion, the early stages of his atoning sacrifice. Patrick Henry Rear-

7. Neal A. Maxwell, Conference Report, April 1985, 92.

8. John MacArthur, *The Murder of Jesus* (Nashville: Word, 2000), 69–71.

9. Brigham Young, *Journal of Discourses*, 26 vols. (Liverpool: F. D. Richards & Sons, 1851–86), 3:205–6.

don, pastor of All Saints Antiochian Orthodox Church in Chicago, has written:

This garden of Jesus' trial was, first of all, a place of sadness, the sorrow of death itself. . . . This sorrow of death is common to the two gardens of man's trial, the garden of Adam and the garden of Jesus. . . . It is common to think of our Lord's prayer in the garden in reference to his fear, but it is significant that the accounts in Matthew and Mark emphasize his sadness more than his fear. Jesus said in the garden, "My soul is exceedingly sorrowful (*perilypos*), even unto death." The context of this assertion indicates that *Jesus assumed the primeval curse of our sorrow unto death, in order to reverse the disobedience of Adam. In the garden, Jesus took our grief upon himself,* praying "with vehement cries and tears" (Heb. 5:7). In the garden he bore our sadness unto death, becoming the "Man of sorrows, and acquainted with grief" (Isa. 53:3, 4).

The author went on to say: "*These prayers and supplications of Jesus are themselves sacrificial,* because Hebrews said that he 'offered' them (*prosenegkas*). They are priestly prayers. That is to say, *Jesus' sacrifice has* [in the garden] *even now begun. The Lord's passion is a seamless whole.*"[10]

In other words, Jesus the Christ's atoning sacrifice began in the Garden of Gethsemane. It was there that he suffered for our sins, our pains, and our infirmities. And it was on the cross, during the hours of darkness, that all of the agonies of the night before re-occurred.[11] Once more the Father's Spirit was withdrawn, causing the Sinless One, the Holy One of Israel, to utter his soul cry: "My God, my God, why hast thou forsaken me?" (Matt. 27:46). It was on the cross that he suffered for our sins, our pains, and our infirmities. To say this another way, what began in Gethsemane was finished, was climaxed on Golgotha. The debt had been paid. The Father's will had been carried out. Following the resurrection it could be said that the victory had been won.

We proclaim, just as the Apostle Paul did, "Jesus Christ and him crucified" (1 Cor. 2:2). In beginning a brief passage on various spiritual gifts, a revelation in the Doctrine and Covenants affirms: "To some it is given by the Holy Ghost to know that Jesus Christ is the Son of God, and that *he was crucified for the sins of the world.* To others it is given to believe on their words, that they also might have eternal life if they continue faithful" (D&C 46:13–14; emphasis added). Joseph F. Smith,

---

10. Patrick Henry Reardon, "The Agony of Gethsemane," *Touchstone* (April 2006): 21, 22; emphasis added.

11. See James E. Talmage, *Jesus the Christ* (Salt Lake City: Deseret Book, 1972), 661; Bruce R. McConkie, *The Mortal Messiah*, 4 vols. (Salt Lake City: Deseret Book, 1979–81), 4:224–28; McConkie, Conference Report, April 1985, 10.

the nephew of Joseph Smith and later the sixth president of the LDS Church, taught that redemption has been "wrought through the sacrifice of the Son of God upon the cross" (D&C 138:35). President Ezra Taft Benson explained: "In Gethsemane and on Calvary, [Christ] worked out the infinite and eternal atonement. It was the greatest single act of love in recorded history. Thus He became our Redeemer."[12] In short, it was necessary that Jesus (1) forgive our sins and thereby deliver us from spiritual death; and (2) die and then rise from the dead, to offer the hope of resurrection, thereby overcoming physical death. One Book of Mormon prophet foresaw the time, some six hundred years ahead, when Jesus would be *"lifted up upon the cross and slain for the sins of the world"* (1 Nephi 11:33; emphasis added).

Notice the language of the risen Lord to the people of the Book of Mormon: "Behold, I have given unto you my gospel, and this is the gospel which I have given unto you—that I came into the world to do the will of my Father, because my Father sent me. And *my Father sent me that I might be lifted up upon the cross*; and after that I had been lifted up upon the cross, that I might draw all men unto me, that as I have been lifted up by men even so should men be lifted up by the Father, to stand before me, to be judged of their works, whether they be good or whether they be evil" (3 Nephi 27:13–14; emphasis added). In that spirit, Joseph F. Smith reminded us that "having been born anew, which is the putting away of the old man sin, and putting on of the man Christ Jesus, *we have become soldiers of the Cross*, having enlisted under the banner of Jehovah for time and for eternity."[13]

We speak reverently of the cross, for so did those whose writings compose a significant portion of the New Testament and those who spoke or wrote what is contained in our own scriptural records. The cross is a symbol of the atonement, a type or shadow of what it cost the Father to give us his Son. On a number of occasions when I have been asked why the Latter-day Saints do not believe in the saving efficacy of the cross, and when I have corrected the false impression by referring to passages like those cited above, a follow-up question comes: "Well then, if you people really do claim to be Christian, why do you not have crosses on your buildings, your vestments, or your literature?" It appears that crosses were seldom if ever placed on our meetinghouses. Inasmuch as many of our early converts came from a Puritan background, they, like the Puritans, were essentially anti-ceremonial, which included not using crosses. For that matter, Baptists did not have crosses on their churches for a long time, at least until they began to move into mainstream Protestantism.

---

12. *Teachings of Ezra Taft Benson* (Salt Lake City: Bookcraft, 1988), 14.
13. Joseph F. Smith, *Gospel Doctrine* (Salt Lake City: Deseret Book, 1971), 91.

Conclusion

Now to be sure, the work of atonement was not finished when the Savior spoke his last words and gave up the ghost on the cross. Rather, his rise from the tomb in glorious resurrected immortality three days later provided the supernal answer to the ancient query of Job: "If a man die, shall he live again?" (Job 14:14). The resurrection also stands, as Paul taught in 1 Corinthians 15:12–17, as the greatest of all witnesses and testimonies of his divine Sonship. Joseph Smith taught that "if there be no resurrection from the dead, then Christ has not risen; and if Christ has not risen He was not the Son of God; and if He was not the Son of God, there is not nor cannot be a Son of God, if the present book called the scriptures is true." Joseph then spoke of an additional undergirding witness of Christ's rise from the tomb: "After the testimony of the scriptures on this point, the assurance is given by the Holy Ghost, bearing witness to those who obey Him, that Christ Himself has assuredly risen from the dead; and if He has risen from the dead, He will by His power, bring all men to stand before Him; for if He has risen from the dead the bands of the temporal death are broken that the grave has no victory."[14]

If there had been no Easter—if Jesus of Nazareth had not suffered and bled and died, if he had not risen from the dead and thus made resurrection and the immortality of the soul living realities for all (1 Cor. 15:21–22)—then there would be no Christmas. Why would we celebrate and rejoice with bells and songs and gifts and merriment the birth of a great moral teacher, a sage philosopher, even a great lover of humankind, if in fact the Man from Nazareth was not who he said he was—God among us? Latter-day Saints join with Christian neighbors throughout the world in affirming that he was and is the Christ, the Promised Messiah, the Prince of Peace, the Lion of the tribe of Judah, and the Lamb of God, our Savior and Redeemer.

14. *TPJS*, 62.

An Evangelical Response
Gerald McDermott

I will never forget the first time I learned that Jesus's death was not just tragic but redemptive. I had grown up in a church with crucifixes. I knew that his death was at the heart of Christianity. But somehow I got the message that I would be saved only if I helped the poor. Hence it was my good works for others that would save me, as long as I was also avoiding egregious sins, especially of the sexual variety. The cross showed something about Jesus (I wasn't sure what), but it seemed to have no direct connection to me.

Then one day when I was eighteen, I was told that Jesus died for my sins on the cross. I knew that I was a sinner by nature and practice, both because I was told that and because I felt it. I also came to learn, after and through a spiritual explosion in my family and finally me, that my sins deserved death. When a young woman (I can't remember her name) told me that Jesus's death on the cross paid the punishment for *my* sins, everything clicked. Suddenly it all made sense—why I had felt guilty, why religiosity never seemed enough, and why the cross was so prominently displayed in Christian churches. But even more, I was blown away by Jesus's love for me. Even though I had become convinced a few months before that Jesus was the Truth, I wept, and decided again that my life must be redirected toward him.

More Pleasant Surprises

This chapter by Professor Millet has been, I suspect, another surprise for many evangelical readers. They were amazed to see such emphasis on the suffering and death of Jesus as *the* events that save you and me. Some might find it hard to believe that the Book of Mormon teaches that "there is no flesh that can dwell in the presence of God, save it be through the merits, and mercy, and grace of the Holy Messiah" (2 Nephi 2:8). Others were probably pleasantly surprised by the Mormon accent on the necessity of the atonement, and LDS belief that the fall caused physical and spiritual death (although I will question their interpretation of these below). They read, perhaps with astonishment, Professor Millet's confession that "every aspect of my life is affected adversely by the fall." Those evangelicals with some knowledge of Mormonism and its relative absence of crosses were no doubt pleased to see the mentions of the cross and crucifixion in both Doctrines and Covenants and the writings of President Benson. Many evangelicals have noted with concern the near-identification or replacement of Calvary with Gethsemane in LDS literature. It will allay their concerns to some degree to learn that Mormons see Calvary as the "climax" of what "began" at Gethsemane.

Was It Really a Fall?

But of course there are still significant concerns for evangelicals. The first is related to the fall, which Professor Millet rightly says is part of the "package deal" that includes the atonement. The fall requires the atonement. Without a real fall, there would be no need for an atonement. Professor Millet agrees with this reasoning: "If there had been no fall, there would have been no atonement."

My problem is with the LDS view of the fall. It seems to so vitiate the severity of the fall that one is left with no logical need for the atonement. The result is that LDS statements about fall and atonement seem incoherent.

Let me try to explain. The LDS view is that the fall was not rebellion or sin per se. In Professor Millet's words, it "was neither selfish nor self-serving; it was neither meddlesome nor megalomaniacal [an attempt by the first humans to be their own gods]." Instead, it was a step "downward, yet forward." It was necessary for humans in order to "be" and "have joy." It enabled us as a race to "make real choices" (Barbara Brown Taylor's words, approvingly cited by Professor Millet). Other LDS literature states that it was the fall that gave us "agency" and so "set [man's] feet upon progression's highway." Furthermore, if not for the fall we would not have had children, for there was no procreation available in Paradise.

First, let me suggest what I see to be three logical problems involved in this view, and then point to what seem to be conflicts with the biblical story. Here's the first logical difficulty: If the fall was neither rebellion nor selfishness, nor, we would presume, disobedience, why are Adam and Eve punished with what Professor Millet says is physical and spiritual death? Why would there be any punishment at all for what was a step of human maturity and indeed the will of God? Why, for that matter, would God want Adam and Eve to do something that would make them "cut off and separated from God"?

Second, if the fall was necessary for the human race to be able to make real choices, that would suggest that Adam and Eve before the fall did not have the capacity for real choices and therefore the fall itself was not a real choice. If the fall itself was not a real choice, how could it make possible further real choices?

Third, if the fall was not rebellion or selfishness or the attempt to usurp deity, and if it in fact enabled us to make real choices, which includes choosing Jesus as Lord, then why would there be an atonement? That is, if the atonement's purpose is to "cover" sin, and "Latter-day Saints do not believe that Adam and Eve 'sinned,'"[15] why in the atonement did Jesus become sin for us? Why would he become a curse for us if there was no sin at the fall to merit a curse?

Biblical Problems

Now for the biblical problems. First, the scriptural portrait of paradise does not seem to support the LDS view that there was no procreation or joy or true humanity there. In the story before the fall, God tells the first pair of humans to "be fruitful and multiply" (Gen. 1:28), which clearly implies the possibility of procreation. The narrator also describes the divine mandate to the first man and woman: "A man shall cleave unto his wife: and they shall be one flesh" (2:24). Becoming one flesh was a Hebrew idiom for complete union, which was not limited to but certainly included sexual union for the purpose of procreation.

Was joy available before the fall? It would seem so. Adam and Eve were told they could have dominion over all other creatures (1:26); God blessed them (1:28), gave them every herb to eat (1:29), and then proclaimed the whole arrangement "very good" (1:31). When Adam was presented with his lovely bride, he exultantly proclaimed that she was "bone of my bones and flesh of my flesh!" (2:23). Joy is suggested in the narrator's statement that "they were both naked, the

15. Millet, *A Different Jesus?* 202; emphasis added.

man and his wife, and were not ashamed" (2:25). What's more, the story implies that they were able to converse with their Maker, who would come into the garden to walk and talk with them "in the cool of the day" (3:8). In contrast, the picture we are given of life *after* the fall is quite the opposite—not joy but sorrow. God told the woman, "I will greatly *multiply* thy sorrow . . . in sorrow thou shalt bring forth children" (3:16). Her husband would "rule over" her, and the implication was that this rule would not be pleasant. The man is told that the ground would be "cursed" because of his disobedience, and he would eat from it "in sorrow" all the days of his life (3:17). Only "thorns and thistles" would spring forth from the earth, and he would eat its bread "in the sweat of [his] face"—not a pleasant prospect indeed (3:18–19). Perhaps worst of all, God "drove out the man" from paradise, never to return (3:24).

What about full humanity? Before the fall, Adam and Eve had all the joys mentioned above, plus the understanding that they had been made in God's very "image, after our likeness" (1:26). There is no suggestion that anything in that image was withheld, or that it increased after the fall. In fact, Paul suggests that something was lost after the fall—if not the image itself, at least some of its powers. Now humans apart from grace have hard and impenitent hearts (Rom. 2:5) and cannot submit to God's law (Rom. 8:7). And by nature they neither understand nor seek God: "There is none that understandeth, there is none that seeketh after God" (Rom. 3:11). Rather than elevating man, as the LDS tradition teaches, the Bible suggests that the fall reduced his powers and vitiated his nature.

There are other biblical problems, particularly with the LDS view that the fall was not rebellion. The Genesis text does not state explicitly why Adam was told not to eat of the forbidden fruit, which lacuna itself suggests that this was a sheer test of obedience. Also, the word for "knowing" in Genesis 3:5 ("Ye shall be as gods, knowing good and evil") is from the Hebrew root *yada*, which connotes "decide for yourself." Hence, a more literal translation of that verse would be, "Ye shall be as gods, deciding for yourselves what is good and evil." The implication is that the essential sin is to decide for ourselves what is good and evil, rather than accepting God's word for it. Adam and Eve heard God tell them not to eat from that tree, but decided for themselves that they could. They decided that what God had said was evil was actually good. This disobedience was therefore rebellion against God's authority over good and evil. They wanted to be their own authority for good and evil, right and wrong—deciding for themselves rather than accepting God's declarations.

If Adam and Eve were not rebellious but were doing what had to be done to progress toward moral agency and full humanity, then why did they sew fig leaves together to hide their nakedness? If this was a case of benign disobedience that in fact was beneficial, why did they hide themselves from God? Why would they try to cast blame elsewhere—on each other, on Satan, and even on God himself (3:12–13)? Why would God punish them and drive them out of the garden? God's own question strongly implies that the fall was indeed rebellion against his authoritative word: "Hast thou eaten of the tree, whereof I commanded thee that thou shouldst not eat?" (3:11).

A Less Important Atonement?

All of this has implications for the atonement, as I suggested in my remarks above about a certain kind of incoherence. Although Mormons teach some wonderful things about the atonement—its necessity and importance—their depiction of the fall makes the atonement seem less important.

If the fall was a step "forward," neither sin nor rebellion, but that which enables us to become human, free to choose liberty and life; and if we are "good by nature," and "it is in the power of man to keep the law and remain also without sin," then I wonder why Jesus had to die.[16] For if by virtue of the fall, I have the power to choose God's will, and there is no defect of will that keeps me in bondage to sin, death, and the devil, then why can't I just do the right thing and work my way into the kingdom? Why would Jesus have to suffer and die?

Jesus's suffering and death then seem superfluous—a nice addition for the weak, to supplement their own natural powers—but not an absolute necessity, and certainly not for the strong of soul. Hence the atonement, which is the power of Jesus's suffering to cover my sins, is not necessary if I am strong enough on my own to keep the law and refrain from sin.

Three Other Reasons for Pause

Professor Millet, as I said at the beginning of this response, affirms important truths about Jesus and the atonement that evangelicals and all orthodox Christians will cheer. He reaffirms LDS belief in the importance and necessity of the cross for salvation. He testifies that Jesus is

16. Ibid., 74, 83–84, 103, 189, 196, 202.

our only Redeemer. And he confesses that Jesus is both fully man and fully God.

Yet his essay makes some minor suggestions that give me pause. The first concerns the relation between Gethsemane and Calvary. Evangelicals may indeed learn something from Mormons about the depth of suffering in the garden. And they can certainly gain from Professor Millet new appreciation for one dimension of that suffering—less fear of physical pain than apprehension over the loss of the Father's presence. But the essay states that Calvary was merely a "re-occurence" of Gethsemane. Evangelicals would point out that the New Testament puts far more emphasis on the cross than the garden, and proclaims repeatedly that redemption and victory and atonement took place at the cross. None of these claims are made for Gethsemane.

Second, I worry that this essay's portrait of the Redeemer detracts from his full humanity. It portrays his suffering in the garden as more "sadness" than "fear." It also states that it was Jesus's "powers of divinity" that enabled him "to resist temptation and remain sinless." Now I am glad Professor Millet, unlike some Christian writers today, emphatically affirms Jesus's sinlessness. But the language I just quoted can be read to suggest that Jesus had latent supernatural power that was used to overcome temptation. (The orthodox tradition has always said that Jesus as a human being fought temptation, not with his divinity, but by the Spirit, just as we are called to do.) It can also imply that Jesus was not as fearful as we would be facing gargantuan pain, but was instead capable of impassive stoicism because of those divine powers. Both of these phrases risk an unbiblical docetism (the heresy that said Jesus's humanity was swallowed up by his deity) and undercut what I take to be the biblical insistence on Jesus's full humanity. They are in danger of denying the scriptural testimony that Jesus was not a Superman or a deified man but one flesh with us, made in the likeness of sinful flesh, clothed with our nature, a high priest endued with a feeling of our infirmities, tempted in all points like as we are, yet without sin.

Finally, LDS President Benson is quoted as saying that because of the atonement, Jesus "became" our Redeemer. This would seem to reinforce the LDS notion that Jesus grew into divinity (see my remarks on this in chapter 3) and was not always the divine Son of God. Yet this seems to conflict with the Book of Mormon's depiction of Jesus as being active as Jehovah in the Old Testament. It also conflicts with (great parts of) the orthodox vision of Jesus as taking up his role of Redeemer just after the fall. Beginning in the second century, Christian theologians taught that Jesus Christ became Mediator once human sin prevented a holy Father from having direct contact with his creation. So Jesus as Redeemer started shielding humans from God's wrath just after the events of Genesis 3. Only because of that redemptive mediation was God able to shed mercy on his sinful creatures. Man survived only because of Christ's intercession—throughout the Old Testament period. During all of these eras, Christ was teaching (thus fulfilling his role as prophet), interceding (hence serving as high priest), and governing both (Jewish) church and world (functioning as king). For these reasons, I would argue that Jesus Christ was Redeemer long before the atonement. And if the Father agreed with the Son and the Spirit, in their eternal counsels before the creation, that the Son would serve as Redeemer once sin appeared, then we would have to conclude that Jesus Christ was the *eternal* Redeemer.

Rebuttal and Concluding Thoughts
Robert Millet

Nothing is more central to the teachings of both evangelicals and Mormons than the doctrine of Christ—that men and women live in a fallen world and are in need of divine aid in order to be lifted from that fallen condition, and that deliverance from the fall comes only through the mediation and atonement of Jesus the Christ. No matter how much men and women might do on their own or how impressive their credentials or accomplishments might be, if there had been no Christ (and thus no atonement), no amount of human good could make up for the loss.

Yes, Latter-day Saints do believe that the fall was a fall. While our view of the purpose of the fall and the motivation for the fall is certainly different from the more traditional viewpoint, the consequences of the fall remain the same. Now, to state that a bit more precisely, Latter-day Saints do not believe in original sin because we believe that God forgave Adam and Eve for their transgression in Eden (Moses 6:53). Moreover, we do not believe that the effects of the fall answered upon our first parents—including physical and spiritual death—represent a curse or a form of punishment that each of us experiences, but rather they represented the natural consequence of choosing to partake of the fruit. Mormons feel that it was necessary for Adam and Eve and their posterity to be cast into a lone and dreary world and to have a veil drawn between humankind and deity in order that men and women might exercise faith in the unseen and learn to trust implicitly in the divine promises of redemption through a Savior. The fall opened the door to the atonement, just as the law of Moses opened the door to the realization that the people simply could not keep every one of the 613 commandments, could not be obedient on their own (Rom. 3:20; Gal. 3:19).

Professor McDermott's argument that God had instructed the first pair of humans to be fruitful and multiply implies the possibility of procreation. I agree. But the question arises: Does it necessarily assure us that procreation was possible in the paradisiacal world of Eden? Do we really know that Adam and Even could have had children at that time? This is an argument from silence. Many times in scripture, especially in the Old Testament, children are called to perform great service in the kingdom of God, but such is not possible, not realizable until they are older and more experienced and prepared. Clearly, however, the doctrinal differences between Latter-day Saints and evangelicals over the fall exist because the LDS position is based on revelation given to Joseph Smith as found in the Books of Moses and Abraham in the Pearl of Great Price, and not just on the biblical account.

As a step downward yet forward, the fall brought men and women into the world and opened the door for difficulty, distress, and temptation, the overcoming of which leads to great joy and satisfaction. In response to Professor McDermott's question regarding the hypothetical possibility of man and woman remaining without sin, I will merely stress that the possibility to live the law of God perfectly is implied by the fact that punishment follows disobedience. God could not in justice condemn us for not keeping a law that was impossible to keep. Then why did Jesus have to die? Because God knew, by his divine foreknowledge, that every man and woman who came to earth would fall short, miss the mark, sin, and that each of us would need deliverance from the effects of our misdeeds through the instrumentality of One greater than death and sin. Christ's atonement was absolutely essential to fulfill the plan and purposes of God, inasmuch as each of us would fall short and never be able to span the chasm between ourselves and a perfect Father in heaven.

Professor McDermott expresses some concern about LDS President Ezra Taft Benson's statement that because of the atonement Jesus "became" our Redeemer, since this seems to imply that Jesus grew into divinity. Though President Benson is not around to consult on his particular choice of words, I seriously doubt that he intended such an idea. He knew, as we know, that Jesus Christ is the Lamb slain from the foundation of the world (Rev. 13:8; Moses 7:47), the one foreordained from eternity to shed his precious blood as a substitutionary offering for sinful humanity (1 Pet. 1:18–20). The act of atonement, performed in the last hours of the Savior's ministry, fulfilled the prophecies and became the realization of Jesus's principal reasons for coming to earth. To be sure, he was our Lord and Savior before he was born, but it was necessary for the act of atonement itself to take place at a moment in history, even though it had taken place in the mind of the Father long before.

5

JESUS OF HISTORY, CHRIST OF FAITH

The Gospels and the Book of Mormon

Gerald McDermott

Sometimes my students ask how we can trust the New Testament. "After all," some of them say, "the authors were biased! They weren't objective. How do we know they weren't just making parts of it up in order to support their own authority?"

These doubts about the reliability of the New Testament, especially the Gospels, go back to the Enlightenment. There were doubts before, but they were sporadic and few. Since the eighteenth century, however, such questions about the Gospels have gained momentum. Their most forceful proponent in the twentieth century was German New Testament scholar Rudolf Bultmann (1884–1976). One reason mainline Protestant churches have declined and Mormon churches have grown in the last few decades is that Bultmann's arguments have found more traction in the Protestant mainline. In this chapter I will discuss both Bultmann's project and a recent, better-known example of similar historical skepticism, the Jesus Seminar. My point is to show that evangelicals and Mormons share substantial agreement on the relationship between the Jesus of faith and the Christ of faith. Without rejecting all historical criticism, both communities trust the basic historical reliability of the Gospels, even after examining well-known attacks on their credibility. At the end of this essay I will look at the claims made for the historical Jesus made by the Book of Mormon, where Mormons and evangelicals differ.

Rudolf Bultmann and the Jesus of History

Bultmann believed that the Gospels give us very little knowledge of the Jesus of history. He was convinced that the early church imported its story of salvation from gnostic, Iranian, and other Hellenistic sources and imposed this framework on what little it knew of Jesus's words and deeds. He was also persuaded by form critics[1] that the authors of the Gospels tailored their accounts to suit the needs of the early church, its *Sitz im Leben* (life setting), rather than being careful to preserve accurately those words and deeds. The result is that in the New Testament we have access not to the Jesus of history but to the beliefs of the early church about the "Christ of faith."

It is not that Bultmann discounted *any* knowledge of the historical Jesus. In his *History of the Synoptic Tradition* (German 1921; English 1963), for example, he sifted, with painstaking detail, the evidence for and against the authenticity of various *logia* (sayings) of Jesus in the Gospels. Some are "more likely" than others, he thought. But only "in very few cases" can "one of the logia be ascribed to Jesus with any measure of confidence." In the vast majority of cases the historian must conclude that whatever was originally from Jesus was so transformed by the early church, in order to make it apply "to a concrete situation," that "it failed in so doing to preserve anything characteristic of him." In sum, "It is frequently impossible to do more than pass a subjective judgment."[2] So the historian must conclude that the historical Jesus, now for the most part lost in the sifting sands of history, was transformed by the early church into the divine "Christ of faith."

Bultmann based these beliefs on flawed exegesis and arbitrary assumptions. He used, as a virtual proof text, Paul's statement in 2 Corinthians 5:16 that "Wherefore henceforth know we no man after the flesh [*kata sarka*]: yea, though we have known Christ after the flesh [*kata sarka Christon*], yet now henceforth know we him no more." Bultmann believed that *kata sarka* meant facts about Jesus's earthly and observable life. Therefore, according to Bultmann, Paul was saying that the gospel has nothing to do with Jesus's earthly ministry or the Jesus of history.

1. These were scholars who attempted to discover the origin, and trace the history, of particular passages by analysis of their structural forms. They assumed the historical setting of the early church determined the various forms.
2. Rudolf Bultmann, *History of the Synoptic Tradition* (Oxford: Blackwell, 1968), 101, 102, 105, 104.

All that matters is the message of the risen Christ speaking through the early church.

Bultmann also assumed that the New Testament's worldview is unintelligible to modern people:

> It is impossible to use electric light and the wireless and to avail ourselves of modern medical and surgical discoveries, and at the same time to believe in the New Testament world of spirits and miracles. We may think we can manage it in our own lives, but to expect others to do so is to make the Christian faith unintelligible and unacceptable to the modern world.[3]

In other words, Bultmann believed that since we moderns supposedly know that spirits do not cause things to happen and miracles do not take place, and since the Gospels are set within a mythical framework that assumes both, we have all the more reason to be skeptical of the historicity of much of what is presented there. We should regard as mythical "the belief that God guides and inspires men; the notion that supernatural powers influence the course of history; the belief that the Son was sent in the fullness of time; the resurrection of Christ regarded as an event beyond and different from the rise of the Easter faith in the disciples; and the belief in the Holy Spirit, if that Spirit be regarded as more than 'the factual possibility of a new life realized in faith.'"[4]

There are problems with both Bultmann's exegesis and these assumptions about worldview. First, his exegesis. N. T. Wright has shown that when Paul said he did not know "Christ after the flesh," he was not rejecting knowledge of the historical Jesus, but instead a certain way of knowing the Messiah (Christ). *Kata sarka* was a "regular Pauline phrase denoting, among other things, the status, attitudes and theology of Jews and/or some Jewish Christians. The sort of Messiah they had wanted would be one who would affirm and underwrite their national aspirations."[5] Paul was saying that the true Messiah would be different, and he said this on the basis of what he knew of the *historical* Jesus in his life as a servant. Paul makes this explicit in Romans 15:1–9, where he says Christ "pleased not himself" and "was a minister [servant]," so that we might learn from his example.

Bultmann's assumption that we who believe in electricity cannot also believe in a God of miracles seems silly to most of us today. But his rejec-

3. Rudolf Bultmann, "New Testament and Mythology," in *Kerygma and Myth: A Theological Debate*, ed. Hans Werner Bartsch (New York: Harper Torchbooks, 1961), 5.

4. David Cairns, *A Gospel Without Myth? Bultmann's Challenge to the Preacher* (London: SCM, 1960), 83.

5. N. T. Wright, *The New Testament and the People of God* (Minneapolis: Fortress, 1992), 408.

tion of the historicity of the Gospels actually goes deeper and resonates with many today. Bultmann's skepticism about knowing the Jesus of history was shaped by neo-Kantian philosophy (based on the thought of eighteenth-century German philosopher Immanuel Kant), which proposed that because we know objects of perception only through the lens of our own consciousness, we can never know objects as they are in themselves. Bultmann came to believe that therefore we cannot know or say what God is in himself, but only how he relates to us. We cannot speak about God objectively, since (1) our perception of everything outside us is clouded by our own mental framework, and (2) God is in a transcendent realm completely removed from our phenomenal realm of everyday existence.

The upshot is that God does not act in ordinary history. This means, in turn, that the true Christ is essentially unrelated to the Jesus of history, so it doesn't matter if we cannot know the Jesus of history.

The problem, however, is twofold. First, seeing reality through a mental framework does not keep us from seeing *anything*. We may "see through a glass, darkly" (1 Cor. 13:12), but we still "see."

Second, for the biblical authors, history does matter. The biblical story itself grounds faith in knowledge of history. N. T. Wright writes, "The Israelites retold the story of creation and fall. Jesus retold, in parable and symbol, the story of Israel. The evangelists retold, in complex and multifaceted ways, the story of Jesus. This may suggest, from a new angle, that the task of history, including historical theology and theological history, is itself mandated upon the followers of Jesus from within the biblical story itself."[6] Luke commends his gospel by insisting that he has combed the historical records for the most reliable accounts:

> Forasmuch as many have taken in hand to set forth in order a declaration of those things which are most surely believed among us, Even as they delivered them unto us, which from the beginning were eyewitnesses, and ministers of the word; It seemed good to me also, having had perfect understanding of all things from the very first, to write unto thee in order, most excellent Theophilus, That thou mightest know the certainty of those things, wherein thou hast been instructed. (Luke 1:1–4).

Paul suggested that if Jesus's resurrection is not grounded in real-time history, we Christians are of all humans the most to be pitied (1 Cor. 15:19).

Therefore, we need to be skeptical about Bultmann's historical skepticism. Just because the Gospel authors were concerned about early church problems does not mean they didn't care about the Jesus of

6. Ibid., 142.

history. As we see for Luke, they insisted they were sorting out historical truth from error and were using eyewitness testimony. Paul's gospel
was based on his knowledge of the Jesus of history, Bultmann's faulty
interpretation of 2 Corinthians 5:16 notwithstanding. There is no rational
reason why we should reject the New Testament portrait of a God who
acts in and through history, precisely because there is no clear reason
why we should presume with Bultmann that God exists in a realm removed from ordinary human life. Therefore, the Christ of faith *can* be
the Jesus of history, for the biblical God is a God who speaks and acts
in history. And by using the Gospels, there is no good historiographical
reason why we cannot conduct "genuine historical reconstruction of
actual events in the past, of the 'inside' of events as well as the 'outside.'"[7]
Using the same historical methods that historians of the ancient world
use for work outside of the Bible, we can say with confidence that we can
know as much or more about the Jesus of history as about most other
figures in the ancient world. Bultmann's skepticism about the historical
content of the Gospels rests on shaky foundations. On this, evangelicals
agree with Professor Millet's sage warning that we should be "critical
of the criticism," particularly when it rules out the supernatural from
"ordinary human affairs."[8]

The Jesus Seminar

Most Mormons and evangelicals may not have heard of Bultmann,
but most Americans have read about the Jesus Seminar. This collection
of Bible scholars has brought the results of Bultmannian assumptions
to the front page of daily newspapers since the mid-1980s.

Yet while the Jesus Seminar is like Bultmann in casting doubt on the
historicity of most of the material in the Gospels, Seminar members do
not share his skepticism about historians' ability to find out what Jesus
really said and did. Like Thomas Jefferson and David Friedrich Strauss
(a nineteenth-century German theologian who denied everything supernatural in the Gospels), to whom their first major book was dedicated, the
Jesus Seminar scholars are confident that their methods can determine
which words in the Gospels are authentic, and which are not.

Before we get to their methods, a word about these scholars. They have
selected themselves, and so are not representative of the top professional
organization in American biblical scholarship—the Society for Biblical
Literature. Instead of being a typical sampling of the best scholars in

7. Ibid., 137.
8. Millet, *A Different Jesus?* 30, 32.

their fields, these seventy or so writers generally think alike, at least in their most important assumptions, such as the debatable Bultmannian presumption that the Gospels are mostly about the early church and not Jesus. Their intent is to "liberate" Jesus from the "Christ of creed and dogma, who had been firmly in place in the Middle Ages, [but who] can no longer command the assent of those who have seen the heavens through Galileo's telescope."[9]

Now for a look at the Jesus Seminar's methods. These seventy-plus scholars cast colored beads to vote on the authenticity of each saying or deed that the Gospels claim for Jesus. A red bead means "Yes, definitely authentic"; pink is "Maybe"; gray, "Probably not"; and black, "Definitely not."

One can see immediately that this manner of determining authenticity is problematic. What if a minority decides on red, but the majority votes black or gray? Doesn't that subject the New Testament to the shifting winds of scholarly debate? Or suggest that the divine authority of the Savior's words are decided by a (scholarly) Gallup poll?

The answer is yes. Consider Matthew 25:29 ("For unto every one that hath shall be given, and he shall have abundance: but from him that hath not shall be taken away even that which he hath"). Twenty-five percent of the Jesus Seminar scholars cast red beads, believing it was definitely authentic, and 11 percent said "probably." But since everyone else cast gray and black beads, this *logion* (saying) was cast into the outer darkness of "inauthentic."

Consider some other *logia* deemed inauthentic:

"This night, before the cock crow, thou shalt deny me thrice." (Matt. 26:34)

"Verily I say unto you, That ye which have followed me, in the regeneration when the Son of man shall sit in the throne of his glory, ye also shall sit upon twelve thrones, judging the twelve tribes of Israel." (Matt. 19:28)

"Blessed are the peacemakers: for they shall be called the children of God." (Matt. 5:9)

By the time the Jesus Seminar was done voting, only 18 percent of Jesus's sayings in the Gospels emerged unscathed. The other 82 percent were "inauthentic."

What is most revealing are the criteria by which a majority of these scholars decided these *logia* never came from Jesus's mouth. The first is

---

9. Robert Funk et al., *The Five Gospels: The Search for the Authentic Words of Jesus* (New York: Macmillan, 1993), 2.

the criterion of "dissimilarity." This is the idea that we can know that a saying was really from Jesus only if it is different from (a) what his Jewish contemporaries said, and (b) what the early church taught. As Richard Hays has put it, this turns Jesus into a "free-floating iconoclast,"[10] with no relation to Judaism or the early church. (I am tempted to say that only academics are foolish enough to believe this!)

One of the underlying assumptions here is similar to Bultmann's—that the early church put words into Jesus's mouth in order to support positions that it knew Jesus himself never took. Yet, as preeminent New Testament scholar James Dunn has said, "The earliest tradents [those who passed on the tradition] within the Christian churches [were] preservers more than innovators, . . . seeking to transmit, retell, explain, interpret, elaborate, but not to create *de novo*."[11]

A second criterion used by the Jesus Seminar is the non-eschatological Jesus. This means a Jesus who never talked about God's future purposes for this world. Yet most scholars have agreed for a long time that Jesus talked repeatedly about the "Son of Man" and the "kingdom of God."[12] Both of these terms are full of eschatological significance.

A third criterion used by the Jesus Seminar is their assertion that the Gospel of Thomas, understood by nearly all scholars to be a gnostic document, was from the first century, perhaps even before some of the four canonical Gospels. Therefore it can be used as a baseline from which to measure the authenticity of sayings in the Gospels. Yet this dating flies in the face of nearly all other scholarly estimates,[13] which therefore undermine many Jesus Seminar conclusions about the authenticity of Jesus's sayings.

So what about my students who think the Gospels are hopelessly biased because their authors were believers? This is part of what drives Jesus Seminar scholars to presume that because the early church had its own interests, it could not have accurately transmitted stories about Jesus. Yet as Craig Blomberg argues, this leads to the silly conclusion

10. Richard Hays, "The Corrected Jesus," *First Things* 43 (May 1994), 49.

11. Cited in Ben Witherington III, *The Jesus Quest: The Third Search for the Jew of Nazareth* (Downers Grove: InverVarsity Press, 1995), 48.

12. See, for example, C. F. D. Moule, *The Origin of Christology* (Cambridge: Cambridge University Press, 1977); George W. E. Nickelsburg, "The Son of Man," in *The Anchor Bible Dictionary* 6:137–50; Norman Perrin, *The Kingdom of God in the Teaching of Jesus* (Philadelphia: Fortress, 1963); N. T. Wright, *Jesus and the Victory of God* (Minneapolis: Fortress, 1996), chs. 6–10.

13. Bart D. Ehrman, for example, who is not an orthodox Christian, writes, "The theology implicit in the more Gnostic teachings [of the Gospel of Thomas] cannot be dated with confidence prior to the beginning of the second century." Ehrman, *Lost Scriptures: Books That Did Not Make It into the New Testament* (New York: Oxford University Press, 2003), 20.

that only someone who was unconvinced by Jesus's claims could have been objective, and a disciple cannot be trusted to pass on what Jesus said.[14]

If that is true, why do we believe that some of the best accounts of the Holocaust were from participants? Do we dismiss histories of feminism that are written by feminists? Or histories of Marxism written by historians sympathetic to Marxist ideals?

Quite the opposite. We tend to think that those who are sympathetic can give us inside accounts that are more attuned to the internal dynamics of a movement or event. They can see and sense things that outsiders often cannot. Outsiders, in fact, have their own prejudices that can cause them to misunderstand the inner workings. For example, one of the leaders of the Jesus Seminar is Robert Funk, who is committed to philosophical naturalism. This is the worldview that chooses to see the universe of matter and energy as all there is. If God exists (and most philosophical naturalists don't believe he does), he has nothing to do with the operations of this world. It is no wonder that the Jesus of the Jesus Seminar does not predict the future or do miracles. He is a charismatic wise man who operates within the world of nature but does not change it.

Interestingly, some leading Jewish scholars have more confidence in the historical reliability of the Gospels than Bultmann or the Jesus Seminar do. Geza Vermes and David Flusser, for example, famously said, "We know more about Jesus than about almost any other first-century Jew," and the other Jew they had in mind was the Apostle Paul![15] At the end of his illustrious scholarly career Flusser wrote, "I am confident that the first three Gospels reliably reflect the reality of the 'historical' Jesus. . . . The Jesus portrayed in the Synoptic Gospels is . . . the historical Jesus, not [simply] the 'kerygmatic Christ.'"[16] Jacob Neusner, the most prolific Jewish scholar of our era, once remarked acidly that the Jesus Seminar is "either the greatest scholarly hoax since the Piltdown Man or the utter bankruptcy of New Testament studies—I hope the former."[17]

My point in this discussion of the Gospels is that Mormons and evangelicals have not traveled the road carved out by Bultmann and the Jesus

14. Craig Blomberg, "Where Do We Start Studying Jesus?" in Michael Wilkens and J. P. Moreland, eds., *Jesus Under Fire: Modern Scholarship Reinvents the Historical Jesus* (Grand Rapids: Zondervan, 1995), 39.

15. James H. Charlesworth, "The Foreground of Christian Origins and the Commencement of Jesus Research," in *Jesus' Jewishness: Exploring the Place of Jesus Within Early Judaism*, ed. James H. Charlesworth (New York: Crossroad, 1991), 81 n.29.

16. By "kerygmatic Christ" Flusser meant the "preached" Christ or "Christ of faith." David Flusser, *Jesus*, 3rd ed. (Jerusalem: The Hebrew University Magnum Press, 2001), 15, 20.

17. Richard Ostling, "Jesus Christ, Plain and Simple," *Time* (January 10, 1994), 38.

Seminar. For reasons of their own, but now supported by some of the best biblical scholars of the late twentieth century, they see no good reason to separate the Jesus of history from the Christ of faith. Many of them support the careful use of selected higher critical tools for the purpose of "historical reconstruction" of Jesus and the early church but reject the presuppositions that led Bultmann and the Jesus Seminar to regard the Gospels as basically untrustworthy. On this road of "faith seeking understanding," regarding the Gospels as ancient documents no less reliable than other ancient histories and in fact chosen by God through which to reveal Jesus Christ, evangelicals and Mormons have walked together. But they have parted company at the fork in the road marked "The Book of Mormon."

The Jesus of History and the Book of Mormon

The Book of Mormon proclaims itself "another testament of Jesus Christ."[18] It is indeed, for it purports to give us, among other things, another Jesus of history. By that I mean it gives another history of what Jesus said and did—not one to replace the Jesus of the Gospels, but to supplement that record. This new record contains the stories of Jesus's three visits, just after his ascension in AD 34 (according to marginal notes in the 2004 Doubleday edition, approved by the LDS Church), to the Nephites in the Americas. According to this third testament, this was the primary group descended from Lehi and his son Nephi. Lehi was the patriarch and prophet who led his family from Jerusalem to the Western Hemisphere about 600 BC. He was also the progenitor of the two major Book of Mormon peoples, the Nephites and the Lamanites. Most of the Book of Mormon traces the rise and fall of the Nephite nation as they "either choose to obey God or yield to the enticings of riches and pride."[19]

The story of Jesus's visits to North America is in 3 Nephi. Here we are told that between AD 33 and 34, over the course of three hours, Jesus Christ destroyed many cities in the Americas by fire and earthquake because of their wickedness in casting out prophets and saints sent to them by God. This was followed by three days of darkness. Many Nephites and Lamanites were killed, but those who did not join in wickedness were spared (3 Nephi 8–10).

"Soon after the ascension of Christ into heaven" (3 Nephi 10:18), Christ showed himself to a crowd of 2,500. He let them put their fingers into

18. *The Book of Mormon: Another Testament of Jesus Christ*, trans. Joseph Smith, Jr. (New York: Doubleday, 2004).
19. Millet, *A Different Jesus?* 11.

the hole in his side and touch the nail holes in his hands and feet. He called and commissioned twelve disciples as leaders and teachers, who were given authority to baptize with water, confer the Holy Ghost, and pass on his teaching (3 Nephi 11:14–15, 21–22; 18.37).

Jesus taught the crowds something very close to the King James version of the Sermon on the Mount, prayed for their children one by one, administered Communion with "bread and wine" several times, healed their sick, and raised a dead man (3 Nephi 12–14; 17:21; 18:2–4; 20:1–7; 17:9; 26:15).

Jesus also made some statements and promises unfamiliar to most who read the New Testament. He said the law of God was fulfilled in him but also "hath an end" (3 Nephi 15:5); he said America was specially destined as this new Israel and was the "new Jerusalem" (3 Nephi 16:16; 20:22); he praised these American disciples for their "great faith" (greater than "all the Jews"; 3 Nephi 19:35), and promised that three Nephites would remain on earth until Jesus returned at the end of the age. They would not suffer pain or sorrow (save that for the sins of the world), they would be cast into prison and a furnace and the den of wild beasts and emerge unscathed, and their bodies would be transformed into an immortal state (3 Nephi 28).

What are we make of this Jesus of history? Can we believe that the same Jesus who preached and healed and was crucified in Palestine came just a year or so later to the Americas and said and did all these things? Is *this* Jesus of history the same as the Christ of faith proclaimed by the orthodox Christian tradition, or at least the Jesus of the New Testament?

I have a hard time believing that he is, for four reasons. First, there are many voices testifying to the one I will call the "Palestinian" Jesus, but only one voice (finally) to the "American" Jesus. We have four Gospels in the New Testament, each written by someone with close connection to the Palestinian Jesus. Both tradition and many modern scholars tell us that Matthew was indeed the tax collector called by Jesus to a new life. Bishop Papias of Hierapolis, writing at the beginning of the second century, assures us that Mark was Peter's interpreter, who "wrote down accurately all that Peter remembered."[20] Other early sources inform us that Luke was the physician who accompanied Paul on some of his missionary journeys.[21] And Irenaeus and Clement of Alexandria (both from the second century) say that the author of John's Gospel was the "beloved disciple" (John 21:20) known to be closest to Jesus.[22]

---

20. Eusebius, *The History of the Church*, 3.39.
21. Irenaeus, *Against Heresies*, 3.1.1.
22. Irenaeus, *Against Heresies*, ibid.; Clement, *Fragments* IV.

In contrast, there is only one voice testifying to the authenticity of the American Jesus—the translator of the gold plates that comprise the Book of Mormon, Joseph Smith. To be sure, the Book of Mormon purports to be the testimony of more than several ancient prophets, and eleven witnesses say they saw the golden plates. But while there are many extant manuscripts from the ancient world attesting the existence of four gospels that arose independently—hence at least four independent voices—there is no other record from the ancient world outside the Book of Mormon that speaks of the American Jesus, and none of the eleven witnesses claimed to be able to translate the writing on the plates. So ultimately there was only one voice speaking with authority about this other Jesus of history: Joseph Smith.

Second, the testimonies we have to the Palestinian Jesus date from the same century as that of Jesus, but the single testimony to the American Jesus comes from eighteen centuries later. Not only do we have manuscripts containing one or more gospels that date to within just a few centuries of the Palestinian Jesus, but evidence within those gospels and some epistles go back to within just a few decades (and for some units of the tradition, *years*) of the crucifixion and resurrection of Jesus. We saw in chapter 1 that by AD 130 all four Gospels were already being recognized as authoritative in the churches (and there is little doubt that all four were penned during the first century). Paul's assertion in 1 Corinthians 15:3–7 that he was delivering to his readers what he had received from his predecessors suggests that he had received a basic Christian creed about the meaning of Jesus's death and resurrection that had been formulated by AD 32 or even before.[23] In other words, we have evidence within the Palestinian Jesus's own century, either coming from eyewitnesses or being circulated at a time when eyewitnesses were still alive and able to corroborate or refute such testimony.[24] But for the American Jesus, the first public record we can find is not until the nineteenth century. If Jesus came to a flourishing civilization in the Americas, why are there no other extant records of these appearances?

Third, there are inconsistencies between the Palestinian Jesus and the American Jesus. The Jesus who is said to have come to the Americas said things that seem out of character for the Jesus of the New Testament. For example, while the American Jesus promises the land of America to the new Israel (who seem to be Mormons; 3 Nephi 16:12) as a "New

23. Peter Kearney, "He Appeared to 500 Brothers (1 Cor. XV 6): *Novum Testamentum* 22 (1980), 264–84.

24. In a new monograph, Richard Bauckham argues that the gospels are indeed based on eyewitness accounts, not simply transmuted oral tradition that was several stages removed from eyewitness testimony, as form critics have charged. Bauckham, *Jesus and the Eyewitnesses* (Grand Rapids: Eerdmans, 2006).

Jerusalem" (3 Nephi 20:22; Ether 13:3), the Palestinian Jesus speaks only of a kingdom of God that is open to people of every land. His promise to the meek is that "they shall inherit the earth" (Matt. 5:5). His apostles write that Jesus's followers still seek a "country" (Heb. 11:14), and "should be the heir of the world" (Rom. 4:13). People will bring into the New Jerusalem "the glory and honor" not of a single nation but of all the nations (Rev. 21:26). So the Palestinian Jesus seems to think of the coming kingdom as a worldwide phenomenon not limited to one geographical part of the earth, but the American Jesus is fixated on America.

There are other discrepancies. The Palestinian Jesus insists he did not come to abolish the smallest letter of the law (Matt. 5:17–20) and warns his followers that they must conform to the law even more than his legalistic opponents (Matt. 5:20; 23:3). The American Jesus affirms that he both fulfills and *is* the law (3 Nephi 15:5–8) but at the same time "the law which was given unto Moses hath an *end* in me" (3 Nephi 15:5).[25] The Palestinian Jesus frequently criticizes the faith of the twelve apostles,[26] all of whom were Jews, but the American Jesus praises the faith of his twelve disciples for being greater than that of "all the Jews" (3 Nephi 19:35). Finally, the only mention in the Gospels of the Palestinian Jesus about anyone not dying is explicitly denied. John says that there was a rumor that Jesus had promised he would not die before Jesus returned, but that Jesus had been misunderstood: "Jesus did not say to him that he would not die, but, 'If it is my will that he remain until I come, what is that to you?'" (John 21:23). Yet the American Jesus promises that three of his disciples will remain on earth until he returns, never tasting death, and they will be thrown into the earth, a furnace, and a den of wild beasts, and yet "[receive] no harm" (3 Nephi 28:20–22).

A fourth reason that keeps me from identifying the Jesus of the Book of Mormon with the Jesus of the New Testament is that there are intra-textual inconsistencies, if you will, between the Jesus of the Book of Mormon and the Jesus of later Joseph Smith prophecies. The greatest of these concerns the Trinity and henotheism. While we saw in chapter 3 that Joseph Smith prophesied at the end of his life against the Trinity, saying that the Father, Son, and Holy Ghost are three separate Gods and this is now official LDS doctrine,[27] there are no signs of this henotheism

---

25. Emphasis added. In v. 5 Jesus says that because the law is fulfilled in him, "therefore it hath an end." This language suggests not simply that Jesus fulfills the Old Testament law, but also that the law no longer has any use.

26. See, for example, Mark 7:18; 8:17–21; 9:32; 14:31.

27. The EOM declares, "Joseph Smith saw for himself that the Father and the Son were two separate and distinct beings," and "the Father alone [not the Son or the Holy Ghost] existed before the beginning of the universe as it is known." Stephen E. Robinson, "God the Father," EOM 2:548–49.

or rejection of the Trinity in the Book of Mormon. In fact, quite the opposite. More than several times, the Book of Mormon affirms traditional Trinitarian language. Take, for example, 3 Nephi 11:27: "And after this manner shall ye baptize in my name: for behold, verily I say unto you, that the Father, and the Son, and the Holy Ghost *are one*; and I am in the Father, and the Father in me, and the Father and I are one." Mosiah 15:5 is even more explicit: "And thus the flesh becoming subject to the Spirit, or the Son to the Father, *being one God*." So also Alma 11:44: "Every thing shall be restored to its perfect frame, as it is now, or in the body, and shall be brought and be arraigned before the bar of Christ the Son, and God the Father, and the Holy Spirit, *which is one Eternal God*, to be judged according to their works."[28] There are similarly explicit testimonies to the oneness of God in 3 Nephi 11:36 and Mormon 7:7.

This language, by the way, suggests a unity of nature and being among the three in the Godhead, not simply "a oneness of mind, purpose, power and intent."[29] In other words, "one eternal God" appears to point to one being, not merely unity in thinking among three different beings.

I can find no trace in the Book of Mormon of the henotheism and anti-Trinitarianism of later writings by Joseph Smith. I draw two conclusions from this. First, Smith seems to have changed his view of the Trinity over the course of his career. In the period during which he wrote the Book of Mormon, he writes explicitly and repeatedly that the Father, Son, and Holy Ghost are only one God, not three. But near the end of his life he says they are three Gods (and that there are even more). This is not a trivial change, but one that has done more than most others to separate LDS believers from other believers in Christ.

Second, this seems to me to undermine claims for the historicity of the Book of Mormon and therefore the history of the American Jesus. If the prophet responsible for the Book of Mormon made cosmically significant changes in his view of God(s) over the course of his prophetic career, one has less confidence in the reliability of his prophecies, particularly those that purport to provide a new history of God on earth. When one adds this to the absence of corroborating voices from the ancient world of these other trips by Jesus to the Americas, one is hard-pressed to believe in this other historical Jesus.

Other critics have found other problems with the Book of Mormon. Thomas Finley and David Shepherd, for example, have pointed to linguistic aspects of the text that suggest that Joseph Smith was imitating the style of the KJV rather than translating an ancient Hebrew original.[30]

---

28. All emphases in this paragraph are added.

29. Robinson, *How Wide the Divide?* 129.

30. Thomas J. Finley, "Does the Book of Mormon Reflect an Ancient Near Eastern Background?" and David J. Shepherd, "Rendering Fiction: Translation, Pseudotranslation,

But my concerns are more historical and theological. Why is there only one voice testifying to the ministry of Jesus in the Americas two thousand years ago, and why are there no historical evidences coming from any time close to that ministry? If the same Jesus ministered in both Palestine and the Americas, within the same three- to four-year span, why do the teachings on one continent seem oddly different from the teachings on the other? And if the same inspired prophet translated the Book of Mormon who prophesied near the end of his life about three different Gods, and in fact more, why does the Jesus of the Book of Mormon seem to deny that later teaching?

For these reasons I cannot affirm with my Mormon friends that the Jesus of the Book of Mormon history is the Christ of faith proclaimed by the New Testament. But at the same time, I am thankful for the joint witness I share with my Mormon friends that the Jesus of New Testament history is credible and that there are no good historiographical reasons for us to doubt the Christ of faith who emerges from those New Testament pages.

and the Book of Mormon," in Francis J. Beckwith, Carl Mosser, and Paul Owen, eds., *The New Mormon Challenge: Responding to the Latest Defenses of a Fast-Growing Movement* (Grand Rapids: Zondervan, 2002), 337–95.

A Latter-day Saint Response
Robert Millet

There is no doubt in my mind but that Jesus of Nazareth was born at about the time of the death of Herod the Great, lived and ministered during the reign of Tiberius Caesar, and died by crucifixion at the hands of Pontius Pilate, procurator of Judea. In other words, I know with an absolute assurance that Jesus was an actual, historical figure, a real person living in real time. Now that's no huge announcement, nothing worthy of a press conference, for most people around the world, even those who do not accept the divine Sonship of Christ, accept the fact that he actually lived, even if they see him as no more than a kindly gentleman who loved people and turned some great phrases, a Samaritan Socrates, a Galilean guru.

Professor McDermott has provided an excellent summary of the teachings and work of Rudolf Bultmann and his fellow travelers, including Bultmann's modern disciples that we know as the Jesus Seminar. For most of us who profess a belief in and commitment to the Savior, there is the tendency—and I encounter it regularly—to smile, shake our heads, and dismiss the Jesus Seminar and their Scholars Version of the four Gospels with a wave of the hand, for few seriously acknowledged New Testament scholars give them even a second look. The problem, of course, is that these men and women who make up the Seminar are teachers or church leaders, persons of influence who have students and parishioners and followers. While their work hasn't given me (or I would say the vast majority of Latter-day Saints) even a slight pause, it is having an impact on a world that has already slid into snide cynicism. Furthermore, a liberal media loves controversy and especially the kind of controversy that in any way casts doubt upon what has been received and believed for millennia. Even scarier, one day the students and research assistants of the Seminar personnel will be professors, and some will choose to work in the ministry. And skepticism and even agnosticism cannot help but influence not only the content but also the spirit of what is taught or preached.

None of this should surprise the Christian world. Mormons certainly are not blown away by it. In 1966 Gordon B. Hinckley, at the time an LDS apostle and later a president of the Church, said: *"Modern theologians strip [Jesus] of his divinity and then wonder why men do not worship him. These clever scholars have taken from Jesus the mantle of godhood and have left only a man. They have tried to accommodate him to their own narrow thinking. They have robbed him of his divine Sonship and taken from the world its rightful King."*[31] Some five years later, Church leader Harold B. Lee explained to a group of students at Utah State University: "Fifty years ago or more," he said, "there were the unmistakable evidences that *there was coming into the religious world actually a question about the Bible and about the divine calling of the Master himself*. Now, fifty years later, our greatest responsibility and anxiety is to defend the divine mission of our Lord and Master, Jesus Christ, for all about us, even among those who claim to be professors of the Christian faith, are those not willing to stand squarely in defense of the great truth that our Lord and Master, Jesus Christ, was indeed the Son of God."[32]

So I gladly proclaim, along with my friend Gerry McDermott, that the scriptures mean what they say and say what they mean, especially as it pertains to the person and work of Jesus of Nazareth. He is who he and others proclaimed he was—the Son of God, God the Son, the second member of the Godhead or Trinity. He did what the Bible said he did—he lived a perfect life and thereby became our exemplar; he spoke as one having authority, even the authority of God, and thereby became our Master Teacher; he suffered in ways that mere mortals cannot comprehend, gave himself a ransom for our sins, and thereby became our Mediator, the one who pleads our cause in the courts of glory before the Father; he was crucified, died, lay in a borrowed tomb for three days, and then rose triumphantly from the dead in glorified immortality, thereby becoming the "first fruits of them that slept" (1 Cor. 15:20).

I love the New Testament, cherish its truths, and rejoice in its central message—the message of hope and salvation to be found only in and through the atoning blood of Christ. I have taught and written of the New Testament for thirty years, and there's just nothing I would rather

31. Conference Report, April 1966, 86; emphasis added.
32. LDS Student Association fireside, Utah State University, October 10, 1971; emphasis added.

do than sit down and have lengthy conversations about the Gospel of John or Paul's epistles to the Galatians and the Romans. These truths are timely and timeless.

And yet, as a professing and practicing Mormon, I believe in the prophetic call of Joseph Smith and of the revelations and scriptural records that came through him, including the Book of Mormon, Another Testament of Jesus Christ. I love reading the Book of Mormon, cross referencing verses both within its covers and related biblical passages, and pondering soberly upon its central message—that fallen men and women are in desperate need of redemption and deliverance that can come only through the mediation and atonement of Jesus Christ.

I want to comment on some of Professor McDermott's lesser points and then focus in conclusion on his major concern, namely, the historical veracity of the Book of Mormon. First of all, I certainly do not see the Book of Mormon as a book about "another Jesus of history" any more than Luke's Gospel is "another Jesus of history" than Mark's or, perhaps more poignantly, any more than the magnificent and weighty Gospel of John is a testimony of "another Jesus of history" than Matthew's. The Book of Mormon is an additional witness, a second witness of Christ. Does it contain details, even historical insights that are not found in the canonical Gospels? Of course, because it is a record of our Lord's ministry to "other sheep" in the New World. I return to the concept I sought to establish in my response to chapter 1: to provide additional testimony of the Savior is *not* to detract from or lessen the established and received testimonies of the Bible.

Second, Professor McDermott points up what he terms "inconsistencies between the Palestinian Jesus and the American Jesus." He illustrates this by making reference to Christ's teachings in the Book of Mormon to the effect that America is a promised land, a choice land, the site of the New Jerusalem, while the Christ of the New Testament speaks of the coming kingdom of God as a worldwide phenomenon. While I appreciate the question, I feel that Professor McDermott has misunderstood the overall message of the Book of Mormon. To be sure, the Nephites and Lamanites were taught that God had chosen the land of America to be the recipients of the testimony of Jesus and given to them the weighty responsibility to preach the salvation of Christ to all the world. A later statement by Moroni, the last Nephite prophet, points up the responsibility resting on the people of America:

> And now, we can behold the decrees of God concerning this land, that it is a land of promise; and whatsoever nation shall possess it shall serve God, or they shall be swept off when the fullness of his wrath shall come upon them. And the fullness of his wrath cometh upon them when they

are ripened in iniquity. . . . Behold, this is a choice land, and whatsoever nation shall possess it shall be free from bondage, and from captivity, and from all other nations under heaven, *if they will but serve the God of the land, who is Jesus Christ*, who hath been manifested by the things which we have written." (Ether 2:9, 12; emphasis added)

This statement does not, however, negate the fact that Jesus the Christ is the Messiah and Lord of the whole earth. Early American colonists spoke often of America as a "promised land" and a "New Jerusalem," a place set apart by God for the accomplishment of his divine purposes. In the very chapter describing the first appearance of the risen Lord to the Nephites in AD 34, the following words are spoken by the "American Jesus": "Behold, I am Jesus Christ, whom the prophets testified shall come into the world. And behold, *I am the light and the life of the world*; and I have drunk out of that bitter cup which the Father hath given me, and have glorified the Father in *taking upon me the sins of the world*, in the which I have suffered the will of the Father in all things from the beginning." Now note this verse: "Arise and come forth unto me, that ye may thrust your hands into my side, and also that ye may feel the prints of the nails in my hands and in my feet, that ye may know that *I am the God of Israel, and the God of the whole earth, and have been slain for the sins of the world*." (3 Nephi 11:10–11, 14; emphasis added). Jesus is not "fixated on America" any more than he was, in the Old World, fixated on the gospel going first to the Jews and later to the Gentiles (Matt. 10:5; 15:24).

Professor McDermott points toward another seeming inconsistency in the Christ of the Book of Mormon: that in him the law of Moses has been fulfilled and that it has an end in him, while the Christ of the four Gospels makes repeated mention of the need for keeping the law. This is simply a matter of timing. The law of Moses was in effect until Jesus made his substitutionary offering, his atonement; it was requisite that the Jews keep the law until Jesus's mortal ministry was finished. The Christ who visits the Nephites is the resurrected Jesus Christ who may now speak of the law in past tense, as having been fulfilled in him. In the Sermon on the Mount Jesus explained: "Think not that I am come to destroy the law, or the prophets: *I am not come to destroy, but to fulfil*" (Matt. 5:17; emphasis added). Is this not why Stephen was martyred—because he taught that the law of Moses had been fulfilled in Christ (Acts 6:9–14)? Is this not the same message the Apostle Paul sought to impress upon both his listeners in Antioch of Pisidia and the Judaizers, those Jewish Christians who sought to hold on to a law that was already fulfilled (Acts 13:38–39; Acts 15)?

Professor McDermott's point about what he perceives as Trinitarian theology in the Book of Mormon—and that theology being at odds with Joseph Smith's later teachings on the Godhead—has certainly come up before and is worthy of careful attention, much more attention than I am able to offer here. But I will respond briefly to this concern, one I have treated at greater length elsewhere.[33] To begin with, there's a very practical question to be raised: if in fact Joseph Smith made all of this up, if he simply had a fertile imagination, if he was enough of a religious genius to produce thousands of pages of scripture and teachings and set in motion the most successful indigenous American religion, wasn't he bright enough to recognize those seeming contradictions?

If Joseph wrote the Book of Mormon himself, with no divine aid, and dictated by sheer mental effort the material in the Doctrine and Covenants and Pearl of Great Price, and if he delivered later sermons or doctrinal instructions, wouldn't he try to avoid or at least minimize what future detractors or investigators would see as inconsistencies in his thought, especially on something as significant as the Godhead? I am not aware of any statement in LDS literature where the Mormon Prophet says something like: "Well, I may have said this and such in 1830, but I'm telling you now that the real truth is so and so" or even "I know that I have taught you in the past that this is the case, but since that time (or over the years) I have gained deeper insights into the matter and now assure you that this new way of seeing things is the way it is." In regard to the Godhead, Joseph said only eleven days before his death, "I have always declared God to be a distinct personage, Jesus Christ a separate and distinct personage from God the Father, and that the Holy Ghost was a distinct personage and a Spirit; and these three constitute three distinct personages and three Gods."[34] Surely, if the early Mormon missionaries had thought that the Book of Mormon presented Trinitarian theology, they would have reacted or spoken up or rebelled against what is found in the Doctrine and Covenants or what is set forth in later sermons. From my perspective, the members of the LDS Church did not so react because they sensed no inconsistency.

Nor do I. There were, in fact, large groups of people in the nineteenth century who believed in the oneness of the Godhead but rejected what they perceived to be mystical views regarding the Trinity. One religious

---

33. See Millet, "Joseph Smith, The Book of Mormon, and the Nature of God," in *"To Be Learned Is Good If . . ."* (Salt Lake City: Bookcraft, 1987), 59–76; "Joseph Smith and Modern Mormonism: Orthodoxy, Neo-Orthodoxy, Tension, and Tradition," in *Brigham Young University Studies*, vol. 29, no. 3 (Summer 1989), 49–68; "By What (Whose) Standards Shall We Judge the Text? A Closer Look at Jesus Christ in the Book of Mormon," in *Review of Books on the Book of Mormon*, vol. 6, no. 1 (1994), 1887–99.

34. Smith, *Teachings of the Prophet Joseph Smith*, 370.

leader, David Millard, a minister who organized an Eastern Christian Church, published a pamphlet in 1818 in which he took serious issue with the prevailing doctrine of the Trinity. He undertook an analysis of the New Testament to prove his point. "The whole tenor of scripture," he asserted, "concurs in the testimony, that Christ is verily the Son of God, as really so as Isaac is the son of Abram." He further stressed the illogical nature of the Nicene formulation: "Three Gods are not one God, any more than three times one are one or two and one are one: which not only destroys the rules of multiplication and addition, but is flat inconsistency."[35] Similarly, William Ellery Channing, the father of Unitarianism, contended in a famous 1819 sermon in Baltimore that God can no more be three persons than man can be.[36]

In short, I do not believe Joseph Smith ever believed in the doctrine of the Trinity (at least not after his First Vision in 1820) or that what we find in the Book of Mormon is Trinitarian. It does establish clearly what I stated in an earlier chapter, that the Father, Son, and Holy Spirit are one in mind, one in purpose, one in glory and attributes—infinitely more one than separate. The references from the Book of Mormon that Professor McDermott cites do not mean what he thinks they mean, at least as far as mainline and mainstream Latter-day Saints are concerned. Again, such passages (e.g., 2 Nephi 31:20; Mosiah 15:5; Alma 11:44; 3 Nephi 11:27, 36; Mormon 7:7) speak of the Godhead as "one God," but very few Mormons would consider this to refer to anything other than one infinitely united Godhead.

Now to the final matter, the issue of the historical evidence for the Book of Mormon. One Mormon scholar noted that "The Book of Mormon is perhaps the most religiously influential, hotly contested, and, in the secular press at least, intellectually under-investigated book in America."[37] On the other hand, within the last few decades, much work has gone forward by LDS academicians—investigations into ancient literary devices, Hebraisms, name studies, treaty-covenant patterns, word print analyses that focus on single or multiple authorship within the Book or Mormon, warfare, and geography—all of which are intended to establish Book of Mormon antiquity and an ancient meso-American milieu for the narrative.[38] Latter-day Saints are also quick to suggest that time

35. Millard, *The True Messiah Exalted, or Jesus Christ Really the Son of God, Vindicated; in Three Letters to a Presbyterian Minister* (Canandaigua, 1818), 5–8.

36. *The Works of William E. Channing* (Boston, 1886), 371; cited in Milton V. Backman, Jr., *American Religions and the Rise of Mormonism* (Salt Lake City: Deseret Book, 1970), 210.

37. Terryl L. Givens, *By the Hand of Mormon* (New York: Oxford, 2002), 6.

38. See, for example, *Book of Mormon Authorship*, ed. Noel B. Reynolds and Charles D. Tate (Provo, UT: BYU Religious Studies Center, 1982); John W. Welch, *The Sermon at the*

and patience are needed when it comes to "proving" Book of Mormon historicity. Biblical scholars have had centuries to establish the historical veracity of the people and events of the Old and New Testaments, and some things have only been corroborated within very recent years. Should people of the Book have hesitated to believe in the man Abraham until sufficient archaeological evidence existed? Should Christians have refused to accept the resurrection itself until physical evidence was uncovered that substantiated it? Joseph Smith's golden plates are not available for scholarly examination, nor are the Urim and Thummim. Mormons are not, however, rushing forward in great numbers to toss their copies of the Book of Mormon into a bonfire.

Latter-day Saints believe that spiritual realities are investigated and confirmed first and foremost in a spiritual way, that, as the Apostle Paul wrote, the things of God are known only in and through the power of the Spirit of God (1 Cor. 2:11–14). People can indeed "know" of the truthfulness of a spiritual reality, can possess "an inward conviction that is perfectly valid to him in whom it arises." The decision to accept a spiritual matter without current physical evidence can "carry with it an incontrovertible inner endorsement that is worth any amount of argument."[39] While there must be an actual physical referent upon which faith is built (a moment in real time, an event such as the resurrection of Jesus, or a set of golden plates), to exercise faith is to believe in the reality of the unseen and to accept as evidence the hope in that which cannot, for the time being, be proven empirically.

"If Joseph Smith did not translate the Book of Mormon as a work of ancient origin," LDS Apostle Jeffrey R. Holland has written, "then I would move heaven and earth to meet the 'real' nineteenth-century author. After one hundred and fifty years, . . . surely there must be someone willing to step forward—if no one else, at least the descendants of the 'real' author—claiming credit for such a remarkable document and all that has transpired in its wake. After all, a writer that can move millions can make millions. Shouldn't someone have come forth then or now to cashier the whole phenomenon?"[40] Gordon B. Hinckley likewise affirmed:

Temple and the Sermon on the Mount (Salt Lake City: Deseret Book and FARMS, 1990); *Re-exploring the Book of Mormon*, ed. John W. Welch (Salt Lake City: Deseret Book and FARMS, 1992); Roger R. Keller, *Book of Mormon Authors* (Provo: BYU Religious Studies Center, 1996); John Sorenson, *An Ancient American Setting for the Book of Mormon* (Salt Lake City: Deseret Book and FARMS, 1996); *Book of Mormon Authorship Revisited*, ed. Noel B. Reynolds (Provo: FARMS, 1997); Richard Rust, *Feasting on the Word: The Literary Testimony of the Book of Mormon* (Salt Lake City: Deseret Book and FARMS, 1997); *King Benjamin's Speech*, ed. John W. Welch and Stephen D. Ricks (Provo: FARMS, 1998).

39. J. B. Phillips, *Your God Is Too Small* (New York: Touchstone), 83, 86.

40. Holland, *Christ and the New Covenant* (Salt Lake City: Deseret Book, 1997), 345–47.

I can hold [the Book of Mormon] in my hand. It is real. It has weight and substance that can be physically measured. I can open its pages and read, and it has language both beautiful and uplifting. The ancient record from which it was translated came out of the earth as a voice speaking from the dust. . . .

The evidence for its truth, for its validity in a world that is prone to demand evidence, lies not in archaeology or anthropology, though these may be helpful to some. It lies not in word research or historical analysis, though these may be confirmatory. The evidence for its truth and validity lies within the covers of the book itself. The test of its truth lies in reading it. It is a book of God.[41]

I was once sitting with a group of evangelical professors at a seminary, responding to their questions about Mormonism. After about an hour and a half of theological conversation, one of their number asked a question that startled me a bit. He inquired: "What can we do for you?" I indicated that I wasn't sure what he meant. He said: "Okay, let me put the question this way: What can we evangelicals do to help the Latter-day Saints?" A score of ideas raced through my mind, but I found myself answering: "Well, for one thing you can cut us a little slack. You can be patient with us as we struggle to articulate the principles of Mormonism and as we search for empirical evidences for the Book of Mormon. You have been at this business of apologetics, of defending the faith, for two thousand years; we're just a little over halfway to Nicaea, in terms of years, when it comes to providing a reason for the hope within us."

"The words of the prophets," said Hugh Nibley, perhaps the most beloved Mormon apologist of the twentieth century,

> cannot be held to the tentative and defective tests that men have devised for them. Science, philosophy, and common sense all have a right to their day in court. But the last word does not lie with them. Every time men in their wisdom have come forth with the last word, other words have promptly followed. The last word is a testimony of the gospel that comes only by direct revelation. Our Father in heaven speaks it, and if it were in perfect agreement with the science of today, it would surely be out of line with the science of tomorrow. Let us not, therefore, seek to hold God to the learned opinions of the moment when he speaks the language of eternity.[42]

I believe in the importance of evidence. I agree with Austin Farrer, friend and colleague of C. S. Lewis, who stated in 1965: "Though argu-

41. Hinckley, *Faith: The Essence of True Religion* (Salt Lake City: Deseret Book, 1989), 10–11.
42. Nibley, *The World and the Prophets* (Salt Lake City: Deseret Book and FARMS, 1987), 134.

ment does not create conviction, the lack of it destroys belief. What seems to be proved may not be embraced; but what no one shows the ability to defend is quickly abandoned. Rational argument does not create belief, but it maintains a climate in which belief may flourish."[43] In that spirit, Latter-day Saints will continue to read and study the Book of Mormon, paying particular attention to the witness of the Spirit that assists us in discerning truth from error, but never relying wholly upon scientific support. While physical evidence may fan the flame of conviction, I refuse to allow my faith to be held hostage to what science has or has not discovered.

43. Farrar, "The Christian Apologist," *Light on C. S. Lewis* (New York: Harcourt and Brace, 1965), 26.

Rebuttal and Concluding Thoughts

Gerald McDermott

It's nice to have so much to agree on with Professor Millet—that while we should not neglect the best of what historical criticism can provide us, we can still affirm that scriptures say what they mean and mean what they say, and that, like any other product of human scholarship, biblical criticism is a very mixed bag. There are some helpful tools, but there are also sometimes arbitrary assumptions that control the questions and therefore also the answers. This is especially the case for Bultmann and the Jesus Seminar, who do not get us to the Jesus of history. Therefore, we should be critical of the critics, as Bob has put it so aptly. The better historical critics have shown us that the New Testament documents are no less reliable than other ancient histories, and in fact, in some respects are *more* reliable because of their connections to eyewitness accounts.

Bob also raises some good points about Mormon faith and America. I am encouraged to see that the Book of Mormon makes use of what the Puritans called the "national covenant." This was the idea that God makes covenants with other peoples besides the ancient Jews and that these covenants entailed both blessing for obedience and wrath for disobedience. They also suggested that with enough disobedience, God might withdraw the covenant entirely and give it to another people.[44] The Book of Mormon does indeed point to an American New Jerusalem (3 Nephi 16:16; 20:22), but I have now learned that its national covenant

---

44. For more on national covenant, see McDermott, "Jonathan Edwards and the National Covenant: Was He Right?" in D. G. Hart, Sean Lucas and Stephen Nichols, eds., *The Legacy of Jonathan Edwards: American Religion and the Evangelical Tradition* (Grand Rapids: Baker Academic, 2003), 147–60.

is conditional and that the overall vision of Smith's prophecies is international rather than American.

On Jesus and the law, I think the Book of Mormon and I are still at odds. For, as Bob puts it, the Christ of the Nephites speaks of the law "in the past tense," as if to say that the law has no place in the Christian life. But New Testament scholar Douglas Moo argues that while Jesus says he is superior to the law and that entrance to the kingdom is through him, not through the law, he "never attacks the Law and, indeed, asserts its continuing validity."[45] When Jesus promises that "till heaven and earth pass, one jot or one tittle shall in no wise pass from the law, till all be fulfilled," and condemns those who "break one of these least commandments" (Matt. 5:18–19), he seems to point to what Calvin called the third use of the law—helping to guide the Christian believer in daily life.[46]

Again, as in so many of our chapters, we come back to the Trinity. As in chapter 3, Bob contends the doctrine is "illogical" and "mystical." Once more I ask how a Mormon can make such an argument without a little smile. For Bob himself at the end of his response appeals to non-historical, "spiritual" proofs for the authenticity of the Book of Mormon. I know he realizes that there are plenty of Mormon doctrines—such as the eternal pre-existence of matter and human spirits—that seem illogical and mystical to non-Mormons. I am surprised that he uses William Ellery Channing for support here, for Channing, the founder of *Uni*tarianism had far worse words than "illogical" for those who believed in more than one God—not to mention his arguments for the unity of the Godhead and *against* the deity of Christ. On all three scores Channing would be vehement in his "rational" opposition to Mormonism, and I doubt that Professor Millet would find these Channing arguments logical or compelling.

I do not find convincing Bob's arguments against my charges of inconsistency on the Trinity. By the latter I mean Book of Mormon statements that seem to point unambiguously to God's oneness and later Mormon statements that flatly deny such oneness. Was Smith bright enough to realize such inconsistency, and wouldn't he therefore have avoided them or minimized them if he believed there was a problem? Yes to the first, and "no, not necessarily" to the second. Smith was no doubt a very bright man. But he may have changed his mind on the Trinity over the years, and simply decided that his earlier affirmations of God's unity should be interpreted "in the light of" later revelation that the Godhead

45. Douglas Moo, "Law," in Joel Green, Scot McKnight and I. Howard Marshall, eds., *Dictionary of Jesus and the Gospels* (Downers Grove: InterVarsity Press, 1992), 450.

46. The first is the religious use, which drives us to Christ by our realization we cannot keep it; the second is the civil use, which restrains sin in the world.

is really three Gods. He apparently did this in his interpretation of the many biblical proclamations of God's unity.

Bob asks if Mormon missionaries would not have reacted against this discrepancy. They might have done so privately, without giving voice to their doubts. But most disciples in new religious movements throughout the history of Christianity, convinced on spiritual rather than rationalistic grounds, follow the lead of a religious founder. In this case, the founder seems to have interpreted the earlier statements in the light of later ones. Or they stay in the faith despite questions because of strong social and psychological cohesion within the group.

Finally, Bob appeals for time and "slack" to answer some of my historical questions. Mainstream Christians have had two thousand years to make an apologetic case against critics, but Mormons have had less than two hundred. Fair enough. I agree with Bob's own words about the superiority of the witness of the Spirit to rationalistic and historical "proofs." Yet at the same time, without my claiming sure-fire arguments for the Trinity or any other orthodox Christian doctrine, I am still impressed with the difference in historical evidence for orthodoxy after its first 170 years (AD 200) vis-à-vis that for Mormonism after the same period of time. Early Christian orthodoxy had far more testimony, and from a greater variety of sources, than the Book of Mormon—as I tried to show at the end of my opening essay in this chapter.

6
THE KEYS
OF THE KINGDOM

The Church and the Sacraments
Robert Millet

Conversion to Christ is a personal experience. One woman begins to sense her plight, her sinfulness, and then turns to God. One man realizes that despite his education and training and competence, he is absolutely helpless and incapable of changing his nature. Another seeker after truth learns of Jesus Christ, senses that he is the last chance, the only hope. Finally, a broken soul cries out to the Lord in prayer, surrenders her will to the Almighty, and commits to a life of discipleship. While others may and almost always do assist in the conversion process, it is an individual heart that is stirred and an individual soul that is saved.

A Community of Believers

Joseph Smith taught his people, however, that "the greatest temporal and spiritual blessings which always come from faithfulness and concerted effort, never attended individual exertion or enterprise. The history of all past ages abundantly attests this fact."[1] In other words, while individual persons establish individual relations with God, there is a growth and a spiritual maturity that come only through corporate worship, through establishing and engaging the body of Christ, the church. A favorite passage for Mormons is found in Paul's epistle to the saints at Ephesus:

> And he gave some, apostles; and some, prophets; and some, evangelists; and some, pastors and teachers; for the perfecting of the saints, for the

1. *TPJS*, 183.

work of the ministry, for the edifying of the body of Christ: till we all come in the unity of the faith, and of the knowledge of the Son of God, unto a perfect man, unto the measure of the stature of the fulness of Christ: that we henceforth be no more children, tossed to and fro, and carried about with every wind of doctrine, by the sleight of men, and cunning craftiness, whereby they lie in wait to deceive; but speaking the truth in love, may grow up into him in all things, which is the head, even Christ (Eph. 4:11–15).

Let's take a few moments and analyze briefly these insightful verses. From an LDS perspective, the church of Jesus Christ, with its gifts and offices, has been established to accomplish at least the following:

1. The church seeks to assist in the *perfection of the saints*. None of us will navigate life's course without committing sins, either of commission or omission. Jesus alone was able to keep the law of God perfectly and to stand innocent and pure before the heavens. The saints of God, those who have come out of the world by covenant, may, however, become *perfect* in the sense that the original word is intended: whole, complete, fully formed, mature. First and foremost, we become "perfect in Christ" in that through our union with him our unrighteousness is transformed into righteousness, our deficits are covered, and our deficiencies are compensated for. As the Spirit works upon us, we begin to gain "the mind of Christ" (1 Cor. 2:16) and to have our minds and hearts conformed (Rom. 12:1–2) to the image of the grand Prototype of saved beings, the Lord Jesus Christ. We also become perfect as we join with men and women of similar convictions, as we sing and praise and pray and preach and work side by side in projects intended to bless others.

2. The church involves the congregation in the *work of the ministry*. There are mourners to comfort, lonely people to be visited and warmed, houses to clean, lessons to be taught, missions to serve, community projects in which to engage, voices to be sounded in the public square, money to be raised—all as a part of the work of the ministry.

3. Meetings are held and sermons are preached and scriptures are searched and studied in an effort to *edify the body of Christ*, the church. The word *edify* is from the same root as the word *edifice*, something we erect— in this case, a sacred domicile, a house of faith. People are edified when they are built up, encouraged, given new vision, provided with an elevated perspective, and infused with enthusiasm. "And now, behold, I give unto you a commandment, that when ye are assembled together ye shall instruct and edify each other, that ye may know how to act and direct my church, how to act upon the points of my law and commandments, which I have given. And thus ye shall become instructed in the law of my church, and be sanctified by that which ye have received, and ye shall bind yourselves to act in all holiness before me" (D&C 43:8–9).

4. The church seeks to establish *unity in the faith* among its members. There is a crying need for the people of Christ to be united in Christ, to speak the same language, to teach the same doctrine, and to be sufficiently orthodox in their beliefs, so that they will not be an easy prey to the perverse or the misled. It is no great compliment, at least in my mind, that a virtue like academic freedom would camouflage underlying dissension, varied and disparate doctrinal disputes, or theological chaos. Christ calls on his people to subscribe to "one Lord, one faith, one baptism" (Eph. 4:5).

The Apostle Paul chastened the saints at Corinth who had divided themselves into personality cults and spiritual schisms: "Now I beseech you, brethren, by the name of our Lord Jesus Christ, that ye all speak the same thing, and that there be no divisions among you; but that ye be perfectly joined together in the same mind and in the same judgment. . . . Now this I say, that every one of you saith, I am of Paul; and I of Apollos; and I of Cephas [Peter]; and I of Christ. Is Christ divided? Was Paul crucified for you? Or were ye baptized in the name of Paul?" (1 Cor. 1:10, 12–13.) Again, while the strength of the church of Jesus Christ derives largely from the solid core of individual witness and conversion, there is power, consummate power, in unity. There is power in numbers, power in people with "like precious faith" (2 Peter 1:1) who join together to lend their gifts and talents and energies to the supernal cause of our Savior and Redeemer.

LDS Clergy

As to the manner in which the work of the LDS Church is carried on by a lay clergy, Rex E. Lee, former U.S. Solicitor General and later president of Brigham Young University, has written:

> The dominant characteristic of almost all Church service is that nonprofessionals donate it. There is no such thing as a professional Mormon cleric who has trained for the ministry and then gone into it because he chose to do so. All ecclesiastical positions in the LDS Church, at all levels, are callings, and the calling comes to the individual, through inspiration, from someone else who has the authority and responsibility to make the calling. . . .
>
> How can a church be run efficiently like this? How can it afford to entrust not only the organization, management, and policy making to amateurs, but also the expounding of doctrinal principles? I have two answers to these questions. The first is pragmatic: the system works. The Church has been run this way since its organization in 1830. And quite well. The second is that the fundamental gospel principles of governance,

cooperation, participation, and direction by the Spirit are plain and simple. They are principles that can be understood without the benefit of specific, college-level training, by the young and the old. They can be understood and taught today by people from all walks of life because they are the same principles that were understood and taught by carpenters and fishermen two thousand years ago.[2]

At the general level, the Church of Jesus Christ of Latter-day Saints is presided over by a group of men known as the General Authorities. These men are headquartered in Salt Lake City, Utah, but in recent years some have assumed administrative responsibilities in different countries throughout the world. The President of the Church is acknowledged and upheld by the people as the presiding Prophet, Seer, and Revelator. He is the senior apostle, the one who has held the apostolic office the longest. He holds the same position in regard to the LDS Church that Joseph Smith held. He has two counselors who officiate with him jointly; they constitute the First Presidency of the Church.

Working closely with the First Presidency are twelve men who form the Quorum of the Twelve Apostles. The counselors in the First Presidency and the Twelve Apostles are sustained by the church membership as prophets, seers, and revelators. Mormons believe that the apostolic power held anciently by Peter, James, and John and restored to Joseph Smith in 1829, is now held by the First Presidency and the Twelve. "The twelve traveling councilors are called to be the Twelve Apostles, or special witnesses of the name of Christ in all the world." This traveling council is called "to officiate in the name of the Lord, under the direction of the Presidency of the Church, agreeable to the institution of heaven; to build up the church, and regulate all the affairs of the same in all nations." (D&C 107:23, 33.)

Other general authorities include the Seventy, priesthood ministers mentioned by Jesus in the New Testament (Luke 10), and the Presiding Bishopric. The Seventy have apostolic callings in the sense that they are called to be special witnesses of the name of Christ in all the world and to build up the church and regulate its affairs in all the world, under the direction of the Twelve Apostles (D&C 107:25, 34). The Presiding Bishopric are responsible for temporal affairs—for real estate, buildings and maintenance, welfare resources and projects, etc. The First Presidency, the Twelve Apostles, and the Presiding Bishopric constitute the Council on the Disposition of Tithes, a group responsible for the expenditures of the church (D&C 120). The General Authorities travel throughout the earth and are to be found in meetings and conferences of the Saints most every Sabbath.

2. Rex E. Lee, *What Do Mormons Believe?* (Salt Lake City: Deseret Book, 1992), 74–76.

I remember distinctly the feeling of personal loss and even a bit of fear as our family moved from the Baton Rouge, Louisiana, area to a small community to the north called Baker. New neighbors. New friends. A new world—and of course, a new branch of the church. I recall asking Mom and Dad why we couldn't continue to attend our ward (congregation) in Baton Rouge, one in which I had essentially grown up, one whose members I had come to trust and love. It was then that I learned for the first time that as Latter-day Saints we are counseled to attend church according to our geography, not our preferences. We found ourselves within the boundaries of what was a brand new branch of the Church of Jesus Christ of Latter-day Saints. Although I did recognize a few faces, most of the folks were total strangers.

What was really unsettling was that we were also asked to leave our beautiful little chapel on Hiawatha Street and hold our meetings elsewhere; in this case, we did not have a chapel. Instead, we attended church in the girl's gymnasium at the high school where I was beginning the ninth grade. In a gym! Because the community was largely Baptist, I was asked quite often through the next couple of years, "Where is your church located?" and I would answer timidly, embarrassingly (and in quiet tones), "In the girl's gym." I don't remember anyone laughing out loud, but I did receive my share of strange looks. Our goal, as a small group of Saints, was, of course, to raise enough money to build our own chapel. The familiar "building fund" was forever before us; we must have had a hundred chicken dinners, spaghetti dinners, donut sales, softball tournaments (where we handled the concessions), car washes, and other activities with one aim in mind—to build the first phase of a three-phase church building in Baker. At first it seemed a strange thing to be asked to do, but as time went by and as we began to rub shoulders with one another in the endeavor, it became both fun and fulfilling.

Now, almost fifty years later, there burns in my soul a firm conviction that there is power in unity, sweet power in toiling together in the work of the Almighty, dynamic power associated with acting as a group in the name of the Lord. And of course, after we had raised the funds, we began work on the chapel, which we did almost every day. This was a work that has left me with scars (from sliding down the roof), deformed toenails (from heavy weights being dropped on my feet), and a weak back (from lifting much more weight than I should have at that young age). But it has also left me changed in more poignant ways: there is an indelible seal of satisfaction in my soul, a quiet but overwhelming sense of accomplishment, and above all, a penetrating love for my fellow followers of Christ. I am not the same now because of the united power I witnessed and contributed to then.

A few years ago while visiting my mother, I drove out to the Baker Ward with my youngest son. I reminisced about how that beautiful campus had once been nothing but swampland and how that a few weak and simple people had, in a southern setting "made the desert to blossom as a rose." As I went on and on to Stephen about what that building represented (and, bless his heart, he was trying to be courteous and attentive), I realized that there was something of me in that edifice, that whatever puny sacrifice I had made in time and energy had been transformed into commitment and conviction and dedication to the work of the kingdom of God. Those who invest themselves in a righteous cause come to be filled with love and loyalty to that cause.

The older I get, the less prone I am to believe in coincidence. Like you, I believe that God has a divine plan, not only for the ultimate establishment of the kingdom of God on earth, but also an individualized plan for you and me. I gladly and eagerly acknowledge his hand in all things, including the orchestration of events in our lives and the interlacing of our daily associations. I believe he brings people into our path who can bless and enlighten us, and I know that he brings us into contact with people whose acquaintanceship will, down the road, open doors, dissolve barriers, and make straight the way of the Lord. And yes, he brings people into our path who may challenge us, prove our patience, and push us to the limit of our Christianity. The prayer of Elisha for the young lad seems particularly pertinent to our work: "Lord, I pray thee, open [our] eyes that [we] may see" (2 Kings 6:17).

There is much said in our expanding world about the need to celebrate diversity. Of course, each of us is a part of a diverse community, even within our respective religious denominations. But strength is not to be found in diversity; power to influence the world for good will not come through diversity. No, we are to strive to achieve unity in spite of our diversity. John Taylor observed,

> We are seeking to establish a oneness under the guidance and direction of the Almighty. . . . To the world this principle is a gross error, for amongst them it is every man for himself . . . But the Lord dictates differently. We are under his guidance, and we should seek to be one with him and with all the authorities of His Church and kingdom on the earth in all the affairs of life. . . . Then, when men say unto us, "you are not like us," we reply, "we know it; we do not want to be. We want to be like the Lord, we want to secure his favor and approbation and to live under His smile, and to acknowledge, as ancient Israel did on a certain occasion, The Lord is our God, our judge, and our king, and He shall reign over us."[3]

3. John Taylor, *Journal of Discourses*, 26 vols. (Liverpool: F. D. Richards & Sons, 1851–86), 11:346–47.

Priesthood and the Sacraments

With the introduction of the concept of a "priesthood of all believers" by Protestants after the Reformation and a reliance on scripture as sole authority, it is little wonder that the doctrinal necessity for ordinances should cease or at best become clouded and uncertain. Questions arose regarding such matters as the saving efficacy of ordinances (sacraments), the place of ordinances as a channel for divine power, and the need to maintain the divinely revealed mode and manner of performance of the ordinances. It was thus early in the work of Joseph Smith's restoration that the sacraments of the church, including those we know as the ordinances of salvation, were dealt with directly. Joseph claimed, first of all, to have been visited in May-June 1829 by heavenly messengers—specifically John the Baptist and Peter, James, and John—and ordained to the priesthood, granting him and the church the same apostolic power promised to Peter and the Twelve in New Testament times (Matt. 16:18–19; 18:18).

Latter-day Saints believe that the first principle of the gospel is *faith* in the Lord Jesus Christ. We have faith in Christ when we acknowledge him not only as a great moral teacher but as the Savior and Redeemer of all mankind, when we trust in and rely upon his merits and mercy and grace. Once we come to know of him—of his majesty and greatness and holiness—it is but natural that we would begin to sense our own inadequacies and sins. And thus *repentance* is the second principle of the gospel. We repent when we literally "turn away" from our wrongdoings, when we confess and forsake them, when we come to have a new way of thinking and viewing the world. Forgiveness comes only from God through Jesus Christ.

Baptism. The first ordinance or sacrament of salvation is baptism by immersion. Baptism is not optional; it is mandatory. It is an evidence of one's acceptance of the death and resurrection and atonement of Jesus. As the initiate is immersed completely beneath the baptismal waters, he or she participates symbolically in Christ's descent into the tomb of death and his rise to newness of life in the resurrection (Rom. 6:3–5). Water baptism satisfies the first half of the Savior's commission to be born of water and of the Spirit (John 3:5).

Confirmation, the laying on of hands by those with proper authority for the reception of the Spirit, is the second ordinance and the complement to water baptism. The gift of the Holy Ghost is the right to the companionship of the Spirit, the third member of the Godhead, based on personal worthiness (see 1 Cor. 3:16–17; 6:19–20). Joseph Smith taught that one may receive promptings or impressions of the Spirit prior to baptism, but that the gift of the Holy Ghost, or constant companionship, is granted only after an authorized baptism. "There is a difference," he said, "between the Holy Ghost and the gift of the Holy Ghost. Cornelius [see Acts 10] received the Holy Ghost before he was baptized, which was the convincing power of God unto him of the truth of the gospel, but he could not receive the gift of the Holy Ghost until after he was baptized. Had he not taken this sign or ordinance upon him, the Holy Ghost which convinced him of the truth of God, would have left him."[4]

The Lord's Supper. As an outgrowth of the Passover meal at the Last Supper, Jesus introduced what Christians have come to know as the Lord's Supper, Communion, or the Eucharist. Like their Christian counterparts, Mormons partake of the sacrament of the Lord's Supper (they use bread and water) in remembrance of his suffering and death, and more specifically, of his broken body and spilt blood. The prayer offered upon the broken bread illustrates the nature of the covenant, of man's promises to God as well as God's promised blessing: "O God, the Eternal Father, we ask thee in the name of thy Son, Jesus Christ, to bless and sanctify this bread to the souls of all those who partake of it, that they may eat in remembrance of the body of thy Son, and witness unto thee, O God, the Eternal Father, that they are willing to take upon them the name of thy Son, and always remember him and keep his commandments which he has given them; that they may always have his Spirit to be with them. Amen." (D&C 20:77.)

The sacrament is distributed during the Sacrament Meeting, the main worship service in the LDS Church on Sundays, as well as on other special occasions. It is a solemn and sacred period of devotion, a time of reflection, introspection, and covenant. It is a time for men and women to examine their lives, consider their commitment to Christ, and renew their covenants with God made at the time of baptism.

Ordination to the Priesthood. The priesthood is essential to the operation of the LDS Church and vital to the promulgation of the gospel itself. Men must be ordained to the priesthood in order to participate in the sacraments and general oversight of the church.

When I say that Latter-day Saints believe that certain ordinances of the gospel such as baptism, confirmation and bestowal of the Holy Spirit, and the Lord's Supper are *essential*, let me be more specific. As we will discuss at length in chapter 7 and in the response to it, God does for us what we could never do for ourselves; these are acts of pure grace. We are called upon to do one major thing—to exercise faith in the Lord Jesus Christ, a faith out of which flows such actions as repentance, baptism, and obedience. While the scriptures speak occasionally of baptism "washing away our sins" (Acts 22:16; D&C 39:10), in

4. *TPJS*, 199.

reality our sins are washed away by the precious blood of Jesus Christ; in other words, baptism doesn't forgive my sins, Christ does. Baptism is an ordinance, a sacrament, a channel of divine grace, an outward manifestation or witness of my inner covenant to come unto Christ and be saved. The ordinances are not essential because they supplement in any way what our Redeemer did for us on the cross (for his is a finished work), but rather they manifest, complement, complete, and round out my faith.

The Lord's house is a house of order (D&C 132:8), and he expects his earthly servants to maintain that order. "Organize yourselves," he instructed some early Latter-day Saints; "prepare every needful thing; and establish a house, even a house of prayer, a house of fasting, a house of faith, a house of learning, a house of glory, a house of order, a house of God; that your incomings may be in the name of the Lord; that your outgoings may be in the name of the Lord; that all your salutations may be in the name of the Lord" (D&C 88:119–120). "Wherefore, as ye are agents, ye are on the Lord's errand; and whatsoever ye do according to the will of the Lord is the Lord's business" (D&C 64:29).

An *ordinance* is a law, a statute, a commandment. It is a regulation, a guide, a means of ordering things or putting matters in place or in their proper relationship to other matters. In short, an ordinance is that which helps to maintain order. The ordinances of God are thus the commandments and rules for governing and ordering our lives. This is the broad definition of ordinance. Thus, in the Preface to the Doctrine and Covenants are found these words describing the world of the nineteenth century: "They have *strayed from mine ordinances*, and have broken mine everlasting covenant" (D&C 1:15; emphasis added). In addition, the Mormons were provided with a pattern for discerning between pretenders and true servants of God. We will know that a man is who he says he is "if he obey mine ordinances" (D&C 52:15–16). That is, obedience to the laws of God are prerequisite to the approbation of heaven. Should one come among us claiming divine authority to speak or demonstrating miraculous power, we need only attend to the manner in which he or she observes the laws and statutes of God.

"And the keys of the mysteries of the kingdom shall not be taken from my servant Joseph Smith, Jun., through the means I have appointed, while he liveth, *inasmuch as he obeyeth mine ordinances*" (D&C 64:5; emphasis added). This does not seem to be a reference to Joseph's willingness to be baptized or confirmed or ordained or sealed, but rather an expression of his need to keep the commandments of the Lord. Similarly, in a revelation to Brigham Young concerning the exodus of the Camp of Israel, the word of the Lord came: "And this shall be our covenant—that we will walk in all the ordinances of the Lord" (D&C 136:4).

"Among his laws and commandments," Bruce R. McConkie has written, "the Lord has provided certain *rites* and *ceremonies* which are called *ordinances*. These *ordinance-rites* might be pictured as a small circle within the larger circle of *ordinance-commandments*. Most of these rites and ceremonies, as illustrated by baptism and celestial marriage, are essential to salvation and exaltation in the celestial kingdom; some of them, such as the blessing of children and the dedication of graves, are not ordinances of salvation, but are performed for the comfort, consolation, and encouragement of the saints."[5] The ordinances serve as a channel between the heavens and the earth, a means by which God can convey his power and deliver divine grace and understanding to his people. Many of the ordinances serve as marvelous teaching devices, tokens, or reminders, conveying sacred truths as well as sacred powers or privileges. For this reason Latter-day Saints believe they have been, are, and forever will be performed in a designated manner.

For example, we know that baptism by immersion is symbolic of the death, burial, and rise to newness of life of our Redeemer (Rom. 6:3–5; D&C 128:12). It must be done by immersion in order to answer to the type, to carry out its symbolic meaning. Thus the Mormon Prophet taught:

> God has set many signs on the earth, as well as in the heavens; for instance, the oak of the forest, the fruit of the tree, the herb of the field, all bear a sign that seed hath been planted there; for it is a decree of the Lord that every tree, plant, and herb bearing seed should bring forth of its kind, and cannot come forth after any other law or principle. Upon the same principle do I contend that *baptism is a sign ordained of God, for the believer in Christ to take upon himself in order to enter into the kingdom of God. . . . Those who seek to enter in any other way will seek in vain; for God will not receive them, neither will the angels acknowledge their works as accepted, for they have not obeyed the ordinances, nor attended to the signs which God ordained for the salvation of man*, to prepare him for, and give him a title to, a celestial glory. . . . Baptism is a sign to God, to angels, and to heaven that we do the will of God, and there is no other way beneath the heavens whereby God hath ordained for man to come to Him to be saved, and enter into the Kingdom of God, except faith in Jesus Christ, repentance, and baptism for the remission of sins, and any other course is in vain; then you have the promise of the gift of the Holy Ghost.[6]

From an LDS perspective, obedience to the ordinances of salvation, meaning both the ordinance-commandments and the ordinance-rites, is prerequisite to the receipt of the full power of God, for "the powers

5. McConkie, *Mormon Doctrine*, 548–49; emphasis in original.
6. *TPJS*, 198; emphasis added.

of heaven cannot be controlled nor handled only upon the principles of righteousness" (D&C 121:36). In this sense, Latter-day Saints are probably closer to Roman Catholics and Eastern Orthodox Christians, where the prescribed sacraments are a vital part of the sacred whole. A modern revelation thus declared that the "greater priesthood administereth the gospel and holdeth the key of the mysteries of the kingdom, even the key of the knowledge of God. Therefore, *in the ordinances thereof, the power of godliness is manifest. And without the ordinances thereof, and the authority of the priesthood, the power of godliness is not manifest unto men in the flesh.*" (D&C 84:19–22; emphasis added.) Those rites or ceremonies that we know as the sacraments or ordinances of salvation must be received in righteousness if they are to be of eternal worth to us. That is to say, worthiness and the companionship of the Holy Spirit are the seedbed for efficacy in regard to the ordinances.

Joseph Smith delivered his "last charge" to the Quorum of the Twelve Apostles before his death. In that charge, he explained: "I have sealed upon your heads all the keys of the kingdom of God. I have sealed upon you every key, power, [and] principle that the God of heaven has revealed to me. Now, no matter where I may go or what I may do, the kingdom rests upon you. But, ye apostles of the Lamb of God, my brethren, upon your shoulders this kingdom rests; now you have got to round up your shoulders and bear off the kingdom. If you do not do it you will be damned."[7] Thus, Latter-day Saints speak regularly of such concepts as apostolic succession and their right to bear the priesthood, as traced through their "line of authority." For example, my son was ordained by me, and I was ordained by Roy Warburton, who was ordained by Delbert L. Stapley, and so forth, back to Joseph Smith and then to Peter, James, and John.

Because Mormons believe that the great plan of happiness is eternal and that salvation in any age is accomplished only in and through the mediation of the Redeemer, we also believe that the covenants and ordinances are likewise eternal and unchanging. It is in this light—the eternal nature of things—that the restored gospel is called the new and everlasting covenant. Modern revelations affirm: "Wherefore, I say unto you that I have sent unto you mine everlasting covenant, even that which was from the beginning" (D&C 49:9). "Verily I say unto you, blessed are you for receiving mine everlasting covenant, even the fulness of my gospel, sent forth unto the children of men, that they might have life and be made partakers of the glories which are to be revealed in the last days, as it was written by the prophets and apostles in days of old" (D&C

7. Smith, quoted in *Discourses of Wilford Woodruff*, selected by G. Homer Durham (Salt Lake City: Bookcraft, 1946), 72.

66:2; compare 1:22; 39:11; 45:9; 49:9; 133:57). The new and everlasting covenant is the sum total of all gospel covenants and obligations. The gospel covenant is *new* in the sense that it is revealed anew following a period of falling away. It is *everlasting* in the sense that it was had from the beginning.

"Now taking it for granted that the scriptures say what they mean and mean what they say," the Prophet Joseph noted, "we have sufficient grounds to go on and prove from the Bible that the gospel has always been the same; the ordinances to fulfill its requirements, the same, and the officers to officiate, the same; and the signs and fruits resulting from the promises, the same." He continues with an illustration of this principle: "Therefore, as Noah was a preacher of righteousness he must have been baptized and ordained to the priesthood by the laying on of the hands."[8] Earlier in his ministry Joseph had spoken concerning Abel, the son of Adam:

> It is said by Paul in his letter to the Hebrew brethren [see Heb. 11:4], that Abel obtained witness that he was righteous, God testifying of his gifts. . . . Then certainly God spoke to him: indeed, it is said that God talked with him; and *if He did, would He not, seeing that Abel was righteous, deliver to him the whole plan of the Gospel?* And is not the Gospel the news of the redemption? How could Abel offer a sacrifice and look forward with faith on the Son of God for a remission of his sins, and not understand the Gospel? . . . And *if Abel was taught of the coming of the Son of God, was he not taught also of His ordinances? We all admit that the Gospel has ordinances, and if so, had it not always ordinances, and were not its ordinances always the same?*"[9]

That is, "Ordinances, instituted in the heavens before the foundation of the world, in the priesthood, for the salvation of men, are not to be altered or changed. All must be saved on the same principles."[10]

In that spirit, and believing what we do about the everlasting nature of the gospel, the church and kingdom, and the covenants and ordinances pertaining thereto, Mormons teach that many of the ancients had the gospel (as discussed in chapter 2). Many of them knew the Lord, taught his doctrine, and officiated as legal administrators in his earthly kingdom. Isaac, Israel, Joseph, and all the patriarchs enjoyed personal revelation and communion with their Maker. We would suppose that Eve and Sarah and Rebekah were baptized, that Micah and Malachi stood

8. *TPJS*, 264.
9. Ibid., 59; emphasis added.
10. Ibid., 308; see also 168.

in the prophetic office by divine call and not because they assumed that role on their own.

Joseph Smith wrote to John Wentworth: "We believe that the first principles and ordinances of the Gospel are: first, Faith in the Lord Jesus Christ; second, Repentance; third, Baptism by immersion for the remission of sins; fourth, Laying on of hands for the gift of the Holy Ghost" (Articles of Faith 1:4). Truly, "all the ordinances and duties that ever have been required by the Priesthood, under the directions and commandments of the Almighty in any of the dispensations, shall be had in the last dispensation."[11] We are not free to pick and choose which of those sacraments we will abide by, for "All men who become heirs of God and joint heirs with Jesus Christ will have to receive the fulness of the ordinances of his kingdom; and those who will not receive all the ordinances will come short of the fulness of that glory, if they do not lose the whole."[12]

Additional Blessings of the Church

Because the church is less a sanctuary for the sanctified than it is a hospital for the spiritually sick, we will always be working alongside those who make mistakes, who do their jobs half-heartedly, who gripe and complain, who are simply a pain to work with. (And certainly each one of us plays those roles at one time or another.) But as Paul taught, if we claim membership in the church of Jesus Christ, we ought to act like it. If we profess discipleship, people who observe us ought to be able to discern that discipleship without great difficulty. In today's jargon, if we talk the talk, we really ought to walk the walk! The fruits of the Spirit (Gal. 5:22–25) are those characteristics and attributes that flow from a changed heart, the ways that truly Christ-like people feel and act. It's a wonderful thing to be a gospel scholar, to be learned in our theology; it's even more of a blessing to know our doctrine and also to embody pure religion (Jas. 1:27). It's a privilege to possess the gift of teaching, to be able to speak the word of God with power and persuasion; it's a treasure beyond price to be able to lift and love others after the manner of our Master and witness the healing power of that love.

I am haunted every time I read the Gospels by the Savior's warnings against self-righteousness. Again and again he attacks the craft of those who profit on others' weakness and poverty and chides those who are scrupulous in their observance of ritual but heartless and unforgiving

11. Ibid., 171.
12. Ibid., 309; see also 331.

toward those who fall short. As Philip Yancey has rightly observed, "The more unsavory the characters, the more at ease they seemed to feel around Jesus. People like these found Jesus appealing: a Samaritan social outcast, a military officer of the tyrant Herod, a quisling tax collector, a recent hostess to seven demons.

"In contrast, Jesus got a chilly response from more respectable types. Pious Pharisees thought him uncouth and worldly, a rich young ruler walked away shaking his head, and even the open-minded Nicodemus sought a meeting under the cover of darkness." Yancey then makes this chilling observation: "Somehow we have created a community of respectability in the church. . . . The down-and-out, who flocked to Jesus when he lived on earth, no longer feel welcome. How did Jesus, the only perfect person in history, manage to attract the notoriously imperfect? And what keeps us from following in his steps today?"[13]

One of the ways we know that we are growing up spiritually, maturing in the qualities of holiness and preparing ourselves to be with our Maker, is the extent to which we become more and more sensitive to people—to their plights, to their challenges, to their silent struggles. When I was a boy, my family was not active in church. We only attended off and on, and my only continuing contact was a caring teacher who picked me up every Thursday afternoon for children's activities. A small branch of the church was begun in a city several miles from where I grew up, and my family was asked to attend there. I suppose my dad felt that it was time to get into gear spiritually, and, maybe sensing that a new beginning would be the best thing, we started back to church.

We came home from Sunday school, and I overheard my father share some tender feelings with my mom. Dad explained that someone had come up to him at church and said: "Well, my goodness! What do we have here? You mean *you* decided to come to church? I think the walls are going to fall down!" I heard my remarkable father, through his tears, utter these words, words that I will never forget, words that are emblazoned upon my soul: "This is my church too, and no man is going to run me out of my church." Dad was soon called to serve in a number of responsible church positions, which he did honorably and faithfully until just before he died.

I will be forever grateful that Dad had the courage of his convictions and that he did not allow another's insensitivity and coarseness to deter him. There is something very special about associating with people who feel about life what you feel, who want for their families what you want, and who know who they are and Whose they are. The household

13. Philip Yancey, *The Jesus I Never Knew* (Grand Rapids: Zondervan, 1995), 147–48.

of faith, the body of believers—the church—is where we grow in faith and commitment and love; where we are encouraged and enabled to get outside ourselves, to be stretched beyond our comfort zone; where we begin the lengthy process of establishing the city of God.

Conclusion

Latter-day Saints are often heard to bear witness that "the church is true." This is bothersome to some Christians, since they feel that a person's witness should be, first and foremost, of the reality of God and the divinity of his Beloved Son. To be sure, those matters are fundamental and foundational, and they are also testified of in LDS settings on a regular and consistent basis. But to state that the church is true is to state that the church is a divinely ordained organization, an aid and an auxiliary for individuals and families to come to Christ and be saved. The church is the custodian of the gospel, the guardian of the ordinances, and the gathering place for worship and fellowship. Joseph Smith taught: "When the Savior shall appear we shall see him as he is. We shall see that he is a man like ourselves. And that same sociality which exists among us here will exist among us there, only it will be coupled with eternal glory, which glory we do not now enjoy" (D&C 130:1–2).

An Evangelical Response

Gerald McDermott

I have been troubled for a long time by the Lone Ranger Christian mentality of so many in the evangelical community. This is the attitude that "all I need is Jesus and the Bible, and since the church is so full of problems and hypocrites, I am perfectly fine without it. I can take my Bible to the top of the local mountain on Sunday morning, have my evangelical Quiet Time, and be fully equipped for the work of the kingdom, free from the pestiferous church people who just get in my way."

One problem with this attitude is that most of these Lone Rangers rarely get to the top of the mountain (we live in the Blue Ridge mountains of Virginia) on Sunday morning anyway. Instead they sleep in, read the paper, and sip their coffee. They miss out on the Word of God coming through preaching, which Paul suggests has a special power beyond what comes simply by reading the Bible on our own (Rom. 10:8, 17). That Word has the added advantage of coming through another person, and so it often challenges our own presumptions and prejudices.

The Lone Rangers also avoid the threat of being challenged by fellow believers at church, whether in Sunday school lessons or simply over coffee. They forego the comfort and encouragement we often need when going through crises.

When I think of how Christ has grown me over the years, nearly every enlargement of my vision of God has been through hearing a sermon, or studying a book with other believers, or being challenged or comforted by others in the church. I know from experience that when I have been absent from fellowship for a while, usually because of travel or other necessity, I have been more tempted to stray off the narrow path. This has reminded me of why we see no Lone Rangers in the New Testament, and why instead all the believers we see there are active in local churches.

Church Not Optional

I therefore resonate deeply with Professor Millet's emphasis on the necessity of church. I like his delineation of the purposes of the church: the perfection of the saints, the work of ministry, edifying the body of Christ, and establishing unity in the faith (more on the last in a bit). I would add the benefit of discipline, which is politically incorrect today. But as I mentioned above, my brothers and sisters in Christ at my church keep me accountable. When I wander off the path, particularly in ways that I do not recognize because of my own blind spots, they let me know. I am thankful for their correction and reproofs because they warn me when I am beginning to cut myself off from the life that feeds me. "Without me, ye can do nothing . . . every branch that beareth fruit, he purgeth it, that it may bring forth more fruit" (John 15:5b, 2b).

I also appreciate Bob's warning that we will experience less life in the church, and therefore less growth in Christ, to the degree we are disobedient to what the living Christ is telling us through his body, the church. This too is not popular and is often misunderstood as legalism or even works righteousness—the idea that we are saved by our works. Yet the same Jesus who taught that the prodigal son was saved by his father's mercy also said we would abide in his love *if* we keep his commandments, and would remain his friends only if we do what he commands (John 15:10, 14).

Are Sacraments Central Only for Mormons?

Professor Millet thinks the Mormon view of the sacraments is more similar to Roman Catholic and Eastern Orthodox than to evangelical perspectives. Since there are so many different varieties of evangelicals, this is only partly true. His emphasis on the necessity of sacraments is indeed different from certain pietistic evangelical traditions, especially those descending from the Radical Reformation such as the Spiritualists, who questioned the means of grace and stressed an unmediated contact with Christ by means of the Holy Spirit. For many evangelicals, the life of personal relationship with Christ through the Bible and prayer and fellowship overshadows or denies the sacraments as means of grace. But for many other evangelicals, especially those in sacramental communities such as Lutherans, Anglicans, or Presbyterians, the means of grace are essential to a full life in Christ.

Let me try to explain my more Reformed version of this evangelical view of sacraments. In this perspective, a sacrament is a visible word of God's grace, a seal of the covenant of grace. It is a means of grace that supplies the mind with ideas of the things of God and thus gives opportunity for grace to act in the soul, just as Elijah's putting wood on the altar gave opportunity for the fire to burn when God sent it down from heaven.

But a sacrament is not just something that God has put "out there" as a pedagogical aid. Far more, it is a representation of Christ in which Jesus Christ is actually present, speaking and communing with believers. Sacraments are re-presentations of Christ.

In another sense, the real sacrament is Christ's death and resurrection. The human rite of baptism, for example, incorporates a person into that real sacrament when it is used by the Holy Spirit, in God's freedom, to make the objective (Christ's saving work) become subjectively real. While for Professor Millet and Arminian evangelicals, baptism points to the work ("is a sign") of the Spirit in the believer, for Reformed evangelicals, baptism points to the objective work of Christ in his death and resurrection. So the true work of baptism is the work of Christ, not a subjective work of cleansing.

Baptism

Baptism is therefore the sacrament of the covenant of election in which Jesus calls people into his body: "Ye have not chosen me, but I have chosen you" (John 15:16). This is seen in Jesus's baptism, where the Father proclaimed Jesus to be his elected Son, and also in baptisms of the church, which seal the redemption of the elect. Hence, the beginning of salvation is to be sought, not in a decision that we make, but in a prior decision that God has already made. God's election, not our faith, is the ground of our adoption into the family of God. Because of that decision we are *given* repentance and faith, which come in many different ways, sometimes by a steady and almost imperceptible process and sometimes in striking and dramatic fashion.

For the elect, therefore, baptism does not merely attest the grace of God (as for most Baptists and, it seems, Mormons), nor is it merely associated with the grace of God, but it is itself, in the Holy Spirit, a means of grace. To the non-elect (those who are baptized but never become disciples) divine things are only offered. For that reason there can be no automatic or *ex opere operato* (the Catholic belief, "in the doing, it is done") efficacy. But to the elect, they are applied and sealed by the gracious working of the Holy Spirit. For them, therefore, baptism will always have its effect through repentance and faith, but the effect cannot be tied rigorously in time to the administration of the rite—as seems to be suggested by the Mormon sacrament of "bestowal of the Holy Spirit." Against the charge of injustice to the non-elect, one can say that even to them the promises are offered through baptism, but they have demonstrated their rejection of those promises by their refusal to convert. Against those who protest the concept of election as an arbitrary selection of individuals, I would say that this is the Father's election of Christ and all those who are his members by his prevenient grace working in them. Everyone who is not in his church has chosen freely not to join.

This last part about election will frustrate many readers, for it does not answer all of our questions. But then neither does the view that baptism is simply the outward sign of our autonomous decision to follow Jesus. There are too many scriptures (one of which we just saw and others I will cite in chapter 7) about God's prior choice of us before we choose him. I have to conclude that there is an irreducible mystery about baptism and regeneration (the new birth): they are inextricably connected, and the Spirit blows where he wills (John 3:8) to connect them, but one cannot say which will come first or the way in which one is tied to the other. In the eternal counsel of God and in Christ, the regeneration and salvation of a person make up an already-accomplished work—therefore the sacrament and its fulfillment do not have to take place at the same time in history.

To assume that the grace of God is always given through the rite (which the Mormon sacrament of bestowing the Holy Ghost seems to suggest) is to bind the divine sovereignty and to exalt the human administrator who disposes the means. The baptismal promises are always declared when baptism is conducted with gospel preaching, and to that extent, grace is present. But the promises are perceived and known and therefore effective, only when the Spirit works through the means to convey union with Christ's death through faith and repentance.

Baptism is always a call to accept the death and resurrection of Christ in our stead—that is, to accept Jesus's baptism of death and resurrection as our own. In other words, our baptism is a baptism into Jesus's baptism, which he said was his death for sinners (Mark 10:38; Rom. 6:1ff.). So baptism is not primarily a sacrament of repentance and faith, which makes it a sign of our work rather than that of the Trinity on our behalf. Rather, baptism is a proclamation of the objective work of Christ and not merely a sign of subjective experience.

This Reformed evangelical understanding of baptism seems to have three advantages: (1) it refuses to postulate purely imaginary effects of baptism that are not borne out in real life; (2) it allows for a truly supernatural work in which God himself has primacy; and (3) it maintains a truly sacramental view of baptism within an evangelical interpretation of the work of God. It is sacramental because it asserts that grace is really imparted in baptism. Christ is always presented, but not all respond to Christ. The elect do, while others don't. And the Holy Spirit is often present before he is perceived. It is evangelical because it insists that faith and repentance are required.

But they must be properly understood. As I will argue in the next chapter, faith is a response to God's act in Christ, not a condition of it. I did not make the first move toward God; God moved first toward me, just as he came to Israel in Egypt when she was helpless. Our faith is God's gift. I am not justified by my faith, but I believe because I am justified by God's work in Christ: "Ye have not chosen me, but I have chosen you" (John 15:16). Christ's death was in some mysterious way the baptism of the whole human race, and by grace led to the faith of some.

Confirmation and the Lord's Supper

Unlike Mormons and most Protestants in sacramental churches, most evangelicals do not see confirmation as essential (although we believe firmly in the necessity of ongoing Christian education and discipleship). Even sacramental Protestants do not regard confirmation as a sacrament, because it does not fulfill the conditions that the sixteenth-century Reformers derived from scripture—that they are commanded by Christ and use material signs.

Yet all evangelicals practice and regard as essential the Lord's Supper. Almost all consider it a sacrament or "ordinance" on par with baptism. They differ on what it means. Some take the "memorial view" that it is just a remembrance of what happened two thousand years ago, thus emphasizing Paul's words in 1 Corinthians 11: "This do in remembrance of me" (v. 24b). Other evangelicals point to Paul's words in the previous chapter ("The cup of blessing which we bless, is it not the communion of the blood of Christ? The bread which we break, is it not the communion of the body of Christ?" v. 16), noting that "communion" is *koinonia* or sharing, and therefore see it as the real presence of Christ. Not only that, but they see the Eucharist as a time where we encounter the Living Christ through the Spirit—in, with, and under the elements—and receive afresh Jesus Christ's forgiveness, righteousness, and eternal life. In this mystical encounter, we participate in the love of the Trinity one for another and join the fellowship of the "great cloud of witnesses," both living and dead in the body of Christ.

All evangelicals note that through the breaking of the bread the inward eyes of the disciples on the road to Emmaus were opened to the identity of Jesus as the risen Christ (Luke 24:30, 31).

Because nearly all evangelicals see baptism and the Lord's Supper as essential to the faith, they would not understand why Professor Millet thinks their convictions about the priesthood of all believers and the authority of scripture would undermine their belief in these two sacraments. Some evangelicals do not use the word "sacrament" because they associate that word with the real presence, which they reject. But they nonetheless think these two ordinances to be essential in full Christian life. And while they believe all believers are priests (1 Pet. 2:4, 5; Rev. 5:10), almost all evangelical communities (Plymouth Brethren are among the few exceptions) believe in special gifts and offices of ministry given to some but not to all. They note that Jesus instituted an apostolic office through his commissioning of the Twelve, and Paul envisioned permanent ministries of apostles, pastors, evangelists, and teachers (Eph. 4:11). In the pastoral Epistles it is clear that the ministry is regarded as a special office in the church.

Unity More Important Than Diversity

I appreciate Bob's underscoring the importance of unity of doctrine in the church. In society today, diversity tends to be prized more than unity. We in the church also celebrate diversity of gifts and perspectives. We appreciate the fact that the church is made up of members from every tribe and nation and color. But we tend to forget, as Bob helpfully urges, that it is also founded on unity of doctrine. He reminds us that Paul calls us to "one faith" (Eph. 4:5) and called on the church at Corinth to "all speak the same thing" (1 Cor. 10).

Recently a minister suggested to me that true Christian faith has nothing to do with believing certain doctrines. It is more, he suggested, a matter of feeling love for Jesus and serving the unfortunate. While it is true that a Christian is to love Jesus and serve others, I find this rejection of doctrine impossible to square with Jesus and the early church. All of Jesus's teachings presume doctrine. He says that he is the Way, the Truth, and the Life (John 14:6). That statement by itself is doctrine. It is a truth claim that sets out what is true from what is not. If Jesus is *the* way to the Father, that means there are no other ways to the Father. If he is the Truth, he is Truth in a way that no one else is. If he is life, other persons are not *the* life in the unique way he is.

Jesus says, "Ye shall know the truth, and the truth shall make you free" (John 8:31). Presumably, then, if we don't know the truth, we won't be set free. That's another truth claim—another doctrinal statement.

The early church believed doctrine was essential to Christian life. Paul said the gospel is all about the "obedience to the faith" (Rom. 1:5; 16:26). What are we to obey unless we believe certain things need to be obeyed?

Doctrine defines who and what we are to obey. The early church "continued steadfastly in the apostles' doctrine" (Acts 2:42). Paul commends the Romans for having obeyed from the heart "that form of doctrine which was delivered you" (Rom. 6:17). That means a set of teachings that were part and parcel of faith.

I would go even further: not only is doctrine part of Christian faith, but Christian faith is *impossible* without doctrine. When ministers preach the parable of the Pharisee and the publican, what do they conclude from it? Invariably they (even my minister friend who doesn't think doctrine is important) conclude something about the grace of God. That something is a doctrine, which simply means a firm teaching about God and life, in this case the idea that God saves by grace and not by works of the law.

Doctrines are taught by every hymn, every sermon, every creed, and every reflection on scripture. Consider the creeds, which as I argued in a former chapter both Mormons and evangelicals possess, even if they call them "statements" or "articles" of faith. They consist of declarations about God and Christ and life with God. We are joining the saints of the ages in proclaiming what is to be believed. In a word, doctrine.

Even those who believe doctrine is unimportant often criticize those who prize doctrine for teaching a wrong view of God. In other words, for teaching the wrong doctrine. The real question, then, is not *whether* doctrine will be taught in the church, but *which* doctrine.

But I have to admit that, in a sense, Mormons have a certain advantage. Not unlike Catholics, they have an institutional authority that sets and enforces doctrine. Catholics have what they call the "magisterium," the teaching office and authority of the bishops that define and enforce orthodox doctrine in "matters of faith and morals."[14] Mormons have the Presidency and Twelve Apostles, who set the boundaries for proper Mormon belief and practice.

Evangelicals have nothing quite so formal and universal. Individual churches often set those limits, and sometimes evangelical denominations do the same. But there is no pope or college of bishops, or anything equivalent, to determine once and for all what is properly believed by all evangelicals. It is this lack of institutional authority that in fact has caused many evangelicals to "swim the Tiber" to Rome or "cross the Bosphorus" to Eastern Orthodoxy. In these communions many former

14. Richard P. McBrien, ed., *The HarperCollins Encyclopedia of Catholicism* (San Francisco: HarperSanFrancisco, 1995), 805.

evangelicals treasure the sense that there is a final answer about what is true and right—something they missed as Protestants when so much of the faith seemed up for debate. I imagine some converts to Mormonism appreciate this same sense of authority they find in Salt Lake City.

For better or for worse, evangelicals reject institutional over-all authority. This rejection probably has something to do with the parallel rejection, by some evangelicals, of creeds. These evangelicals feel that only the Bible should have such final authority. To give final jurisdiction to human beings would, in their view, compromise *sola scriptura*. But as I argued in chapter 1, all evangelicals already implicitly accept the authority of some tradition. These traditions already function as intermediaries between the scripture and the church—not a set of bishops, but a body of doctrine that serves, however imperfectly, as its own kind of magisterium for the myriad of evangelical sub-groups around the world.

Some Basic Differences

Needless to say, there are still some differences between Professor Millet and me on church and sacraments, despite my emphatic appreciation for the basic direction of his argument. While I support his emphasis on unity of doctrine and his insistence that active church membership is not optional, he and I would disagree on the foundation of the church. As I already argued in chapter 1, evangelicals point to Paul's declaration that the church is founded "upon the foundation of the apostles and prophets" (Eph. 2:20), and limit those apostles and prophets to those who wrote the classical Christian canon. This means their doctrines will not admit anything coming from the "modern revelation" of Joseph Smith and later LDS prophets—which means, in turn, that some basic evangelical doctrines about God and Jesus will conflict with LDS views of the same. We have detailed many of these differences in previous chapters and will point to some more in later chapters. So, for example, evangelicals do not admit as doctrine the LDS notion of three heavens, and so see no biblical reason to say, with Professor Millet, that exaltation to that highest heaven is open only to those who have been married, or for that matter, in a Mormon marriage "sealed" in a Mormon temple.

And while I agree with Bob that there is far more continuity between the two Testaments than most Christians have realized and that Jesus was active in the Old Testament era, I think he goes too far to assume that Eve and Sarah and Rebekah were baptized. Nor do I agree with Joseph Smith that all the "ordinances [were] always the same."

Reformed evangelicals agree that there was really only one covenant, but they also see two dispensations in the administration of the one covenant. The two modes were integrally related, so that they shared the same mediator; the same medium of salvation (the incarnation, suffering, righteousness, and intercession of Christ); the same Spirit applying Christ's redemption; the same external means (the word of God, prayer, praise, Sabbath); and the same condition (faith expressed in humility and repentance).

But there were also differences. While each Testament teaches grace, the surface text of the Old Testament at many points appears to teach salvation by works. I see this as a pedagogical tool God used to point his people to the deeper meaning of grace. By pointing them to works, he showed them they could never achieve the righteousness he demanded, so they might despair of their own efforts and throw themselves on his mercy, who is Christ. Jesus worked similarly, offering the rich young ruler the covenant of works in order to teach him to despair of it and cry for mercy. Yet at other points both Jesus and Paul taught grace more clearly and directly than in the Old Testament. My point is that while there are similarities between the two Testaments, there are also differences.

A second difference is that in the Old Testament era God taught his people to make animal and plant sacrifices for their sins, but in the New he revealed that all those sacrifices prefigured the final and perfect sacrifice. Third, the older dispensation promised land, prosperity, and other public tokens of favor, while the new promises eternal life.

Therefore, we would expect to see differences in sacraments. The most obvious is the change from circumcision to baptism, which Paul suggests in Colossians 2:11–12 is precisely the change made between the old and new dispensations of the one covenant. Scripture gives no indication whatsoever that anyone in the Old Testament era was baptized, much less that Old Testament saints had any inkling of Christian baptism per se. The only ground for such belief is faith in the authenticity of Joseph Smith's revelations, which we see once again is the core issue that divides us.

Rebuttal and Concluding Thoughts
Robert Millet

I was pleased to learn that Professor McDermott and I have so many beliefs in common relative to the work of the church and its significance in the saving of souls. Although I may not have made it clear in my essay, I too believe, with Professor McDermott, that the sacraments or ordinances are in fact a means of grace, a channel through which the Almighty blesses and endows and empowers and enables his needy children. It seems to me that far too many Latter-day Saints feel that the most significant purpose for attending the Sacrament Meeting or main worship service on the Sabbath is to be inspired by the sermons delivered that day. Mormons do speak of "renewing their covenants" through the ordinance of the sacrament, but often there is not the depth of soul-searching, the personal introspection, the spiritual stretch or bending of the soul in an effort to commune with the Infinite during the Lord's Supper. This is something I feel Latter-day Saints could learn from some of our Roman Catholic, Orthodox, and Protestant brothers and sisters.

It was not my intention to convey that those who subscribe to a priesthood of all believers and the authority of scripture cannot feel the importance of either confirmation or communion. What I was trying to indicate is that from our perspective these rites must be performed by one holding sacred authority, priesthood authority that has been conferred by the laying on of hands. There is no question in my mind but that many of my evangelical associates enjoy special giftedness and an endowment of God's strength and direction in their specific duties. I suppose it is here that we come face to face with what may in the long run be the greatest of all differences between our two faith communities, namely, the question of divine authority—from whence it comes and how it is conveyed.

One final point that I would like to address is the Apostle Paul's declaration that the Christian church is built upon the foundation of the apostles and prophets (Eph. 2:20). I know that all of my Christian friends are in full accord with Paul's teachings, but again, the LDS posture that the Lord's living church is built on a foundation of current, modern, and living apostles and prophets is where the difference lies. Professor McDermott suggests that Paul's statement has reference to the apostles and prophets during the first century of the Christian era and no more. I would simply ask, Why? What indication is there in the Bible that the church will one day be able to operate without the support and divine direction of those charged as special witnesses of Jesus Christ?

Paul is very direct in his expression in Ephesians 4 that the officers of the Lord's church will be necessary until we all come to the unity of the faith and until we mature spiritually to the point where we have been conformed to the image of our Master. While I acknowledge much of goodness in the Christian world, my assessment is that we aren't there yet. I agree wholly with the idea that we are to abide by the principles taught by the leaders of the church as found in the New Testament, but I do not see that we are anywhere given the scriptural disclaimer that the need for apostolic and prophetic direction would cease after the first generation of apostles are gone. Indeed, that the early apostles felt the need to fill the vacancy in the twelve with the defection and suicide of Judas (see Acts 1:13–26) and that Paul and Barnabas are later called as apostles (see Acts 14:4, 14) is evidence enough for me: Peter and his associates sensed that apostolic authority, not that which we learn about in the record of those ordained in the past but that which we witness in living color, now, in our own day and time, was necessary in order for the church to have its full impact.

7

SALVATION
IN CHRIST

Grace, Faith, and Works
Gerald McDermott

In 2004 many of us watched *The Fog of War,* a documentary about Robert S. McNamara, the American secretary of defense during the Vietnam War. One of the lessons of the film was that in the hurly-burly of war and politics, original purposes and insights get lost and distorted. Even the most principled can lose their way.

So too in evangelical-Mormon debates. In the "fog of theological war" we evangelicals often accuse Mormons of teaching salvation by works, even when they protest they don't and try to prove it with passages from the Book of Mormon or Doctrine and Covenants. Hearing evangelicals insist that all you need is faith, sometimes Mormons get the impression evangelicals think you can be saved as long as you believe Jesus died for your sins, even if you're living like the devil.

One purpose of this chapter is to show that both of these are false stereotypes. But I also want to demonstrate that there is a kernel of truth in each, that each community can learn something from the other, and that both need to move to a more biblical view of grace and salvation.

But first I want to tell two stories. One is about Martin Luther (1483–1546), the other about Jonathan Edwards. Each theologian has something pertinent to say to this debate—Luther to Mormons and evangelicals who are in danger of works-righteousness (thinking our salvation comes from our making a righteous decision), and Edwards to evangelicals (and many mainline Protestants today) who are in danger of thinking works are irrelevant to salvation.

Luther's Struggle for Salvation

Luther was a Catholic monk for many years before his evangelical breakthrough at the age of 35.[1] At some point during these years he was struck with terror when he read Romans 1:17: "For therein is the righteousness [in Luther's Latin translation, "justice"] of God revealed from faith to faith: as it is written, The just shall live by faith." All his attempts to satisfy God—hours-long prayers, rigorous fasting, all-night vigils, endless good works—failed to quiet his guilty conscience. He felt he could never satisfy this all-demanding God. Luther's mood swung from despair to rage toward God: "I did not love, yes, I hated the righteous God who punishes sinners, and secretly, if not blasphemously, certainly murmuring greatly, I was angry with God."

Luther kept reading Paul, anxiously scanning his letters for help, meditating night and day. Finally light broke forth:

> Then I began to understand that the righteousness of God is that by which the righteous lives by a gift of God, namely by faith. This is the meaning: the righteousness of God is revealed by the gospel, a passive justice with which the merciful God justifies us by faith, as it is written, "He who through faith is righteous shall live" [Hab. 2:4]. Here I felt that I was altogether born again and had entered paradise itself through open gates.[2]

There were several reasons why Luther had such spiritual torment for all those years in the monastery, but two are important for our purposes. Both were theological. The first was the medieval belief that God will give grace only to those who try their best. The assumption behind this was that God's grace is based on what we do. He waits until we have done the right thing, then he moves in with his grace.

You can imagine Luther's problem with this. Since he was spiritually conscientious, he would ask himself, "Am I trying my best? How would I know if I am, since I also know 'the heart is deceitful above all things, and desperately wicked: who can know it?' (Jer. 17:9). I know from past experience that because of my desire to justify myself, I allow my heart to believe the best even when it is in sinful shape. So how can I trust myself to know when I am trying my best?"

Medieval theology had also taught that faith was formed by love. But again Luther, who knew his mind often worked to rationalize sin, wondered how he would know if he ever had enough love. Sure, he

---

1. My rendition of this story is indebted to Timothy George, *Theology of the Reformers* (Nashville: Broadman, 1988), 51–107.
2. Martin Luther, "Preface to Latin Writings," in *Luther's Works*, vol. 34 (Philadelphia: Muhlenberg Press, 1960), 336–37.

might think so in his heart and mind. But how could he trust his own heart and mind? The Pharisees thought they were right before God, but Jesus declared they were self-deceived. How could he know he wasn't also self-deceived?

It was only after these tortured self-doubts that Luther had his "Damascus Road experience." He came to see, as if by revelation, that what preceded the experience of grace and salvation was not trying one's best or achieving a state of love, but instead, active rebellion against God. Luther was struck by Romans 5:8: "While we were yet sinners, Christ died for us."

Then he remembered Paul's own experience. Christ found Paul, not when he was trying his hardest to find Jesus or living a life of love, but quite the opposite—Paul was on the road to hunt down and kill Christ (as Christ himself later implied by his statement to Paul, "I am Jesus whom thou persecutest" [Acts 9:5]). Christ "justifieth the *un*godly" (Rom. 4:5), not the godly.

Luther realized that it didn't matter how hard he was trying or whether he had reached the perfection of love. All that mattered was that Christ specialized in saving sinners, people who were *not* godly or trying their best or living a life of love. Christ loved to save those who knew they were *not* doing their best and *not* being very loving. It is faith in *this* Christ—the Christ who saves religious and moral failures—that saves.

Luther's story speaks to both Mormons and evangelicals, who alike believe that while we are all sinners and need saving, only some of us reach out and take the gift of salvation being offered to us. And it is that reaching out and taking that distinguishes those who are saved from those who are not. I will discuss this in more detail later in this chapter, but for now, suffice it to say that Luther's breakthrough suggests that any view of salvation that makes it finally up to us—and our "virtuous" receiving (the gift of salvation)—misunderstands the gospel of a Christ who "justifieth the *un*godly."

Edwards's Struggle for Discernment

My second story is about Jonathan Edwards (1703–58), the eighteenth-century American theologian. Many know his "Sinners in the Hands of an Angry God" sermon, preached at the beginning of the Great Awakening (1741–42), an enormous revival that eventually swept up and down the eastern seaboard from Maine to Georgia and changed the colonies not only religiously but also politically. During an awakening several years before this sermon (1734–35), and then again during this time of religious revival (1741), hundreds of new believers joined Edwards's church in Northampton, Massachusetts. But a few years later Edwards came to conclude that not all the new "believers" were truly regenerate. They all had had some sort of religious experience, often emotional and attended with dramatic signs. But some of these folks proceeded to depart from their newly awakened ways and go back to their carnal and worldly lives.

As a result, Edwards came to what he believed to be a deeper understanding of what the Bible has to say about faith and works. He previously had thought that the sincere profession of faith, especially if accompanied with deep religious feeling, might be a certain sign of regeneration. But after the Great Awakening he came to conclude that faith is living faith only if it "worketh by love" (Gal. 5:6) and that love, which is the "essence" of faith, is shown to be genuine only over the course of time.

Edwards went on to write *Religious Affections* (1746), his magnum opus, which has been called the greatest work on spiritual discernment in the history of the church. In this volume he delineates twelve "positive" or reliable signs of grace. The last and greatest of all, and the one to which he devotes four times as much space as to any of the others, is "Christian practice." In other words, the practice of the faith in works of love and obedience is the greatest final test of true faith.

The upshot of Edwards's discovery for us, as we will see, is the inextricability of faith and works. One cannot be separated from the other without doing violence to each. Hence the question of whether we are saved by faith or by works is the wrong question, as Professor Millet has suggested.[3] The better question, as I will propose at the end of this chapter, is "Who is saving us?"

The Inseparability of Faith and Works

"The last time I saw Mo that year, he was being carried out of a bar, feet first, by Virginia Beach's finest. Mo's tanned, muscular body was contorted with rage. He was cursing the officers and shouting something about the other guy starting the fight.

"So I had a difficult time believing it was the same Mo whom I saw just six months later, fully clothed and in his right mind. He was the picture of serenity. After exchanging a hug and the usual greetings, I asked Mo what in the world happened to him. He looked so different.

"Mo said that he'd become a Christian. He didn't try to convert me, but the change I saw in him made me think long and hard about the life I was leading."

3. Millet, *A Different Jesus?* 87.

My former pastor, who told me this story, was transformed by Jesus a few months later, in part because of the change he saw in his friend Mo, who abandoned the hedonistic, uncommitted lifestyle he had flaunted for years and settled down to a disciplined pursuit of holiness. Instead of chasing women, Mo gave himself faithfully to his wife, children, and church. In the years since his conversion, Mo has become a physician with a difference. He takes extra time with his patients rather than rushing them in order to make more money. He waives his fees if he knows a patient is destitute. And he cares about them after they finish treatment. He sees his patients, in other words, not as diseased organs or sources of income, but as fellow creatures of God whom he is privileged to serve.

Mo illustrates the inextricability of faith and good works. One cannot go without the other—unless one or the other is a cheap imitation. True faith will always work when it has a chance (some brand-new believers die before they get that chance). Works that are not inspired by faith do not please God.

Paul wrote that true faith "worketh by love" (Gal. 5:6). Its nature is to produce works of love. Mo's new faith naturally produced a lifestyle of loving service. Paul told the church at Ephesus that this is why God created us—that we would do "good works" inspired by faith: "For we are his workmanship, created in Christ Jesus *unto good works*, which God hath before ordained that we should walk in them" (Eph. 2:10).

Luther, who coined the term "faith alone" in an effort to combat the notion that we are saved by good works, nevertheless insisted that true faith always results in good works because it is the nature of true faith to work.

> O, it is a living, busy, active, mighty thing, this faith. It is impossible for it not to be doing good works incessantly. It does not ask whether good works are to be done, but before the question is asked, it has already done them, and is constantly doing them.[4]

Not only does true faith work, but it keeps working until the end. Jesus said, "He that endureth to the end shall be saved" (Matt. 10:22; 24:12–13). In the parable of the sower and the seed, only the seed that endured through trouble, persecution, the cares of the world and the lure of wealth was pronounced "good" (Matt. 13:4–8). In another parable Jesus declared, "Blessed are those servants, whom the lord when he cometh shall find watching" (Luke 12:37). And in John's Gospel, Jesus teaches, "If ye *continue* in my word, then are ye my disciples indeed" (8:31).

4. Martin Luther, *Works of Martin Luther* (Philadelphia: Concordia and Muhlenberg Press, 1960), 35:370.

Jesus also teaches that works are the best evidence of true faith to our own conscience. At the end of the Sermon on the Mount, he distinguishes true from false disciples by their practice: "Therefore whosoever heareth these sayings of mine, and doeth them, I will liken him unto a wise man. . . . And every one that heareth these sayings of mine, and doeth them not, shall be likened unto a foolish man" (Matt. 7:24, 26). So we can know what kind of disciples we are by looking at our works.

In John's Gospel, Jesus teaches the same thing: "He that hath my commandments, and keepeth them, he it is that loveth me. . . . If a man love me, he will keep my words. . . . He that loveth me not keepeth not my sayings. . . . Herein is my Father glorified, that ye bear much fruit; so shall ye be my disciples. . . . Ye are my friends, if ye do whatsoever I command you. . . . If ye continue in my word, then are ye my disciples indeed" (John 14:15, 23–24; 15:8, 14; 8:31).

Does this imply we are saved by our good works? Does it rob glory from Christ by placing so much emphasis on our works? Isn't this inconsistent with the grand Protestant doctrine of justification by grace through faith alone?

I don't think so, and for two reasons:

1. This emphasis on works might suggest these things only if the basic point were not taught by the scriptures that works are not the price of God's favor but instead the *sign* of faith and therefore God's favor. The scriptures I have quoted above, when placed in the context of the whole biblical message of salvation, teach us that works are the sign of true faith. They are what faith *does*, not what we do to gain faith or favor.

If I give a student a dollar bill (I sometimes do this to teach this very point) simply because I feel like it, she will look at the dollar in her hand as a sign of my generosity. Her possession of the dollar says nothing about her. I could have given it just as easily to the student sitting beside her. And it says nothing about her character—whether she is studious or lazy, friendly or obnoxious. But it does say something about me. It says that either I am generous or I just wanted to make a point to my class that day.

Similarly, the presence of works in believers' lives does not mean they are better than unbelievers or more deserving, or that those works have earned them a place in God's kingdom. It simply indicates that God has freely poured his grace on them. The result of that grace is faith which in turn has produced works, for faith is always active and will produce Christlike character.

In theological terms, this is the idea of justification without works. We are justified (accepted by God and received into his kingdom) only by the righteousness of Christ, not by our own righteousness. In other words, we are saved by Christ's works, not by our own. But once we are saved, we are filled with the Holy Spirit, who inevitably does works through us.

2. If justification by grace through faith alone is contradicted by the necessity of works as a sign of true faith, then it is also contradicted by the necessity of *anything* as a sign of true faith and grace—joy, love, gratitude, a softened heart, conviction of sin, or any kind of holy practice. Any of these can be regarded as human works that earn salvation. But just as a believer typically will see these spiritual experiences as signs of (not payments for) grace, the believer, when properly instructed, will see works as a sign of grace.

Faith, then, cannot be separated from works of obedience. To emphasize the fact that we are saved by a free gift, evangelicals say that we are saved by faith and not by works. But as I have argued, all true faith produces works. If faith does not produce works, it is not true faith. Lutheran martyr Dietrich Bonhoeffer explained, "From the point of view of justification it is necessary thus to separate [faith and works], but we must never lose sight of their essential unity. For faith is only real when there is obedience, never without it, and faith only becomes faith in the act of obedience."[5]

Mormons on Grace

My point in all of this is to try to defuse some evangelical hostility and misunderstanding. Many of us have wrongly accused Mormons of teaching salvation by works because they have put such strong emphasis on works. We have become convinced that Mormons do not understand or teach grace—the vision of God saving us by God's work—because they talk so much about the necessity of works.

One of the problems with this evangelical view of LDS teaching is that, as I have just tried to show, Jesus also teaches the necessity of works. By "necessity," I mean the idea that true faith will *necessarily* produce works of love.

Another problem is that Professor Millet and other Mormon leaders teach salvation by Christ's work of grace. They draw upon—this will be surprising to most evangelicals—rich language in the Book of Mormon:

There is no flesh that can dwell in the presence of God, save it be through the merits, and mercy, and grace of the Holy Messiah. (2 Nephi 2:8)

For we know that it is by grace that we are saved, after all we can do. (2 Nephi 25:23)

5. Dietrich Bonhoeffer, *The Cost of Discipleship* (New York: Macmillan, 1959), 69.

And since man had fallen he could not merit anything of himself; but the sufferings and death of Christ atone for their sins, through faith and repentance. (Alma 22:14)

Professor Millet explains that "after all we can do" in the second quotation above means that "no matter how much we do, it simply will not be enough to guarantee salvation without Christ's intervention. . . . There is a very real sense in which 'all we can do' is come before the Lord in reverent humility, confess our weakness, and plead for his forgiveness, for his mercy and grace."[6]

In his 2005 book on Jesus, Professor Millet cites approvingly the radical statements on grace by Andy Stanley, an evangelical writer:

> "Jesus taught that good people *don't* go to heaven. . . . Jesus claimed that God desires to give men and women exactly what they do *not* deserve." The sobering fact is that Jesus "declared that even the best among them was not good enough to reach God on his own merit." Further, "the reason good people don't go to heaven is that there aren't any good people. There are only sinners. . . . Good people don't go to heaven. *Forgiven* people go to heaven."[7]

Professor Millet also quotes Mormon apologist Bruce McConkie, "All salvation is free; all comes by the merits and mercy and grace of the Holy Messiah; there is no salvation of any kind, nature, or degree that is not bound to Christ and his atonement."[8]

BYU professor Stephen Robinson asserts that "there are no prerequisites for being born again."[9] He observes that evangelicals naturally stumble when they hear Latter-day Saints "talk about works all the time and . . . even use the phrase 'salvation by works.'" But what they mean, says Robinson, is that *after* conversion they want to continue serving Christ with their whole lives.[10]

The Encyclopedia of Mormonism makes a similar point. It proclaims that faith is "in, and only in, Jesus Christ. It is not sufficient to have faith in just anything; it must be focused on 'the only true God, and Jesus Christ' whom he has sent (John 17:3). Having faith means having complete confidence in Jesus Christ alone to save humankind from sin and the finality of death. By his grace 'are ye saved through faith'" (Eph. 2:8).[11]

6. Robert L. Millet, *Grace Works* (Salt Lake City: Deseret Book, 2003), 131–32.
7. Millet, *A Different Jesus?* 86; quotations are from Andy Stanley, *How Good Is Good Enough?* (Sisters, OR: Multnomah, 2003); original emphasis.
8. Bruce McConkie, *Promised Messiah* (Salt Lake City: Deseret Book, 1978), 346–47; cited in Millet, *Grace Works*, 14.
9. Robinson, *How Wide the Divide?* 156.
10. Ibid.
11. Douglas E. Brinley, "Faith in Jesus Christ," *EOM* 2:483.

So let's put some old staples of evangelical anti-Mormon apologetics to rest. Let's stop saying incessantly that Mormons teach unadulterated salvation by works and that they have no conception of grace. The latter may be true of some Mormons in the pews. But then I would say the same is true of some people in the pews of evangelical churches. We need to compare apples with apples, which in this case means official statements with official statements, scriptures with scriptures. Not apples with oranges, which means official statements in one community with popular anecdotes about the other community.

The Real Issue: Who Makes the First Move?

This does not mean, however, that Mormon understandings of grace are precisely the same as evangelical views. Mormons tend to view grace as God giving the individual the *opportunity* to accept his free gift of salvation. Some evangelicals, particularly Arminians,[12] agree with this. But other evangelicals, those influenced by the Reformed tradition, say this still makes Christ only a partial savior. According to these Reformed evangelicals, this view gives unbiblical autonomy to the individual; the individual still is the one who makes the first move toward God and therefore is the one finally responsible for whether she is saved.

As you can see, this criticism is directed against not only Mormons but also some Arminian evangelicals.[13] In just a bit I will explain what I think is a more biblical view of salvation. But first let us look more closely at Mormon views and focus on what I think to be the critical question—Who makes the first move?[14]

12. Arminians are influenced by James Arminius (1560–1609), who rejected Calvin's view of predestination, saying it means, not that God chooses some for salvation irrespective of their own choices, but instead that God predetermines for eternal life those whom he foreknows will accept Christ.

13. I say "some" because John Wesley, perhaps the most influential Arminian, taught that God has given "prevenient grace" to every person. This grace is a tendency to "life," and if exercised, leads to further gifts of "convincing grace" or "repentance." Hence, evangelicals using this way of thinking can say it is all by grace. Reformed evangelicals, on the other hand, might reply that God still waits for those who will use that universal gift of prevenient grace. See Henry D. Rack, *Reasonable Enthusiast: John Wesley and the Rise of Methodism* (Nashville: Abingdon, 1992), 389.

14. In his recent *Arminian Theology: Myths and Realities* (Downers Grove, IL: InterVarsity, 2006), Roger E. Olsen argues that classical Arminianism does not believe humans make the first move in salvation. Prevenient grace is the "sole cause" of the first exercise of good will toward God (161). This grace is "regerative" by renewing and liberating the will so that it can accept or resist the gift of repentance and faith (163). But he also shows that Arminius believed the freed will, liberated by grace to be able to accept or resist the gift of faith, was at an "intermediate stage," neither unregenerate nor regenerate

For Professor Millet and the LDS tradition, it seems that we move first. In other words, Christ purchased the gift of salvation for us by his life and suffering and death. He is eager to give us this gift but is waiting for us to repent and believe. It finally depends on us, for we must take the initiative. "There are certain things that must be done in order for divine grace and mercy to be activated. . . . All men and women have the capacity to be saved. . . . The gift of God . . . must be received."[15] We have the power to "have faith in Christ, repent of our sins, be baptized, love and serve one another, and do all in our power to put off the natural man and deny ourselves of ungodliness."[16] But we must put that power to work by choosing to start the whole process. Christ is waiting for us to act.

Bruce McConkie is even more direct. "Those who work by faith must first have faith; no one can use a power that he does not possess, and the faith or power must be gained by obedience to those laws upon which its receipt is predicated."[17] McConkie seems to be saying that we gain faith by obedience, the latter of which starts with our autonomous decision.

To be fair, Professor Millet says that "the power to save us, to change us, to renew our souls, is in Christ." And he wisely reminds us that the real question is not whether we're saved by grace or works, but rather, "In whom do we trust? On whom do we rely?"[18]

But at the same time, "Redeemed man is man who has *partaken* of the powers of Christ through the Atonement, repented of his sins, and been renewed through the sanctifier, who is the Holy Ghost."[19] Professor Millet and other leading Mormon theologians often insist that salvation and power are from Christ, but just as often they make clear that we must make the first move. We must first "partake." The power is ready and waiting, but our will alone has the capacity and authority to access that power. We are the ones to start the process of salvation.

(164–67). At this point, one would think, all the evangelized are on a level playing field, having been given the same grace. At this point—logically if not chonologically—the next move, and the move that will distinguish who is saved and who is not, is up to each person. This is the move that is eternally significant, and that is decided by the free will of each individual. At this point, the first move in salvation is made by those who decide to accept rather than resist the offer. Therefore, even though prevenient grace has come first to enable them to choose, the first move to distinguish the saved from the damned is made by the saved.

15. Millet, *A Different Gospel?* 95–96.
16. Ibid., 97.
17. McConkie, *A New Witness for the Articles of Faith* (Salt Lake City: Deseret Book, 1985), 192; cited in Blomberg, *How Wide the Divide?* 178.
18. Millet, *A Different Gospel?* 97.
19. Ibid., 87; emphasis added.

Yet it seems to me that the Bible suggests otherwise. God in Isaiah says, "I am sought of them that asked not for me; I am found of them that sought me not" (Isa. 65:1). This suggests that God comes to those who *don't* make a first move toward him, such as Paul, who was in fact persecuting his Son (remember Luther's realization).

Paul tells us that salvation "is not of him that willeth, nor of him that runneth, but of God that sheweth mercy" (Rom. 9:16). If, as Mormons and Arminians hold, God is waiting for humans to make the first move, then it *does* depend on "him that willeth." But holy writ here denies this very thing. In his first letter to the church at Corinth, Paul says that everything we have is a gift (1 Cor. 4:7). But if salvation starts with our autonomous decision, that first decision is not a gift but our own achievement.

Jesus said none of us can come to him "except the Father which hath sent me draw him" (John 6:44). Doesn't that suggest that when we think we are making the first move, we have missed the Father's prior drawing us to Jesus? And if Jesus is the "author . . . of our faith" (Heb. 12:2), doesn't that mean he gave it to us in the first place? This would imply that our first decision to accept Christ (which most would say is faith itself) is itself a gift from Christ.

The Mormon and Arminian tendency suggests that the natural man (or, in the Arminian case, the man who has been freed by prevenient grace to be able to accept or resist salvation) can be neutral, coolly considering the prospect of salvation through Christ. The Book of Mormon, in fact, declares, "Men are free according to the flesh. . . . And they are free to choose liberty and eternal life" (2 Nephi 2:27). Doctrines and Covenants teaches that "men . . . do many things of their own free will, and bring to pass much righteousness; for *the power is in them, wherein they are agents unto themselves*" (D&C 58:27–28; emphasis added). Mind you, this picture also talks about "prevenient grace,"[20] but this typically means the Holy Spirit's presenting evidence to the autonomous human mind and will to consider. It is still the human self, even if freed by prevenient grace, that must decide.

Yet the Bible seems to suggest that there is no such thing as a neutral mind or will, able to turn this way or that, toward or away from God. Instead, the picture is of a self that by nature flees from God: "There is none that understandeth, there is none that seeketh after God. They are all gone out of the way, they are together become unprofitable; there is none that doeth good, no, not one. . . . There is no fear of God before their eyes" (Rom. 3:11–12, 18). God *had* to make the first move because

---

20. Grace that "comes before," that is, before one even starts believing, in order to induce faith.

before our eyes were opened, we were "dead" in our sins (Eph. 2:5). A dead person cannot move at all.

Peter Forsyth put it this way: "[God] does more than justify faith, He creates it. It is His more than ours. We believe because he makes us believe—with a moral compulsion, an invasion and capture of us."[21]

The problem with the passage quoted above from Doctrine and Covenants is what the theological tradition has called "synergism," the idea that God and the human will work together as partners. Both Erasmus and Philip Melanchthon made synergistic statements: "Free will is the power of applying oneself to grace" (Erasmus); in conversion "God draws, but draws him who is willing" (Melanchthon).[22]

The Lutheran churches eventually repudiated Melanchthon's position in the Formula of Concord, and for good reason. It gives some of the credit for salvation to man, and some to God. Yet Paul says that if we really understand salvation, we will realize that no man can "boast" (Eph. 2:9; Rom. 3:27). None of us can get any credit at all for our salvation. Yet if salvation comes when I lay hold of God's grace, which is ever waiting for me, hasn't my salvation become, at least in part, my achievement, and something of which I can boast? Doesn't this mean that my salvation depends partly on grace and partly on my free will? Have I not then become, in a sense, a co-savior with Christ?

Some say salvation is both active and passive in the Bible, since we are acted *on* and we also act. True enough. But as I have argued above, the Bible suggests that even when I act, it is only because the Spirit has made me active: "For it is God which worketh in you both to will and to do of his good pleasure" (Phil. 2:13). "But by the grace of God I am what I am: and his grace which was bestowed upon me was not in vain; but I laboured more abundantly than they all: yet not I, but the grace of God which was with me" (1 Cor. 15:10).

Synergism is common in theology because of our natural inclination to reduce mystery and paradox to rationally understandable formulas that are easier to picture. That the Bible presents God as the sovereign first actor in all of existence and also individual existences is not difficult to show. Nor is it hard to show that the Bible presents humans as being free creatures. But what is difficult to explain rationally is how the two cohere. It has been easier in theology to declare one side of the paradox to be the controlling one: either God is so sovereign that we have no

---

21. Peter T. Forsyth, *The Justification of God* (London: Independent Press Ltd., 1948), 47; cited in Donald G. Bloesch, *Essentials of Evangelical Theology*, Vol. 1: *God, Authority, and Salvation* (San Francisco: Harper and Row, 1978), 200.

22. Erasmus, in correspondence with Luther on the *Bondage of the Will*; Melanchthon, in *Loci Communes*.

real freedom, or our freedom is finally sovereign. Mormons and some Arminians[23] have chosen the latter, it seems to me.

A better way to go has been shown by Jonathan Edwards:

> In efficacious grace we are not merely passive, nor yet does God do some, and we do the rest. But God does all, and we do all. God produces all, and we act all. . . . God is the only proper *author and fountain*; we only are the proper *actors*. We are in different respects wholly passive and wholly active.[24]

What Edwards means is that God is the one who moves first. He has created not only us but also our first moves toward him. He has authored our faith, and so was the fountain inspiring our first thoughts about and attraction toward him. At the same time, we are the ones who voluntarily believe and move toward him. Our arms are not being twisted.[25] Perhaps it can be compared to a play. God is the author of the script, and we are the actors who choose to play the roles that have been assigned to us—but only because we feel moved by the author.

How this all works out is a mystery rather than a contradiction. This should not surprise us, since life is full of many other mysteries that we accept (for example, how the human person can be both body and soul, mutually interpenetrating, and how light can appear to be both particle and wave), and we believe in a God who is infinite, which by definition means there would be plenty about him that we cannot conceptualize adequately.

Grace as Union

I have tried to suggest that both Mormons and those Arminians who think we are justified by God because of our faith are mistaken, for this way of thinking about salvation makes faith a work that is meritorious. It suggests that believers are indeed better than unbelievers, because

---

23. I say "some" because classical Arminians insist every move made by humans toward God is by grace. Yet, as I argue above, even with prevenient grace there is a point at which human initiative is the determining factor.

24. Edwards, "Efficacious Grace, Book III" in *Writings on the Trinity, Grace and Faith*, ed. Sang Hyung Lee, vol. 21 of *The Works of Jonathan Edwards* (New Haven, CT: Yale University Press, 2003), 251.

25. Of course, Forsyth spoke above of "compulsion" and "capture." Yet what Edwards means is that we are never coerced against our will—in the end. We might be shocked and overwhelmed and even stunned, but when push comes to shove, we say Yes to what we had previously thought unimaginable. God captures our minds and produces new thinking and therefore new willingness.

they believed, while their neighbors did not, and it was for this reason that God chose to give them the gift of eternal life.

Yet it is more biblical—and beautiful!—to think of salvation as based on union with Christ. Jesus said, "I am the vine, ye are the branches" (John 15:5). Paul said the church is "his body, the fulness of him that filleth all in all" (Eph. 1:23), and suggested that each member of the church is joined to Christ really and mysteriously: "I am crucified with Christ: nevertheless I live; yet not I, but Christ liveth in me" (Gal. 2:20).

Applying this biblical truth to the doctrine of salvation, we can say that we are justified, not because of our faith, but by virtue of our union with Christ. God does not confer union with Christ as a reward for faith, but faith is the very act of uniting itself. Faith justifies because it makes Christ and the believer one, and because God has regard for Christ's righteousness, which is now the believer's because the believer is one with Christ. Therefore, the imputation of Christ's righteousness simply means partaking, by union, of the reward given to Christ for his obedience to the Father. Everything Christ did is reckoned to his members' accounts, since they are one with him.

Marriage is a good image to use for this. God used it for his union to Israel, and Paul uses it of the church in Ephesians 5. Just as a wealthy husband assumes the debts of his impoverished bride, so too Christ's righteousness swallows up the sins of his believers in union with him.

The marriage image, which in fact is the preferred image in scripture for this union of Christ and believers, aptly demonstrates why faith is not meritorious (as in some Arminian and most Mormon theologies) but is the very act of uniting. When a man gives himself to a woman in marriage, he doesn't do it as a reward for her accepting him. Nor is her receiving him considered a virtuous act that he rewards by marrying her. Instead, it is by her receiving his proposal to be joined together that the union itself is made.

Human marriage, then, illustrates the mystical union of believers with Christ and shows that faith is not a work that is then rewarded with salvation. No, faith is itself the sign or badge that shows who is already joined with Christ, for faith is the human side of the joining. It shows that God has already moved to give the gift of union. As Luther put it, faith "unites the soul with Christ as a bride is united with her bridegroom. [By it] Christ and the soul become one flesh."[26]

26. Luther, *Christian Liberty*, trans. W. A. Lambert (Philadelphia: Fortress Press, 1957), 14–15.

What Evangelicals Can Learn from Mormons about Salvation

What I am now about to say may cause all of my evangelical friends to desert me, or think I have lost it. But I think we evangelicals have something to learn from our Mormon friends on this subject that is absolutely integral to faith.

Plenty has been written, and justifiably so, on the Christian church in the West embracing what Bonhoeffer called "cheap grace." This is the idea that as long as we believe Jesus died for our sins or have had an emotional experience that is filled with "Christian" appurtenances, we can do as we please. Because, after all, Jesus freed us from the law (this despite the fact that the New Testament never claims this—only that Jesus freed us from being saved by the law). Or (we are also told by those who believe in this "sloppy agape" and "greasy grace") we have made salvation a work if we believe that true faith will work.

In this context, where unbelievers are scandalized by the laxity and materialism and self-indulgence they see in the lives of all too many in the churches, we need a good kick in the rear. Perhaps the envy some non-Mormon believers feel when they see the order and virtue in Mormon communities is like the holy "jealousy" that God provoked in Jews when they saw the new life in Gentiles (Rom. 11:11). Perhaps we can learn from Mormons that we have wrongly separated faith from works, that we have created a false dichotomy between justification and sanctification, and that while we are saved from being justified by the law, nevertheless the law is still "holy, and just, and good" (Rom. 7:12).

Don't get me wrong. I think Mormons, like some Arminians, have made faith a work and have therefore turned salvation into something of a human achievement. But at the same time, they are not Pelagians, who crudely say we can work our way into the kingdom. And they have a proper understanding of the nature of true faith—an inner disposition that "worketh by love" (Gal. 5:6).

A Latter-day Saint Response
Robert Millet

There's nothing more frustrating and even maddening than to have someone insist that they know exactly what you believe, when in fact their
perception is flawed in some way. On many occasions during the last
decade I have stood before large groups of evangelicals in question and
answer sessions and attempted to explain LDS soteriology, our concept
of salvation in Christ—the nature of the human plight, how salvation
comes, what grace and faith and justification mean from an LDS perspective—only to have someone in the audience reply, essentially: "Well,
we hear what you're saying, and it sounds good. We just don't think you
are representing properly the Mormon position." A second group is a bit
more aggressive: they suggest that I am lying, being disingenuous, trying to make our doctrinal stance sound more appealing. Others are bold
enough to declare: "I think you simply don't understand what Mormons
really believe on this subject." More than once I have retorted: "Well, I
may not be the brightest Latter-day Saint you will encounter. I may not
be as eloquent or articulate in making plain our doctrine as someone
more qualified might. And there's no doubt but that there's a better way
to present all of this. But, if you'll forgive my brashness, I'm an expert
on what I believe. Nobody understands what Bob Millet believes better
than Bob Millet."

It will be a wonderful day when you and I can take one another at our
word, can hear and digest and accept the fact that our evangelical or
Mormon counterpart is stating things as they really are, is representing
honestly and sincerely what they believe. Now, to be sure, I have absolutely no control over what the average Latter-day Saint on the street
may think or say; I'm certain that it's just as tough for evangelicals to get

the water to the end of the row as it is for Latter-day Saints. The difference between the explanation we get from scripture, both the biblical canon and the expanded LDS canon, and what we may receive from our next-door neighbor may or may not be the same. There always seems to be, in any faith community, a slight difference (and sometimes a more pronounced one) between what the doctrine of the church is and how that doctrine is presented by the woman or man in the pew. In that spirit, and with a strong desire to be better understood, I will attempt to set forth the LDS doctrine of salvation as found in scripture and in the teachings of church leaders.

Let's begin with a clear statement that while Latter-day Saints differ somewhat from traditional Christians on the purposes behind the fall of Adam and Eve (whether it was or was not a part of God's overall plan), we do not disagree appreciably on the *effects* of the fall. Every man and woman who comes into mortality is "conceived in sin" (Moses 6:55; cf. Ps. 51:5; 2 Nephi 2:21; Mosiah 16:1–5; Ether 3:2), meaning (1) he or she is conceived into a world of sin; and (2) conception becomes the means, the vehicle by which mortality, a fallen nature, "the flesh" is transmitted to the posterity of Adam and Eve. The effects of the fall are inherited.

In what seems to be the very first reference in the Book of Mormon to the fall, a prophet taught that "six hundred years from the time that my father left Jerusalem, a prophet would the Lord God raise up among the Jews—even a Messiah, or, in other words, a Savior of the world. And he also spake concerning the prophets, how great a number had testified of these things, concerning this Messiah, of whom he had spoken, or this Redeemer of the world. Wherefore, *all mankind were in a lost and in a fallen state, and ever would be save they should rely on this Redeemer.*" (1 Nephi 10:4–6; emphasis added; cf. Alma 42:6.) Truly, as Isaiah declared, "All we, like sheep, have gone astray; we have turned every one to his own way" (53:6). The Good Shepherd thus comes on a search and rescue mission after all of his lost sheep. He who never took a moral detour or a backward step thus reaches out and reaches down to lift us up. We are lost in the sense that we do not know our way home without a guide; in the sense that we are alienated from God and separated from things of righteousness. We are fallen in the sense that we live in a fallen world, in the sense that we must be lifted up, quickened, and resuscitated spiritually if we are to enjoy the presence of God. Men and women are lost and fallen in that they are subject to spiritual death, the separation from God (Alma 42:7, 9), the separation from things of righteousness (Alma 12:16, 32; 40:26).

A modern LDS Church leader, Bruce R. McConkie, wrote: "Adam fell. We know that this fall came because of transgression, and that Adam broke the law of God, became mortal, and was thus subject to sin and disease and all the ills of mortality. We know that the effects of his fall passed upon all his posterity; all inherited a fallen state, a state of mortality, a state in which temporal and spiritual death prevail. In this state all men sin. All are lost. All are fallen. All are cut off from the presence of God. All have become carnal, sensual, and devilish by nature. Such a way of life is inherent in this mortal existence."[27] Similarly, Brigham Young noted that a critical and doubting disposition concerning the work of the Lord "arises from the power of evil that is so prevalent upon the face of the whole earth. It was given to you by your father and mother; it was mingled with your conception in the womb, and it has ripened in your flesh, in your blood, and in your bones, so that it has become riveted in your very nature."[28] On another occasion he explained: "There are no persons without evil passions to embitter their lives. Mankind are revengeful, passionate, hateful, and devilish in their dispositions. This we inherit through the fall, and the grace of God is designed to enable us to overcome it."[29]

Note the following from Joseph Smith:

I have learned in my travels that man is treacherous and selfish, but few excepted.[30]

All are subjected to vanity while they travel through the crooked paths and difficulties which surround them. Where is the man that is free from vanity? None ever were perfect but Jesus.[31]

In this world, mankind are naturally selfish, ambitious and striving to excel one above another.[32]

There is one thing under the sun which I have learned and that is that the righteousness of man is sin because it exacteth over much; nevertheless the righteousness of God is just, because it exacteth nothing at all, but sendeth the rain on the just and the unjust, seed time and harvest, for all of which man is ungrateful.[33]

The propensity for and susceptibility to sin are implanted in our nature at conception, just as death is (Ps. 51:5; Moses 6:55). Both death and sin are present only as potentialities at conception, and therefore neither is

27. McConkie, *The Promised Messiah*, 244.
28. *Journal of Discourses* 2:134.
29. Ibid., 8:160.
30. *TPJS*, 30.
31. Ibid., 187.
32. Ibid., 297.
33. Ibid., 317.

fully evident at birth. Death and sin do, however, become actual parts of our nature as we grow up. Sin comes spontaneously, just as death does. In the case of little children, Mormons believe that responsibility for the results of this fallen nature (sinful actions and dispositions) are held in abeyance by virtue of the atonement until they reach the time of accountability (D&C 29:46; 68:25–27; 74:7; Moses 6:53–54). When children do become accountable, however, they become subject to spiritual death and must thereafter repent and come unto Christ by covenant and through the sacraments or ordinances of the gospel.

Ezra Taft Benson, thirteenth president of the LDS Church, observed: "Just as a man does not really desire food until he is hungry, so he does not desire the salvation of Christ until he knows why he needs Christ. No one adequately and properly knows why he needs Christ until he understands and accepts the doctrine of the Fall and its effect upon all mankind."[34] The fall and the atonement are a package deal; one brings the other into existence. I am not aware, for example, of any discussion of the atonement in the Book of Mormon that is not accompanied, either directly or by implication, with a discussion of the fall. We do not appreciate and treasure the medicine until we appreciate the seriousness of the malady. One cannot look earnestly and longingly to the Redeemer if he or she does not sense the need for redemption. Jesus came to earth to do more than offer sage advice. He is not merely a celestial cheerleader or a wise and benevolent consultant. He is our Savior. He came to search us out, to find us, to bring us back home, to redeem us, to save us. In that spirit and with that understanding, let's proceed to examine the nature of Christ's work and thus our work.

It seems to me that the major purpose of religion is literally to link or tie us back to God. Theoretically speaking, there are two ways by which people may be justified—be pronounced innocent, decreed clean and just and right before God. The first is by keeping the law of God perfectly. That is, to the extent that a person's discipleship and obedience are perfect, flawless, and without the slightest drift from the path of righteousness as set forth by Jesus Christ, to that extent the person could be said to be justified by *works* or by *law*. Jesus certainly called us to the lofty ideal of perfection (Matt. 5:48), did he not? He himself lived a perfect life, never took a spiritual detour or backward step (see 2 Cor. 5:21; Heb. 4:14–15; 1 Peter 2:22). Could he ask anything less of us? I presume that it is hypothetically possible for a man or a woman so to do, but it is practically impossible, beyond the reach of the greatest prophet or the mightiest apostle. As Paul in the New Testament and Lehi

---

34. Ezra Taft Benson, *A Witness and a Warning* (Salt Lake City: Deseret Book, 1988), 33.

in the Book of Mormon both taught, "by the deeds of the law there shall no flesh be justified in his sight" (Rom. 3:20; 2 Nephi 2:3).

Second, because no one of us can in deed and in fact fail to err or sin, because the effects of the fall are such that we cannot walk life's paths without being guilty of either sins of commission or omission, and because one sin against the law of God disqualifies us of justification by law or by works (James 2:10), there must be some other way. And thank God, there is. We may be *justified by faith*. To do so, we must recognize our sinful condition; confess our need for help, for relief, for redemption; and acknowledge freely that the only way we can be made right with God is through having total trust, complete confidence, and ready reliance on one who did live the law of God perfectly. We have faith in Christ in the sense that we trust his word, trust what he said, trust what he has done, and trust that he can deliver us from death, hell, and endless torment. We have faith in Christ in that we have confidence in his own matchless life, confidence in the power of his atoning blood to wash and sanctify us from sin, and confidence in his ability to raise us from the dead and glorify us hereafter. We have faith in Christ in the sense that we humbly acknowledge that we cannot rely on our own un-aided efforts for salvation; we cannot rely on any other mortal to fill in the gaps and cover the debt; and we must rely, as the Book of Mormon teaches, *wholly* and *alone* upon the merits and mercy and grace of Jesus Christ (2 Nephi 31:19; Moroni 6:4).

Salvation or eternal life is the greatest of all the gifts of God (2 Nephi 2:4; D&C 6:13; 14:7). One does not earn a gift; he or she receives it, humbly and gratefully. Do the Latter-day Saints, then, believe in salvation by grace? Of course we do, for our own scriptural works (certainly including the Bible) so attest. Grace is unearned divine assistance. It is unmerited divine favor. It is divine enabling power. I've heard it put this way: grace is God's acceptance of us; faith is our acceptance of God's acceptance of us; and peace is our acceptance of us.

While mercy and grace are words that are quite often used interchangeably, I see them as two sides of the same coin. I sat with a colleague once having an enjoyable theological conversation about life here and life hereafter. Without thinking or evaluating what I was about to say, and certainly without biting my tongue, I made a rather stupid, offhand comment. I said: "I just want to get hereafter what I deserve." My friend, probably twenty years my senior and never more wise than at that very moment, replied quite sternly: "Bob, you'd better pray to God that you never get what you deserve!" Well, he's right, of course. The good news of the gospel, the glad tidings, is that Jesus has come and that through an acceptance of his atonement, we need not receive just what we deserve. The other side of that coin is grace: to receive the grace of God is to receive that which I *do not deserve*. Salvation is free (2 Nephi 2:4) in the sense that it may not be purchased, bartered for, or even earned.

Although there is a very important place for man's good works (which we will consider shortly), it is important that we understand that "since man had fallen he could not merit anything of himself; but the sufferings and death of Christ atone for their sins, through faith and repentance" (Alma 22:14). The Mediator pleads our cause before the Father on the basis of his works, his perfect obedience, his atoning blood (see D&C 45:3–5). In short, Christ does for us what we could never, worlds without end, do for ourselves. This is pure grace. Note the following statements from LDS literature on grace:

> Wherefore, I know that thou art redeemed, because of the righteousness of thy Redeemer. (2 Nephi 2:3)

> Wherefore, how great the importance to make these things known unto the inhabitants of the earth, that they may know that there is no flesh that can dwell in the presence of God, save it be through the merits, and mercy, and grace of the Holy Messiah. (2 Nephi 2:8)

> The Lord showeth us our weakness that we may know that it is by his grace, and his great condescensions unto the children of men, that we have power to do these things. (Jacob 4:7)

> And I also thank my God, yea, my great God, that he hath granted unto us that we might repent of these things, and also that he hath forgiven us of those our many sins . . . which we have committed, and taken away the guilt from our hearts, through the merits of his son. (Alma 24:10)

> And if ye believe on [Christ's] name ye will repent of all your sins, that thereby ye may have a remission of them through his merits. (Helaman 14:13)

> Yea, come unto Christ, and be perfected in him, . . . and if by the grace of God ye are perfect in Christ, ye can in nowise deny the power of God. And again, if ye by the grace of God are perfect in Christ, and deny not his power, then are ye sanctified in Christ by the grace of God, through the shedding of the blood of Christ. (Moroni 10:32–33)

> If thou wilt do good, yea, and hold out faithful to the end, thou shalt be saved in the kingdom of God, which is the greatest of all the gifts of God; for there is no gift greater than the gift of salvation. (D&C 6:13)

> And, if you keep my commandments and endure to the end you shall have eternal life, which gift is the greatest of all the gifts of God. (D&C 14:7)

And we know that justification through the grace of our Lord and Savior Jesus Christ is just and true; and we know also, that sanctification through the grace of our Lord and Savior Jesus Christ is just and true, to all those who love and serve God with all their mights, minds, and strength. (D&C 20:30–31)

We are to understand from these passages [Eph. 2:8–9], that the grace and faith by which man is saved, are the gifts of God, having been purchased by him not by his own works, but by the blood of Christ. Had not these gifts been purchased for man, all exertions on his part would have been entirely unavailing and fruitless. Whatever course man might have pursued, he could not have atoned for one sin; it required the sacrifice of a sinless and pure Being in order to purchase the gifts of faith, repentance, and salvation for fallen man. Grace, Faith, Repentance, and Salvation, when considered in their origin, are not of man, neither by his works; man did not devise, originate, nor adopt them; superior Beings in Celestial abodes provided these gifts and revealed the conditions to man by which he might become a partaker of them. Therefore all boasting on the part of man is excluded. He is saved by a plan which his works did not originate—a plan of heaven, and not of earth.[35]

The word *grace* occurs 252 times in the standard works, while the word *mercy* occurs 396 times. It is apparent that these words are not descriptive of fringe gospel principles. They lie at the core of LDS doctrine, flowing directly from the Atonement of Jesus Christ.[36]

Men and women unquestionably have impressive powers and can bring to pass great things. But after all our obedience and good works, we cannot be saved from death or the effects of our individual sins without the grace extended by the atonement of Jesus Christ. . . . In other words, salvation does not come simply by keeping the commandments. . . . Man cannot earn his own salvation.[37]

My intention has not been to drown the reader with so many passages and doctrinal statements, but rather to point out that "salvation by grace" is neither foreign to nor scarce within LDS literature. This is not an idea that has evolved in the last couple of decades; this central, saving doctrine has been there from the time of Joseph Smith. Professor Gerald McDermott is correct in indicating that Latter-day Saints see the process of being saved as a joint enterprise between man and God.

35. Orson Pratt, "The True Faith," in *A Series of Pamphlets* (Liverpool, 1852), 3–9.
36. Tad R. Callister, The Infinite Atonement (Salt Lake City: Deseret Book, 2000), 310.
37. Dallin H. Oaks, *With Full Purpose of Heart* (Salt Lake City: Deseret Book, 2002), 75; see also 6.

I think that is exactly what is intended in Philippians 2:12–13. Verse 12 states that we are to "work out our own salvation with fear and trembling." But verse 13 states that it is God who is working in us to do his will. Well, which is it, man or God? C. S. Lewis observed: "You see, we are now trying to understand, and to separate into water-tight compartments, what exactly God does and what man does when God and man are working together."[38] That sounds like synergy to me, a concept that is embraced by a huge segment of Christianity today.

The gospel of Jesus Christ is a gospel covenant, a two-way agreement established and revealed by an infinite deity to finite, mortal men and women. God does for us what we could never do for ourselves: he forgives our sins, cleanses our heart, changes our nature, raises us from the dead, and conforms us to the image of Christ, thus preparing us to dwell with him hereafter. These are acts of grace. On our part, we exercise faith in the Lord Jesus Christ, a faith that is in reality a gift of the Spirit, something with which God endows us (1 Cor. 12:9; Moroni 10:11). In some ways, Latter-day Saints are like Arminians in that we do believe that man has a role to play in salvation. Although Mormons believe that salvation is available to all men and women (Articles of Faith 1:3), we acknowledge at the same time that the effects of the fall tend to entice humankind away from God, from godliness, and from an acceptance of the gospel of Jesus Christ. To counteract this influence, there are unconditional blessings and benefits—graces, prevenient graces, that flow from the Almighty. For one thing, Latter-day Saints believe that every man and woman born into mortality possesses the Light of Christ or the Spirit of Jesus Christ, an inner moral monitor that leads us to light and truth. This inner light is given to each of us to lead us to God, to Christ, and to the gospel. If persons are true to this light within them, they will in time be led to higher light and deeper understanding (Moroni 7:12–19; D&C 84:44–48).

A second kind of prevenient grace is that through the mediation of the Master, men and women are empowered to choose good or evil. Note this language from an early Book of Mormon prophet: "Adam fell that men might be; and men are, that they might have joy. And the Messiah cometh in the fulness of time, that he may redeem the children of men from the fall." Now pay particular attention to the following: "And *because that they are redeemed from the fall they have become free forever, knowing good from evil; to act for themselves and not to be acted upon. . . . Wherefore, men are free according to the flesh. . . . And they are free to choose liberty and eternal life, through the great Mediator of all men,* or to choose captivity and death, according to the captivity and power

---

38. C. S. Lewis, *Mere Christianity*, 131–32.

of the devil; for he seeketh that all men might be miserable like unto himself." (2 Nephi 2:25–27; emphasis added; cf. 2 Nephi 10:23.)

Now consider this passage: "And now remember, remember, my brethren, that whosoever perisheth, perisheth unto himself; and whosoever doeth iniquity, doeth it unto himself; for behold, ye are free; ye are permitted to act for yourselves; for behold, God hath given unto you a knowledge and he hath made you free. He hath given unto you that you might know good from evil, and he hath given unto you that you might choose life or death" (Helaman 14:30–31). In the Doctrine and Covenants the early Latter-day Saints were instructed that "men should be anxiously engaged in a good cause, and *do many things of their own free will*, and bring to pass much righteousness; for *the power is in them, wherein they are agents unto themselves*" (D&C 58:27–28; emphasis added).

The passages just quoted are in harmony with early Christian teachings as contained in the collection *The Ante-Nicene Fathers*:

> Neither do we maintain that it is by fate that men do what they do, or suffer what they suffer. Rather, we maintain that each man acts rightly or sins by his free choice. . . . Since God in the beginning made the race of angels and men with free will, they will justly suffer in eternal fire the punishment of whatever sins they have committed.[39]

> But man, being endowed with reason, and in this respect similar to God, having been made free in his will, and with power over himself, is himself his own cause that sometimes he becomes wheat, and sometimes chaff.[40]

> Those who believe, do His will agreeably to their own choice. Likewise, agreeably to their own choice, the disobedient do not consent to His doctrine. It is clear that His Father has made everyone in a like condition, each person having a choice of his own and a free understanding.[41]

> We . . . have believed and are saved by voluntary choice.[42]

> I find, then, that man was constituted free by God. He was master of his own will and power. . . . For a law would not be imposed upon one who did not have it in his power to render that obedience which is due to law. Nor again, would the penalty of death be threatened against sin, if a contempt

39. Justin Martyr, in *Ante-Nicene Fathers* (*ANF*) 1:190.
40. Irenaus, *ANF* 1:466.
41. Irenaus, *ANF* 1:556.
42. Clement of Alexandria, *ANF* 2:217.

of the law were impossible to man in the liberty of his will. . . . Man is free, with a will either for obedience or resistance.[43]

Now what of works? Do not good works matter? Didn't James teach that faith without works is dead and that true faith always manifests itself in faithfulness (James 2), meaning in dedicated discipleship and obedience to the commandments of God? Did not Jesus state, "If any man will come after me, let him deny himself, and take up his cross daily, and follow me" (Luke 9:23)? Do not a score of scriptural passages indicate that we will be judged according to our works, whether they be good or evil? One's repentance, receipt of the ordinances or sacraments, and efforts to keep the commandments are extensions and manifestations of true faith. So on the one hand, LDS scripture and prophetic teachings establish the essential truth that salvation is free and that it comes by grace, through God's unmerited favor. On the other hand, ancient and modern prophets set forth the equally vital point that works are a necessary though insufficient condition for salvation. We will be judged according to our works, *not according to the merits of our works*, but to the extent that our works manifest to God who and what we have *become* through the transcendent powers of Christ. Truly we are saved by grace alone, but grace is never alone.

Reflect on the following statements from early Christian teachings:

The way of light, then, is as follows. If anyone desires to travel to the appointed place, he must be zealous in his works.[44]

We are justified by our works and not our words.[45]

The tree is made manifest by its fruit. So those who profess themselves to be Christians will be recognized by their conduct.[46]

This, then, is our reward if we will confess Him by whom we have been saved. But in what way will we confess Him? We confess Him by doing what He says, not transgressing His commandments. . . . For that reason, brethren, let us confess Him by our works, by loving one another.[47]

If men by their works show themselves worthy of His design, they are deemed worthy of reigning in company with Him, being delivered from corruption and suffering. This is what we have received.[48]

43. Tertullian, *ANF* 3:300–301.
44. Barnabas, *ANF* 1:148.
45. Clement of Rome, *ANF* 1:13.
46. Ignatius, *ANF* 1:55.
47. Second Clement, *ANF* 7:518.
48. Justin Martyr, *ANF* 1:165.

Let those who are not found living as He taught, be understood not to be Christians, even though they profess with the lips the teachings of Christ. For it is not those who make profession, but those who do the works, who will be saved.[49]

The matters of our religion lie in works, not in words.[50]

Whoever obtains this and distinguishes himself in good works will gain the prize of everlasting life. . . . Others, attaching slight importance to the works that tend to salvation, do not make the necessary preparation for attaining to the objects of their hope.[51]

Before I close this chapter, I need to explain a Book of Mormon passage that is generally misunderstood by evangelicals and, unfortunately, too often by Latter-day Saints. "For we labor diligently," one writer declared, "to write, to persuade our children, and also our brethren, to believe in Christ, and to be reconciled to God; for we know that *it is by grace that we are saved, after all we can do*" (2 Nephi 25:23; emphasis added). This does not mean that we must do everything we can do *before* Christ can assist us. This is not about chronology. Further, who do you know who has or will ever do *all* they can do? Grace is not just that final boost into heaven that God provides at the end of a well-lived life, although we obviously will need all the help we can get. Rather, the Almighty assists us all along the way, every second of every minute of every hour of every day, all through our lives. It does not mean that we will carry the bulk of the load to salvation and Jesus will fill in the gaps; he is not the God of the gaps. Our contribution to glory hereafter, when compared to his, is infinitesimal and miniscule. If I might be permitted a paraphrase of what the passage stated, "We are saved by grace, *above and beyond* all we can do, *notwithstanding* all we can do, *in spite of* all we can do." In the words of Brigham Young, "It requires all the atonement of Christ, the mercy of the Father, the pity of angels and the grace of the Lord Jesus Christ to be with us always, and then to do the very best we possibly can, to get rid of this sin within us, so that we may escape from this world into the celestial kingdom."[52]

To be sure, there have been misunderstandings, misapplications, and abuses of these specific truths by both our faith communities. I would be the first to admit that some Latter-day Saints have often been guilty of attempting almost to save themselves, guilty of a kind

49. Justin Martyr, *ANF* 1:168.
50. Justin Martyr, *ANF* 1:288.
51. Clement of Alexandria, *ANF* 2:591.
52. *Journal of Discourses* 11:301.

of works-righteousness that discounts, understates, underappreciates, and even sets at naught the mighty work performed by our Savior and Redeemer.[53] On the other hand, some evangelicals give the impression that all that Jesus asks of us is a verbal acceptance of him as Savior, responding to an altar call, or filling out a card at a revival or crusade. This has given rise to a kind of cheap grace, an easy-believism that separates salvation from discipleship, justification from sanctification, profession from obedience. Some evangelical writers have commented that the result is that many born-again Christians do not tend to live any differently from worldly, nonreligious people.[54]

This is a topic where evangelicals and Latter-day Saints need not have endless squabbles, nor even heated discussions. We both believe we are sinners desperately in need of redemption. We both know we are unable to forgive our own sins or cleanse our own souls. We both know that Jesus is the answer, that his atonement is the solution, that submission and surrender to him is the path that leads to peace in this life and eternal reward in the life to come. We both know that our trust, our confidence, our reliance—in other words, our faith—must, simply must, be in Jesus Christ. We both know that the burden of the New Testament, especially the epistles of Paul, is that salvation comes by the grace of God, comes as we are justified from the penalty of sin, sanctified from the tyranny of sin, and eventually delivered from the tentacles of sin through divine enabling power. This is also the message of LDS scripture, a message that weaves its way in particular through the Book of Mormon like a doctrinal refrain. We ought to know our own doctrine and thus acknowledge where differences exist. But there's no crime, no harm done, no penalty associated with identifying similarities, sweet spiritual similarities that bring joy and rest and respite to both of us.

---

53. See Bruce C. Hafen, *The Broken Heart* (Salt Lake City: Deseret Book, 1989); Stephen E. Robinson, *Believing Christ* (Salt Lake City: Deseret Book, 1992); Robert L. Millet, *Grace Works*, and *Are We There Yet?* (Salt Lake City: Deseret Book, 2005).

54. See John F. MacArthur, *The Gospel According to Jesus* (Grand Rapids: Zondervan, 1988); *Hard to Believe* (Nashville: Thomas Nelson, 2003); Ronald J. Sider, *The Scandal of the Evangelical Conscience* (Grand Rapids: Baker, 2005); Robert Jeffress, *Grace Gone Wild* (Colorado Springs: Water Brook Press, 2005); Dallas Willard, *The Great Omission* (San Francisco: HarperSanFrancisco, 2006).

Rebuttal and Concluding Thoughts
Gerald McDermott

I like Professor Millet's humor. The first page of his response gave me a good guffaw as I heard him explain that No, he was not lying about his own Mormon beliefs, and Yes, he thought he could describe his own thinking. We evangelicals are often guilty as charged, failing to admit the possibility that we could be wrong in our estimation of what Mormons really believe.

I also appreciate Bob's definition of judgment by works, in which I believe, and his ability to thread the needle on this one: "We will be judged according to our works, *not according to the merit of our works*, but to the extent that our works manifest to God who and what we have *become* through the transcendent powers of Christ." He steered between the Scylla of antinomianism[55] and the Charybdis of Pelagianism.[56]

The criticism I made in my essay at the beginning of this chapter still stands—that Mormons regard humans as somewhat autonomous, able to make the first move toward God. On this, as I pointed out, they are like some evangelical Arminians. Bob agrees with this assessment but does not quite do justice to (a common) Arminian approach when he says they "believe that man has a role to play in salvation." Reformed folks also believe man has a role to play, but that role has been initiated, scripted, and empowered by God. The key difference is that while Mormons and (some) Arminian evangelicals believe a man *decides* to play his role, Reformed theology (and scripture, I would add) sees God as moving man

---

55. From *anti* (against) and *nomos* (law), taking the position that the law is no longer necessary or relevant to the Christian.
56. The heresy that one can take the initial and basic steps toward salvation without the help of grace.

in heart and mind to *want* to play the role God has already planned out. As I said in my essay, Arminians say grace frees a person to be *able* to accept, but it is the freed will that finally decides it wants to.

Mormon confidence in man's ability to decide for God goes back to the LDS view of the fall. As I argued in chapter 4, Mormons do not see the fall as either rebellion or producing an impaired will, which combination appears to make the atonement less necessary. For human moral ability remains, and there is therefore a theoretical possibility of remaining sinless without the help of Jesus. Bob's reply is that God foresaw that every last human would sin and therefore need atonement. This is plausible, it seems to me, even if I cannot agree that it is the best reading of the biblical story.

But this seems to produce another problem: if human nature was not morally impaired by the fall, why is it that every human being who has ever lived begins to sin, in Bob's wording, "spontaneously"? Does this historical universality of sin not suggest that the fall went beyond causing death and agency and in fact crippled humans' ability to choose God?

Bob's catena of quotations from early church thinkers on human ability to choose does not necessarily help his case. It has long been recognized that these early, mostly Greek theologians were fighting the notion of Greek fate, which seemed to rob humanity of any meaningful freedom. Even Augustine was caught up by this dynamic, and only later in his career realized it could not be squared with the biblical emphasis on human bondage to sin—and consequent inability to make the first move toward God.

In some ways this chapter has been the most significant in this book. Evangelicals have most typically dismissed Mormonism as unchristian because it was thought to teach salvation by works. I hope this chapter will show the case to be significantly different. Even if Bob and I do not agree on who makes the first move, we both affirm that works are indissolubly connected to living faith, that it is Jesus's suffering and death, not our works, that saves us, and that Jesus is our Lord and Savior, not simply a "wise consultant" or "celestial cheerleader."

8

THE ONLY NAME
UNDER HEAVEN?

The Fate of the Unevangelized
Robert Millet

The story is told of a young mother who went through the trauma of a divorce and then did her very best to support herself and her young son. She investigated and then joined the Church of Jesus Christ of Latter-day Saints. She later learned to her complete horror that her son had contracted a terminal illness, and the mother consequently faced the daunting and heart-rending challenge of preparing her boy and herself for what was coming. Once the boy learned that his death was inevitable, he seemed to have only one thing in mind. Over and over he would ask: "Mama, you won't forget me, will you? I won't be forgotten, will I?"[1]

Engaging the Problem of the Ages

None of us wants to be forgotten, whether by friends or by loved ones. And surely no person who believes in the reality of God or a Providential Head would want to be forgotten in any way or lost track of in the eternal scheme of things. Each of us desires the personal assurance that God knows us, loves us, orchestrates the events of our lives, and will do all he can to bless and care for us. It is in that spirit that Joseph Smith wrote the third article of faith: "We believe that *through the Atonement of Christ, all mankind may be saved*, by obedience to the laws and ordinances of the Gospel" (Articles of Faith 1:3; emphasis added). For Mormons there is no set quota, no ceiling on the number of saved beings, no predetermined election of those who will enjoy heaven hereafter.

---

1. As related by Boyd K. Packer, *That All May Be Edified* (Salt Lake City: Bookcraft, 1982), 172.

God "will have all men to be saved, and to come unto the knowledge of the truth" (1 Tim. 2:4). Truly, our Heavenly Father is long-suffering to us, "not willing that any should perish, but that all should come to repentance" (2 Pet. 3:9). Salvation is freely available to all (2 Nephi 2:4; 26:23–28); no accountable person comes into this life who is not capable of hearing and receiving the gospel of Jesus Christ and basking in the light and life that flow therefrom.

I mention these things to lead into what is beyond doubt one of the most vexing and perplexing issues in the history of Christianity—what has come to be known as the soteriological problem of evil. It might be stated simply as follows: If Jesus Christ is truly the only name and means by which salvation may come to the children of God (Acts 4:12), what do we make of the sobering fact that the bulk of humankind (from the beginning of time to the winding up scenes) will go to their graves never having even heard of him? To be honest, I for one do not find a great deal of comfort or peace, nor do I find very convincing answers, in traditional Christian efforts to address this matter, which strikes at the heart of what we mean when we speak of the infinite love of God, the tender mercies of God, and the consistent justice of God.

Those with an Augustinian or Calvinistic bent would be prone to provide a prompt response to this query: persons who never heard were not predestined to do so from before the foundations of the world; they were not counted among the elect to begin with. Many have chosen to take the position that they simply do not know what will become of some of the great ones before Jesus who never knew of him, except perhaps that God will judge men and women according to how well they attended to the general revelation given them, or how and to what extent they exercised faith in God. Others believe some opportunity to know of Christ will come to each person in this life, even perhaps at the moment of death. A relatively small segment of Christian scholars have chosen to take more seriously scriptural passages and statements of early Christian teachers that Jesus's redemptive labors did not end with his death, but rather that he ministered to the dead after the crucifixion.[2]

Joseph Smith's Discovery

It may be worthwhile to consider how Joseph Smith first came to understand who would and who would not be saved. The Smith family

---

2. I have reviewed some of the attempts to address the soteriological problem of evil in *A Different Jesus?* 120–33; see also John Sanders, *No Other Name* (Grand Rapids: Eerdmans, 1992); *What About Those Who Have Never Heard?* (Downers Grove, IL: InterVarsity Press, 1995); and, finally, *The God Who Risks* (Downers Grove, IL: InterVarsity Press, 1998).

read regularly from the Bible, so the parents and children would no doubt have been familiar with at least the rudiments of the Christian faith. In addition, Joseph's experience with the Book of Mormon (however one chooses to construe its production) was deeply significant and in fact foundational for the young prophet's spiritual education. As noted earlier, the Book of Mormon is filled with redemptive theology—the nature of fallen men and women, the need for a savior, and the sole and singular salvation available to mortals through the mediation of Jesus Christ. It is also worth reinforcing the idea that the Book of Mormon has a strong flavor of what many scholars have called the Deuteronomic Code, the black-white, good-bad, and blessing-cursing dichotomous way of presenting its message. In fact, it almost seems as though there are only two types of beings who will stand before the Almighty at the day of judgment—those bound for the highest heaven and those who have defected from truth and are thus headed for the lowest pits of hell.

For example, one Book of Mormon teacher reminded his wayward audience that "this life is the time for men to prepare to meet God; yea, behold the day of this life is the day for men to perform their labors." He continued:

> And now, as I said unto you before, as ye have had so many witnesses, therefore, I beseech of you that ye do not procrastinate the day of your repentance until the end; for after this day of life, which is given us to prepare for eternity, behold, if we do not improve our time while in this life, then cometh the night of darkness wherein there can be no labor performed. Ye cannot say, when ye are brought to that awful crisis, that I will repent, that I will return to my God. Nay, ye cannot say this; for that same spirit which doth possess your bodies at the time that ye go out of this life, that same spirit will have power to possess your body in that eternal world. (Alma 34:32, 33–34)

My understanding is that Joseph Smith was well aware in his early years of the Savior's Great Commission for followers of the Christ to go into all the world and make disciples in all nations (Matt. 28:19–20). I have great difficulty imagining that the fires of revivalism in the "Burnt-over district" in upstate New York in 1820 would not have been seen as at least a partial fulfillment of that Commission. It is not unimportant to observe that the heralds of Christianity were not only to teach all nations but were also to baptize them in the name of the Father, Son, and Holy Spirit. The first Latter-day Saints took Jesus's directive to Nicodemus to be born of water and of the Spirit (John 3:5) quite literally as the need for a baptismal immersion, followed by a confirmation and bestowal of the Spirit. In other words, Joseph Smith and his followers believed that it was the responsibility of those who took upon them the name of Christ to go into the world, preach the glad tidings of salvation, and perform the necessary ordinances. And they were to do this here and now, in this life, before the time of death. Nothing in Joseph's teachings or in the revelations recorded prior to 1836 would have altered such a perception.

As the membership of the restored church grew, there came a time when two church centers existed at the same time—one in Kirtland, Ohio, and one in Independence, Missouri, although Joseph himself resided in Kirtland in the early 1830s. Plans for the erection of the Kirtland Temple were underway by 1833, and by the end of 1835 the building was nearing completion. Joseph and the early leaders of the church had begun to meet in the temple before its completion. On Thursday evening, January 21, 1836, the prophet and a number of church leaders from Ohio and Missouri gathered on the third or attic floor of the Kirtland Temple in the translating or "President's Room." The history of the church then records the following, which has come to be known as Joseph Smith's Vision of the Celestial Kingdom, now section 137 of the Doctrines and Covenants (added to the canon in April 1976):

> The heavens were opened upon us, and I beheld the celestial kingdom of God, and the glory thereof, whether in the body or out I cannot tell.
> I saw the transcendent beauty of the gate through which the heirs of that kingdom will enter, which was like unto circling flames of fire;
> Also the blazing throne of God, whereon was seated the Father and the Son.
> I saw the beautiful streets of that kingdom, which had the appearance of being paved with gold. (D&C 137:1–4)

Joseph the prophet had recorded in February 1832 the nature of those who would inherit the highest heaven, the celestial. These persons are they who "overcome by faith, and are sealed by the Holy Spirit of Promise," they "into whose hands the Father has given all things" (D&C 76:53, 55).

Joseph's account of the vision continues:

> I saw Father Adam and Abraham; and my father and my mother; my brother Alvin, that has long since slept;
> And marveled how it was that he had obtained an inheritance in that kingdom, seeing that he had departed this life before the Lord had set his hand to gather Israel the second time, and had not been baptized for the remission of sins. (vv. 5–6)

Joseph's vision was a glimpse into the future celestial realm, for he saw his parents in the kingdom of the just, when in fact both were still living in 1836. Mother Smith would live for another twenty years, while Joseph Sr. would not die until 1840. Father Smith was, interestingly, in the same room with his son at the time the vision was received.

Alvin Smith: The Prototype

The prophet also saw his brother Alvin. Alvin Smith was the firstborn of Joseph Sr., and Lucy Mack Smith. He was born on February 11, 1798, in Tunbridge, Vermont. His was of a pleasant and loving disposition, and he constantly sought opportunities to aid the family in their financial struggles. Lucy Mack Smith, Joseph's mother, wrote that on the morning of November 15, 1823, "Alvin was taken very sick with the bilious colic," probably appendicitis. One physician hurried to the Smith home and administered calomel, an experimental drug, to Alvin. The dose of calomel "lodged in his stomach," and on the third day of sickness Alvin became aware that he was going to die. He asked that each of the Smith children come to his bedside for his parting counsel and final expression of love. According to Mother Smith's record, "When he came to Joseph, he said, 'I am now going to die, the distress which I suffer, and the feelings that I have, tell me my time is very short. I want you to be a good boy, and do everything that lies in your power to obtain the Record. [Joseph had been visited by the angel Moroni less than three months before this time.] Be faithful in receiving instruction, and in keeping every commandment that is given you.'"[3]

Alvin died on November 19, 1823, some seven years before the organization of the LDS Church; he had not been baptized by proper authority. Joseph wondered during his vision how it was possible for his brother to have attained the highest heaven. Alvin's family had been shocked and saddened at his funeral when they heard the Presbyterian minister announce that Alvin would be consigned to hell, having never officially been baptized or involved in the church. William Smith, Alvin's younger brother, recalls: "Hyrum, Samuel, Katherine, and mother were members of the Presbyterian Church. My father would not join. He did not like it because Rev. Stockton had preached my brother's funeral sermon and intimated very strongly that he had gone to hell, for Alvin was not a church member, but he was a good boy and my father did not like it."[4] What joy and excitement must have filled the souls of both Joseph Jr. and his father when they heard the voice of an omniscient

3. Lucy Mack Smith, *History of Joseph Smith by His Mother* (Salt Lake City: Bookcraft, n.d.), 87.

4. See an interview with William Smith by E. C. Briggs and J. W. Peterson published in the *Deseret News* (Salt Lake City), January 20, 1894.

and omni-loving God saying: "All who have died without a knowledge of this gospel, who would have received it if they had been permitted to tarry, shall be heirs of the celestial kingdom of God; also all that shall die henceforth without a knowledge of it, who would have received it with all their hearts, shall be heirs of that kingdom; for I, the Lord, will judge all men according to their works, according to the desire of their hearts" (vv. 7–9).

Latter-day Saints believe that God does not hold anyone accountable for a gospel law of which he or she was ignorant. Joseph the prophet learned that every person will have an opportunity—here or hereafter—to accept and apply the principles of the gospel of Jesus Christ. Only the Lord, the Holy One of Israel, is capable of perfect judgment, and thus only he can discern completely the hearts and minds of mortal men; he alone knows when a person has received sufficient knowledge or impressions of the Spirit to constitute a valid opportunity to receive the message of salvation. This vision reaffirmed that the Lord will judge men not only by their actions but also by their attitudes—the desires of their heart (see also Alma 41:3).

Another of the profoundly beautiful doctrines enunciated in the Vision of the Celestial Kingdom deals with the status of children who die. "And I also beheld that all children who die before they arrive at the years of accountability are saved in the celestial kingdom of heaven" (D&C 137:10). This affirmed what earlier prophets had taught. King Benjamin in the Book of Mormon had learned from an angel that "the infant perisheth not that dieth in his infancy" (Mosiah 3:18). And after having described the nature of those who will come forth in the first resurrection, one ancient American prophet said simply, "Little children also have eternal life" (Mosiah 15:25). A revelation given to Joseph Smith in September 1830 had specified that "little children are redeemed from the foundation of the world through mine Only Begotten" (D&C 29:46). And Joseph taught in 1842 that "the Lord takes many away, even in infancy, that they may escape the envy of man, and the sorrows and evils of this present world; they were too pure, too lovely, to live on earth; therefore, if rightly considered, instead of mourning we have reason to rejoice as they are delivered from evil, and we shall soon have them again."[5] By virtue of his infinite understanding of the human family, "we may assume that the Lord knows and arranges beforehand who shall be taken in infancy and who shall remain on earth to undergo whatever tests are needed in their cases."[6]

5. Smith, *TPJS*, 196–97.
6. Bruce R. McConkie, expressing the sentiments of Joseph Fielding Smith, in "The Salvation of Little Children," *Ensign*, April 1977, 6.

The Gospel Preached Hereafter

To state that all who would have received the gospel if they had been permitted to live on earth long enough to find the message is certainly a grand declaration of God's omniscience. As we pointed out earlier, however, Mormons do not believe that the decision as to who will be saved rests solely with God; each man or woman possesses sufficient moral agency to decide for themselves. And if that opportunity is not afforded here, it will come hereafter. Mormons take quite literally the passages in Peter's first epistle (1 Pet. 3:18–20 and 4:6) to the effect that Jesus preached the gospel to those in a post-mortal spirit world, the "spirits in prison" who had been wicked in the days of Noah, as well as those through the generations who had not had a valid chance to hear and receive the gospel; this took place following the time of his death but before his resurrection.

"St. Peter has one doctrine that is almost peculiar to himself," Frederick Farrar wrote in the nineteenth century, "and which is inestimably precious." This doctrine, Farrar adds, is a "much disregarded and, indeed, till recent times, half-forgotten article of the Christian creed; I mean the object of Christ's descent into Hades. In this truth is involved nothing less than the extension of Christ's redeeming work to the dead who died before his coming. Had the Epistle contained nothing else but this, it would at once have been raised above the irreverent charge of being 'secondhand and commonplace.'" Farrar then quotes 1 Peter 3:18–20 and 4:6 and states: "Few words of scripture have been so tortured and emptied of their significance as these." He notes that "every effort has been made to explain away the plain meaning of this passage. It is one of the most precious passages of scripture, and it involves no ambiguity, except such as is created by the scholasticism of a prejudiced theology. It stands almost alone in scripture. . . . For if language have any meaning, this language means that Christ, when His spirit descended into the lower world, proclaimed the message of salvation to the once impenitent dead." And then, in broadening our perspective beyond those of the days of Noah, Farrar writes: "But it is impossible to suppose that the antediluvian sinners, conspicuous as they were for their wickedness, were the only ones of all the dead who were singled out to receive the message of deliverance."

"We thus rescue the work of redemption," Farrar adds, "from the appearance of having failed to achieve its end for the vast majority of those for whom Christ died. By accepting the light thus thrown upon 'the descent into Hell,' we extend to those of the dead who have not finally hardened themselves against it the blessedness of Christ's atoning work."[7]

---

7. Frederick Farrar, *The Early Days of Christianity* (New York: E. P. Dutton & Sons, 1882), 139–42, 169.

In a modern commentary on 1 Peter, the author observes that 1 Peter 3:19 and 4:6 are the only passages in the New Testament that refer to the ministry of Christ to the post-mortal spirit world. "But 1 Peter would not be able," he points out, "to make such brief reference to this idea if it were not already known in the churches as tradition. What 1 Peter says in regard to this tradition is, in comparison with the traditions of the second century, quite 'apostolic.'" Through this means, he points out, "the saving effectiveness of [the Lord's] suffering unto death extends even to those mortals who in earthly life do not come to a conscious encounter with him, even to the most lost among them."[8]

Vicarious Baptism

The Apostle Paul wrote of the necessity of the Savior's rising from the tomb and explained that the physical evidence of the divine Sonship of Christ is the resurrection. If Christ had not risen from the dead, Paul asserted, the preaching of the apostles and the faith of the saints would be in vain. "If in this life only we have hope in Christ," he said, "we are of all men most miserable" (1 Cor. 15:19). After establishing that the Lord has conquered all enemies, including death, Paul added: "And when all things shall be subdued unto him, then shall the Son also himself be subject unto him [the Father] that put all things under him, that God may be all in all. *Else what shall they do which are baptized for the dead, if the dead rise not at all? why are they then baptized for the dead?*" (1 Cor. 15:28–29; emphasis added.) Some recent translations of the Bible have attempted to clarify this passage. The New King James Version has it: "Otherwise, what will they do who are baptized for the dead, if the dead do not rise at all? Why then are they baptized for the dead?" The Revised English Bible translates 1 Corinthians 15:29: "Again, there are those who receive baptism on behalf of the dead. What do you suppose they are doing? If the dead are not raised to life at all, what do they mean by being baptized on their behalf?"

On the subject of baptism for the dead, one non-LDS scholar has recently observed: "Paul had no reason to mention baptism for the dead unless he thought it would be an effective argument with the Corinthians, so presumably he introduced what he thought was an inconsistency in the Corinthians' theology. In this case, some at Corinth might have rejected an afterlife but practiced baptism for the dead, not realizing what the rite implied." In addition, "Because his mention [of the practice] could

---

8. Leonhard Goppelt, *A Commentary on 1 Peter*, ed. Ferdinand Hahn, trans. John E. Alsup (Grand Rapids: Eerdmans, 1993), 259, 263.

imply his toleration or approval of it, many have tried to distance Paul from baptism for the dead or remove features regarded as offensive from it. Some maintain that Paul was arguing *ad hominem* or *ex concessu* in 1 Corinthians 15:29, so that he neither approved nor disapproved of the practice by referring to it. Yet it would have been unlike Paul to refrain from criticizing a practice he did not at least tolerate."[9] Or as an LDS writer has pointed out: "Paul was most sensitive to blasphemy and false ceremonialism—of all people he would not have argued for the foundation truth of the resurrection with a questionable example. He obviously did not feel that the principle was disharmonious with the gospel."[10]

On the afternoon of Tuesday, May 8, 1838, Joseph Smith answered a series of questions about the faith and practices of the Latter-day Saints. One of the questions was: "If the Mormon doctrine is true, what has become of all those who died since the days of the Apostles?" His response: "All those who have not had an opportunity of hearing the Gospel, and being administered unto by an inspired man in the flesh, must have it hereafter, before they can be finally judged."[11] We cannot help but conjecture that Joseph must have spoken of this doctrinal matter since the time of his vision of Alvin over two years earlier, but there is no record of such a conversation.

The first public discourse on the subject of baptism for the dead was delivered on August 15, 1840, in Nauvoo, Illinois, at the funeral of a man named Seymour Brunson.[12] Simon Baker described the occasion:

I was present at a discourse that the prophet Joseph delivered on baptism for the dead 15 August 1840. He read the greater part of the 15th chapter of Corinthians and remarked that the Gospel of Jesus Christ brought glad tidings of great joy, and then remarked that he saw a widow in that congregation that had a son who died without being baptized, and this widow in reading the sayings of Jesus "except a man be born of water and of the spirit he cannot enter the kingdom of heaven," and that not one jot nor tittle of the Savior's words should pass away, but all should be fulfilled. He then said that this widow should have glad tidings in that thing. He also said the apostle [Paul] was talking to a people who understood baptism for the dead, for it was practiced among them. He went on to say that people could now act for their friends who had departed this life, and that the plan of salvation was calculated to save all who were willing to

9. Richard E. DeMaris, "Corinthian Religion and Baptism for the Dead (1 Corinthians 15:29): Insights from Archaeology and Anthropology," *Journal of Biblical Literature* 114, no. 4 (1995): 678, 679.

10. Richard L. Anderson, *Understanding Paul* (Salt Lake City: Deseret Book, 1983), 405.

11. Printed in the *Elders' Journal* 1, no. 2 (July 1838): 28–29; also in *TPJS*, 121.

12. *History of the Church*, 4:231.

obey the requirements of the law of God. He went on and made a very beautiful discourse.[13]

After the meeting the woman referred to, Jane Nyman, was baptized vicariously for her son by Harvey Olmstead in the Mississippi River.[14] It is also worth noting that on his deathbed on September 14, 1840, just one month later, Joseph Smith Sr. made a final request of his family—that someone be baptized on behalf of his oldest son, Alvin. His second son, Hyrum, complied with the wish and was baptized in 1840 and again in 1841.[15]

On March 20, 1842, Joseph stated that if we have the authority to perform valid baptisms for the living, it is our responsibility to make those same blessings available to those who have passed through death.[16] On April 15, 1842, in an editorial in the *Times and Seasons*, the church's newspaper in Nauvoo, Joseph called on the Saints to expand their vision beyond the narrow and protracted views of unenlightened man. "While one portion of the human race is judging and condemning the other without mercy," he said, "the Great Parent of the universe looks upon the whole of the human family with a fatherly care and paternal regard; He views them as His offspring, and without any of those contracted feelings that influence the children of men." He observed that "it is an opinion which is generally received, that the destiny of man is irretrievably fixed at his death, and that he is made either eternally happy, or eternally miserable; that if a man dies without a knowledge of God, he must be eternally damned. . . . However orthodox this principle may be, we shall find that it is at variance with the testimony of Holy Writ, for our Savior says, that all manner of sin and blasphemy shall be forgiven men wherewith they shall blaspheme; but the blasphemy against the Holy Ghost shall not be forgiven, neither in this world, nor in the world to come, *evidently showing that there are sins which may be forgiven in the world to come.*"

In this same doctrinal statement the Mormon Prophet added: "Chrysostom says that the Marcionites practiced baptism for their dead. . . . The church of course at that time was degenerate, and the particular form might be incorrect, but the thing is sufficiently plain in the scriptures." He then quoted once again 1 Corinthians 15:29 and concluded by referring

13. Baker, quoted in *Words of Joseph Smith*, ed. Andrew F. Ehat and Lyndon W. Cook (Provo: BYU Religious Studies Center, 1980), 49.

14. From Alex Baugh, "The Practice of Baptism for the Dead Outside of Temples," *Religious Studies Center Newsletter* 13, no. 1 (September 1998): 3–6.

15. "Nauvoo Baptisms for the Dead," Book A, Church Genealogical Society Archives, 145, 149.

16. *TPJS*, 201.

to the restoration of this vital dimension of the "ancient order of things" as the fulfillment of the words of Obadiah concerning saviors on Mount Zion (Obad. 1:21). "A view of these things reconciles the scriptures of truth, justifies the ways of God to man, places the human family upon an equal footing, and harmonizes with every principle of righteousness, justice and truth."[17] Then on May 2, 1844, he stated: "Every man that has been baptized and belongs to the kingdom has a right to be baptized for those who have gone before; and as soon as the law of the Gospel is obeyed here by their friends who act as proxy for them, the Lord has administrators there to set them free."[18] Such baptisms for the dead are performed in LDS temples.

The LDS hope in Christ is in the infinite capacity of an infinite Being to save men and women from ignorance as well as from sin and death. The God of Abraham, Isaac, and Jacob is indeed the God of the living (Matt. 22:32), and his influence and redemptive mercies span the veil of death. As Joseph Smith explained, "It is no more incredible that God should save the dead, than that he should raise the dead."[19]

A Pressing Question

How do Mormons reconcile the doctrine of the redemption of the dead with the Book of Mormon passage cited earlier that we must not procrastinate the time of our repentance, that the acceptance of the gospel and the living of its precepts must be undertaken in this life (Alma 34:32–34)? We do not suppose, knowing the goodness and justice of our God, that it would be any easier to accept the gospel as a disembodied spirit than it would be as a mortal (1 Pet. 4:6). And yet there are factors that bear upon a person's capacity to see and feel and hear and receive the truth. Some of those factors act on all of us, and some of them are beyond our power to control. "It is my conviction," LDS Apostle Boyd K. Packer declared, "that those wicked influences one day will be overruled."[20]

Surely, at least from my perspective, in the post-mortal spirit world, men and women will have such burdens of abuse, neglect, false teachings, and improper traditions—all of which can deter one from embracing the truth—torn away as a film. Then perhaps in that sphere, free from Lucifer's taunts, they will see as they are seen and know as they are known. Wilford Woodruff, third president of the LDS Church,

17. Ibid., 217–23; emphasis added.
18. Ibid., 367.
19. Ibid., 191.
20. Boyd K. Packer, Conference Report, April 1992, 94.

stated: "I tell you when the prophets and apostles go to preach to those who are shut up in prison, thousands of them will there embrace the Gospel. They know more in that world than they do here."[21] His successor, Lorenzo Snow, also pointed out: "A wonderful work is being accomplished in our temples in favor of the spirits in prison. I believe, strongly too, that when the Gospel is preached to the spirits in prison, the success attending that preaching will be far greater than that attending the preaching of our Elders in this life. I believe there will be very few indeed of those spirits who will not gladly receive the Gospel when it is carried to them. The circumstances there will be a thousand times more favorable. . . . I believe there will be very few who will not receive the truth. They will hear the voice of the Son of God . . . and they will receive the truth and live."[22]

Conclusion

Why then do missionary work? That is, why send our young people and experienced couples into the world to preach the gospel? Why spend so much money and expend so much time and effort when in fact all people will have the opportunity to hear about the gospel eventually in the world to come? First of all, we go into all the world in an effort to reach every creature because our Lord and Savior has commissioned us to do so (Matt. 28:19–20; Mark 16:15–16; D&C 68:8). In addition, we have found one pearl of great price, something worth more than all the silver and gold of the earth; we just want to share it with others. We desire, with all our hearts, to make those same blessings that we enjoy available to all men and women, not only hereafter but here. We don't want people to miss any blessing, any privilege, any joy that could be theirs through the sweet fruits of the gospel. In the end, no one will have been forgotten.

21. As cited in Boyd K. Packer, *The Holy Temple* (Salt Lake City: Bookcraft, 1980), 206.
22. *Collected Discourses*, ed. Brian H. Stuy, 5 vols. (Burbank, CA: B. H. S. Publishing, 1987–95), 3:363.

An Evangelical Response
Gerald McDermott

More than at any other time since the second and third centuries after Christ, Christians are wondering what happens to those who die before they hear the gospel. Those were the centuries of the great Greek theologians such as Justin Martyr, Irenaeus, Clement of Alexandria, and Origen, who developed for this problem elaborate solutions that they thought were grounded securely in scripture and good theology.[23] This has been a problem especially for conservative Christians who have been raised in traditions that have held that all non-Christians go to hell. Sometimes these traditions have suggested that even those who have never heard the gospel will be damned, because the mere fact that they haven't heard is evidence that God knew they would have rejected the gospel had they heard it. It has seemed to many that the God of these traditions is arbitrary and unfair, and the resulting dilemma has led some to question and sometimes lose their faith in the Christian God.

Mormons seem to have an elegant solution to the problem. Not only, they say, does everyone get a second chance after death, but no matter what choice they make, almost everyone will wind up in some degree of heavenly happiness with at least one member of the classical Trinity. Ironically, in this respect Mormonism teaches something close to the modern liberal doctrine that either there is no hell or everyone will eventually be saved.

By way of response, I want to propose three things. First, Joseph Smith's elegant solution to the problem was based on a series of historical and exegetical misunderstandings. Second, there are alternative solutions that also appeal to the biblical narrative and lack the eschato-

---

23. For more on this, see McDermott, *God's Rivals*.

logical (having to do with "last things") pessimism that so horrified the American prophet. Third, the LDS solution to this problem is plausible only if one grants the authenticity of Smith's revelations.

Historical Misunderstandings?

A non-LDS reader of Professor Millet's intriguing chapter would have to conclude that the 1836 revelation of a second chance after death and exaltation to different kingdoms was stimulated, at least in part, by Smith's dismay over the "traditional" evangelical understanding of his brother Alvin's eternal fate. The Smith family's Presbyterian minister told them that since Alvin, who was known to be a "loving" person, had died without being a baptized church member, he was probably roasting in the fires of hell. Both Joseph and his father were incensed by such presumption and rejected the idea, and Joseph Jr. seemed determined to divine God's true purposes in such a situation.

The Presbyterian minister was fairly representative, not only of antebellum evangelicalism[24] but also of Western Christians generally in that period. Most Christians assumed that unless a person confessed Christ with the lips and lived a life of visible discipleship, which would typically involve church attendance, that person would be damned. Even if the person had been raised in outer Mongolia with no chance to hear the gospel, that very fact itself spelled doom. Either God knew she and her fellow Mongolians would never accept a missionary's message and so didn't bother sending one, or she had failed to respond to other revelation coming through nature and conscience and so did not merit supernatural evangelism by dream or angel. So if she didn't hear the gospel, she deserved damnation, not only because all of us do but also because her religious situation proved she was impervious to the Spirit.

Many antebellum evangelicals had trouble with these assumptions and thus joined or at least supported the great nineteenth-century Anglo-American missionary movement, hoping to save at least a small portion of those on the road to hell. Some no doubt questioned whether every unevangelized pagan was going to hell, but they still believed that all but the rare exceptions would burn forever unless they accepted the Christian gospel.

It is understandable that Joseph Smith was discontented with such a theology, but it is unfortunate that he was apparently unaware that

24. Antebellum evangelicalism was not the same as evangelicalism of the early twenty-first century. However, its eschatology, particularly in regard to the fate of the unevangelized, was nearly the same as that of conservative evangelicals today.

the history of Christian thought contained a variety of solutions to the problem, some of which might have alleviated his dismay over his brother Alvin's irreligious death.

Justin Martyr

Smith evidently did not know about Justin Martyr's (c. 100–c. 165) remarkable conclusion that everyone who follows the Logos within is really following Jesus Christ. Here Justin developed an idea first suggested by the Apostle John, that Jesus was the Logos, who not only created the world and holds it together moment by moment but also "lighteth every man that cometh into the world" (John 1:1, 9). John traded on the Stoic concept of a Logos, or rational principle, that gave form to all the creation and is discernible because it is present in the human mind.

Justin pushed this Johannine concept further by relating it to the religions. He argued, in effect, that Christ the Logos was speaking in the philosophical religions of the Hellenistic world. Socrates, he said, knew Christ in part because he had part of the Logos. Christ "was and is the Logos who is in every man," and so inspires whatever truth we find in the world. Therefore, "whatever things were rightly said among all men, are the property of us Christians."[25]

Drawing on Jesus's parable of the sower, Justin contended that the Stoics, the poets, and the historians all "spoke well in proportion to the share [they] had of the seminal divine Logos [*tou spermatikou theiou logou*]." They were all "able to see realities darkly through the sowing of the implanted words that was in them."[26] They could see, for example, Christian truths such as the creation, final judgment, and even the Trinity.

So the word of Christ, speaking to non-Christians, is the source of whatever truth there is in other religions. It also explains why there is error in the religions. "Because they did not know the whole Logos, which is Christ, they often contradicted themselves."[27] With only part of the Logos, they could not see the whole picture. They could see the trees but not the forest. Details without the big picture. Truths taken out of context. Little nuggets of gold, but without the means to cash them in.

Justin went still further, making claims that were daring for the second century. Not only did he say that some non-Christian thinkers had parts of Christian truth, but he also proposed that they were actually Christians!

---

25. 2 *Apology* 10, 13; in *The Writings of Justin Martyr and Athenagoras*, ed. Marcus Dods et al. (Edinburgh: T & T Clark, 1879).
26. 2 *Apol.* 13.
27. 2 *Apol.* 10.

[Christ is the Word] of whom every race of men were partakers; and those who lived reasonably are Christians, even though they have been thought atheists; as, among the Greeks, Socrates and Heraclitus, and men like them; and among the barbarians, Abraham, and Ananias, and Azarias, and Misael,[28] and Elias, and many others whose actions and names we now decline to recount, because we know it would be tedious.[29]

Justin proposed that all poets and philosophers (and others, for that matter) who have truth not only got it from the Christ, but are actually followers of Christ—presumably, at least insofar as they practice such truth. Or, whether or not they follow Christ in a manner recognizable to later "Christians," they are counted as members of Christ's body by Justin. His evidence for such a revolutionary claim? Their tacit embrace of truths that Justin insists came only from the Logos, who is within every person. Most of them never heard of Christ, but they have taken to be true those realities that came (without their knowing it) from him, and apparently have made those truths central to their lives. Justin also appealed to Romans 2:14–15, where Paul speaks of those without the law who nonetheless have the law written on their hearts and show by their lives that they are living by that law. Justin understood this to mean that the Spirit of Christ had called them into his kingdom without their hearing the gospel per se. Once they penetrated the veil on the other side of death, they would recognize that what they had accepted was really Jesus of Nazareth and his good news.

Notice what Justin could have shown Joseph Smith: there was an alternative way to read scripture in the orthodox Christian tradition that provides the possibility of salvation for those who are not members of the church without necessitating an elaborate series of events and stages after death.

Irenaeus

Smith might also have learned from Irenaeus (c. 145–202) that all human beings, from the beginning of the world, have been given revelation of God sufficient for salvation. Revelation has come in different ways and degrees, but every human being has seen enough of God to be able to believe and be saved by Christ.

What about those who came before Christ? This question was asked both by Irenaeus's fellow Christians and by the pagans to whom they were

28. The last three are Greek names for Shadrach, Meshach, and Abednego in Daniel 1:7.

29. 1 *Apol.* 46.

witnessing. Irenaeus's answer was that Christ the Word had revealed the Father through the Jewish prophets to the Jews, and through creation to the Gentiles. Both Jews and Gentiles therefore knew enough to be able to fear and love God and to "desire to see Christ" (*AH* 4.22.2[30]). Even apart from seeing Christ, and, in the case of the Gentiles, even without having the law of Moses, they were justified by faith:

> All the rest of the multitude of those righteous men who lived before Abraham, and of those patriarchs who preceded Moses, were justified independently of [requirements of the Jewish law], and without the law of Moses. (*AH* 4.16.2)

> [Christ came] for all men altogether, who from the beginning, according to their capacity, in their generation have both feared and loved God, and practiced justice and piety towards their neighbours, and have earnestly desired to see Christ, and to hear His voice. (*AH* 4.22.2)

Irenaeus therefore believed in "righteous pagans" who by the Word were given light sufficient to hope for Christ. They "feared God and died in justice and had the Spirit of God within them, such as the patriarchs and the prophets and the just" (*Proof of the Apostolic Preaching* 56). It was to both these pagans and also to believing Jews, who were "sleeping" in Hades before the incarnation, that Jesus came on Holy Saturday, the time between the crucifixion and resurrection. To these souls he preached the gospel, making plain what had to this point been revealed only in shadows and types (*AH* 4.22.2; 4.27.2; 5.31.1). To them all he gave the promise that they would be resurrected at his second coming, at the end of the world, to live on earth with him in bodily form—a new incarnation, as it were—for a thousand years (the "millennium"), and therefore able to live in the fullness of gospel truth. This would give them the same opportunity as the apostles enjoyed at Christ's first coming, to prepare for the vision of the Father in heaven (*AH* 5.32–35).

Since, for Irenaeus, the revelation of God through the Son was given in different ways at different times, he believed the final judgment will take that into account. People will be judged on the basis of what they did with the revelation that they received; God will not assume that all have received the same mode and degree of revelation. But Irenaeus did assume that all human beings had received some revelation of the Son of God the Savior—either through revelation of the Son in creation, or at the time of the incarnation, or at some point after through the preaching of the church. Those who did not know of the incarnation when they lived, but lived in hope of something of the sort, will enjoy the second

---

30. *AH* refers to Irenaeus, *Against Heresies*, in *The Ante-Nicene Fathers*, vol. 1.

incarnation during the millennium, and respond in faith to the Son at that time. For that reason, no one will be saved without accepting the gospel of Jesus Christ, and none of the damned will be able to say they didn't know anything of the Son of God.

The point to be learned from Justin and Irenaeus (not to mention Clement of Alexandria and Origen) is that there were thinkers in the early Christian tradition who would have disagreed with antebellum evangelicals on the fate of the unevangelized. They did not assume that all the unevangelized were damned. They assumed that Christ is the only way to God, but they also believed that God joined people to Christ in a variety of ways across different eras in history.

Joseph Smith need not have despaired over the fate of the unevangelized, nor need he have assumed that more revelation was needed.[31] There was already a history of rich reflection on *biblical* revelation that could have given answers to his troubling questions. Early church thinkers were far more imaginative on these questions than nineteenth-century evangelicals, and their exegesis of the biblical narrative held out far more possibilities than Smith imagined.

Exegetical Misunderstandings

Smith's interpretation of the 1 Peter passages is also problematic. He reads them as teaching a second chance after death to those who rejected the gospel in this life. Since these are among the most difficult passages in all the New Testament (1 Cor. 15:29 on baptism for the dead is another!), no one should be dogmatic in interpretation; however, there is a growing consensus that Peter was not referring to postmortem preaching to human souls.[32]

The critical portions of these texts in 1 Peter 3:18–4:6 are the following: "He went and *preached unto the spirits in prison*; Which sometime were disobedient, when once the longsuffering of God waited in the days of Noah . . . For this cause was *the gospel preached also to them that are dead*, that they might be judged according to men in the flesh, but live according to God in the spirit" (3:19; 4:6). Smith and Mormons have assumed that the "spirits in prison" are human souls awaiting their final

---

31. Of course Alvin may not have been, strictly speaking, unevangelized, for he had probably been exposed to some gospel proclamation. But Joseph could have found some hope for his brother in the nuanced approaches to the problem taken by Justin and Irenaeus.

32. See, e.g., I. Howard Marshall, *1 Peter* (Downers Grove, IL: InterVarsity Press, 1991); Norman Hillyer, *1 and 2 Peter, Jude* (Peabody, MA: Hendrickson, 1992).

destination. But most scholars now think these are fallen angels, for a number of reasons.

First, the Greek word for "preached" is from the verb *kēryssein* (to proclaim or announce) not *euangelizō* (proclaim the good news). This suggests that Christ did not preach the gospel to souls who might be saved, but instead proclaimed his victory and thereby confirmed their judgment to the fallen angels. Second, the intertestamental period was full of Jewish literature that linked the fallen angels of Genesis 6:1–4 to Noah's day, since the story of the "sons of God" (a common term in the Old Testament for angels) immediately precedes the story of the flood. In 1 Enoch 12–14, for example, Enoch preaches to the fallen angels of Genesis 6 who were disobedient in Noah's day—language nearly identical to Peter's. Second Peter actually calls these spirits "the angels that sinned" and were cast "down to hell" (2:4) in the same breath that the writer cites Noah and the flood (2:5). Third, it was widely believed in this period that these spirits were patrons of powerful kings of the earth. This fits what we know to be 1 Peter's historical context: a church of persecuted believers. Peter offers encouragement by reminding them that Christ also "once suffered," and by so doing defeated the evil spirits that inspire this church's persecutors. Therefore, these embattled Christians need not fear, for they will be vindicated at the Judgment, when Christ's victory over the spirits and their political minions will be manifested.

This also helps explain what Peter means by "them that are dead." These are Christian friends who have already died, perhaps by martyrdom. "For this cause was the gospel preached also to them that are dead, that they might be judged according to men in the flesh, but live according to God in the spirit" (4:6). The gospel was preached to them (before they died) so that, even though judged by wicked rulers, they would have the ultimate reward of living with God in the heavenly realm.

This interpretation makes the best sense of the rest of 1 Peter, which is full of encouragement for Christians suffering fierce persecution. They were not concerned primarily with what happens to pagans or those who rejected the gospel (Smith's interpretation), but about whether their suffering was worth it. Peter reassured them that not only they but also their friends who had already died would be vindicated, for Christ had already defeated the evil spirits that were driving those tormenting the church.

It doesn't help the Mormon case for a second chance after death to appeal to Jesus's inference in Matthew 12:32 that there will be forgiveness "in the world to come." Most scholars interpret this to mean the kingdom of God, which Jesus had already inaugurated and would be more visible after the destruction of Jerusalem (Matt. 24, esp. v. 34) and during the church age. Calvin believed this referred to the final judgment. In either case, the passage does not clearly refer to a life after death in which there is a second chance for those who already rejected the gospel on earth.

Smith's use of 1 Corinthians 15:29 ("Else what shall they do which are baptized for the dead, if the dead rise not at all? Why are they then baptized for the dead?") to support vicarious baptism for the dead is also questionable. Once again, we have to be at least a little tentative, for this verse has been called "the most obscure verse in the Bible."[33] According to Anthony Thistleton, it has been explained in at least forty different ways. Ralph Martin says two hundred is more accurate.[34]

The distinguished Pauline scholar Gordon Fee says that while many scholars have tried to explain away the plain sense of the words, it does seem that Paul refers here to vicarious baptism for the dead. The practice seems to have been real, and Paul neither denies nor criticizes it. At the same time, the absolute absence of evidence for this practice anywhere else in the early orthodox churches (only Marcionite heretics mention it) makes its use questionable. "How can such a practice be so *completely* unknown if in fact it had any authorization within the churches of the first century?" Fee asks. "This complete silence in all other sources is the sure historical evidence that, if such a practice existed in fact, it did so as something purely eccentric among some in the Christian community."[35]

Does Paul's failure to criticize this practice mean he recommends it? Hardly, says Fee: "That is not a necessary inference, any more than Jesus's parable about the shrewdness to act on the part of the corrupt household manager implies tacit approval of his financial shenanigans (Luke 16:1–8)."[36]

This practice by *some* Corinthian Christians (Paul's usual practice to refer to the whole community is to use the second person, but in v. 29 he uses the third) seems to indicate among the Corinthian Christians a strong sacramentalism, the idea that baptism is absolutely necessary for salvation (1:13–17 and 10:1–22). But it is significant that in the latter passage, Paul rebuts this view by suggesting that some baptized church members would still be damned: "All our fathers . . . passed through the sea; and were all baptized unto Moses in the cloud and in the sea. . . . But with many of them God was not well pleased: for they were overthrown in the wilderness" (10:1–2, 5).

Martin Luther famously taught from one of the last verses in Mark's Gospel ("He that believeth and is baptized shall be saved; but he that be-

33. Alan F. Johnson, *1 Corinthians* (Downers Grove, IL: InterVarsity, 2004), 295.
34. Ibid.
35. Gordon Fee, *The First Epistle to the Corinthians* (Grand Rapids: Eerdmans, 1987), 764 n.17.
36. Ibid., 764 n.19.

lieveth not shall be damned," 16:16) that while baptism was commanded by Jesus, the failure to be baptized had nothing to do with damnation.

We see this same disconnect between baptism and regeneration (being born again) in the larger New Testament pattern. The Holy Spirit is finally more crucial to regeneration than is baptism: some are saved without baptism (the good thief, for example), some before baptism (Cornelius), and some are not saved though baptized (1 Cor. 10:2–5; Simon in Acts 8; Esau and Ishmael in the Old Testament equivalent to baptism). So the real question about joining the body of Christ is not when or how we were baptized, but whether we have received the Holy Spirit.

Therefore, even if Paul saw nothing wrong with vicarious baptism for the dead, there would be no biblical reason to practice it. Though baptism is commanded for all believers, its absence will not damn anyone.

Of course, Mormons baptize the dead for another reason—to help them ascend to higher kingdoms. To this I would say only that there is no biblical reason for this either. Even if baptism for the dead were permitted, there is nothing in scripture making baptism essential to any heaven. Quite the contrary, in fact: the good thief on the cross, who was not baptized, was told by Jesus he would be in Paradise with him that very day (Luke 23:43).

Quasi-universalism

One final problem with Mormon eschatology is its quasi-universalism. LDS talk about a "few" that are finally damned in total exclusion from any one of the Godhead.[37] Precise numbers are never mentioned, but one gets the impression from LDS literature that we could count the numbers of the "sons of perdition" fairly quickly and easily. These are souls who have committed the "unpardonable sin against the Holy Ghost" by receiving the Spirit, having the heavens opened, knowing God, and then rejecting it all (EOM 4:1499). They continue to reject it all, even after many more chances to change their minds in Spirit Prison after death. The *Encyclopedia of Mormonism* counts Lucifer and Cain among these few, but questions "whether [Judas] had received the Holy Ghost sufficiently to sin against it at the time of his betrayal of Christ" (3:1392).

There are "many" who reject the gospel on earth but later repent in Spirit Prison after hearing it again (and again). Even if they still refuse to "receive the fullness of the gospel" after death but nevertheless "bow their knee and confess their dependence on Christ" in those post-mortal

37. Rodney Turner, "Sons of Perdition," *EOM* 3:1392.

realms, they get to enjoy the Telestial Kingdom where they live in the presence of the Spirit of God.[38]

Evangelicals wonder, then, what Jesus meant when he said, "Wide is the gate, and broad is the way, that leadeth to destruction, and *many* there be which go in thereat" (Matt. 7:13; my emphasis). Or why he talked about hell so often, describing weeping and gnashing of teeth, eternal punishment, undying worms and unquenchable fire, and uncrossable chasms between hell and heaven. One would think he would not have discussed it so often if it were not a real danger to many.

When the disciples asked if only a few were saved, Jesus refused to answer but replied "Strive to enter" (Luke 13:23–24). The point seems to be that we cannot know how many will go to hell. Yet to promise some sort of salvation to all but a "few" seems to err on the side of optimistic presumption, especially in light of the considerable emphasis Jesus gives to the possibility of eternal damnation.

In the end, then, we have come once again to an oft-recurring theme. The "Mormon difference"—in this case, the eschatological difference—is difficult to square with classical biblical revelation. Only if we accept Smith's revelations can we allow the LDS proposal of a second chance for all. Therefore, I cannot agree with Professor Millet that Mormon doctrine—in this case, on the unevangelized—merely supplements biblical revelation. In the history of Christian thought before Joseph Smith there were imaginative solutions to the problem of the unevangelized, particularly among the early Greek theologians. But none except Origen made central any kind of second chance that would reverse the direction of a person's life[39]—and even his (reincarnation) continued to hold that one's earthly life determines the next life beyond. Therefore LDS eschatology appears to represent a significant departure from biblical teaching.

38. "Degrees of Glory," *EOM* 1:368; "Hell," *EOM* 2:585–86.

39. Irenaeus thought righteous pagans from the OT period might hear the gospel in Hades or on Holy Saturday or during the millennium. Clement of Alexandria spoke similarly. But Irenaeus never extended this possibility to pagans after the incarnation, and neither he nor Clement believed that postmortem conversions to Christ would be anything more than recognizing the true name of the God previously seen only dimly. Neither envisioned the radical reversal of direction implied in Mormon eschatology. Irenaeus, *AH* 4.22.2; 4.27.2; 5.31.1; Clement, *Stromata* 6.6.

Rebuttal and Concluding Thoughts
Robert Millet

There seems to be no disagreement about the fact that the soteriologi-cal problem of evil—the question of how a gracious and just God could require all men and women to be saved through Christ, when in fact, the bulk of humanity will pass away without ever having heard of him—can-not be dismissed easily as either unimportant or uncompelling. Fur-thermore, one of the points of clarification I wish to make in replying to Professor McDermott's response is that Latter-day Saints do not look upon Christ's ministry to the world of spirits, baptism for the dead, or the construction of temples as means of providing a "second chance" for people to receive the message of salvation. No, what we believe such principles teach is that every man or woman will be given a valid "first chance" to do the same.

I would hate to think, for example, that the thousands of people who spurned my testimony of Jesus at the doorstep when I was serving as a young Mormon missionary were in fact forfeiting their opportunity for eternal reward hereafter. I would certainly not believe that one en-counter with the truth, either through reading it or making contact with someone who declared it, constituted one's only and final opportunity to find salvation.

We cannot judge or condemn other human beings because we do not know what is going on in their hearts, what struggles they may have had, what tragedies may have been inflicted upon them, what crosses they have been called upon to bear, what ironies they may have been required to endure. So many things, including false traditions transmitted through the generations, can prevent us from being at our best, from discerning clearly the truth from error, from walking in the light when we seem to be drawn so dramatically into the darkness. Thank heavens that God is in charge and that the final judgment will rest with him.

I suppose it would be easy to suggest that because Latter-day Saints believe that only the sons of perdition, those who have sinned against major light and committed the unpardonable sin (the one that will not be forgiven in this world or in the world to come—Matt. 12:31) are the only ones consigned to hell forever, that Mormons believe in a kind of universal salvation. This requires a slight clarification. Yes, we do believe that each person who does not defect to perdition will be assigned to one of three degrees of glory hereafter (D&C 76), but this does not mean that either (a) there will be no consequences or suffering for sin, or (b) everyone will be saved in the presence of God and the Lamb. We believe that when a person passes from this world into the next, into a post-mortal spirit world, it is there that he or she will face up to who he or she is and how he or she has lived. Those who have fought against light and truth, who have denied and defied the Only Begotten Son, will be subject to hell, to the tauntings of conscience, taunting so bitter and exquisite as to be compared to fire and brimstone. Second, only those who attain unto the highest degree of glory, the celestial glory, will enjoy the eternal association of God the Eternal Father and his Beloved Son, the Lord Jesus Christ.

Recently, I read two books by two Quaker theologians who truly believe in universal salvation, that God is perfect and just, loving and everlastingly patient.[40] They both contend that God's divine purposes will not be accomplished until he has so worked on the souls of every man, woman, and child that they accept him and qualify for salvation. While I do not subscribe to this view of universal salvation (or to their view of atonement), I am haunted by the question that underlies both of their books: What difference would it make in today's world if each of us believed that every person on earth will eventually be saved? Would it promote greater respect among human beings? Would it help us to avoid the kinds of division and segregation that seem to follow naturally on the heels of believing you have the truth while someone else does not?

One final comment. As a believing Latter-day Saint, I do not perceive that Joseph Smith and his scribes went through the Bible, ticking off concepts and ideas like 1 Peter 3:18–20; 4:6 (on Christ preaching to the spirits in prison) or 1 Corinthians 15:29 (on baptism for the dead) so that they could be implemented into the newly organized Church of Jesus Christ of Latter-day Saints. Rather, Mormons believe that Brother

40. Philip Gulley and James Mulholland, *If Grace Is True: Why God Will Save Every Person* (San Francisco: HarperSanFrancisco, 2003); *If God Is Love: Rediscovering Grace in an Ungracious World* (San Francisco: HarperSanFrancisco, 2004).

Joseph received independent revelation on these matters, announced them to the church over time, and then only later began to recognize biblical allusions to the same. For example, in his Vision of the Celestial Kingdom, recorded in January of 1836, an occasion where Joseph learned that his brother Alvin would enter the highest heaven because that had been the desire of his heart, he does not quote or refer to either 1 Peter or 1 Corinthians 15 as scriptural support for his novel doctrinal ideas. As I indicated, it was some four years before Joseph ever delivered his first public address on baptism for the dead and actually quoted 1 Corinthians 15:29 in that light.

I once again express my own love and respect for the Holy Bible. It is the Book of books. More people have been led to forsake their sins and commit their lives to the Almighty through the reading and preaching of the Bible than any other book. In the last few decades the Bible has become a trusted and tender friend, a treasure house of spiritual understanding for me. And yet I am bold enough to suggest that not all truth, not all divine direction, not all holy practices or teachings are contained within the collection from Genesis to Revelation. I do believe the Bible to be the word of God, but I do not believe it to be the *only* written word of God and the *only* divine directive by which to govern our lives. Thus, over and over again, as Gerry McDermott or my other evangelical friends may suggest that this or that LDS doctrine is "not biblical," I am forced to reply in as kindly a manner as I know how: Yes, I am aware that this teaching is not found in the Bible. Yes, I am aware that this particular doctrine is neither confirmed nor condemned by the Bible. And yes, I know that a number of things taught in Mormonism are unbiblical.

For me there are deeper questions: Is the teaching true? Does it answer our questions truthfully? Is the concept or doctrine from God? Can it be confirmed through prayer and through asking God, who is the Fount of all knowledge and understanding (Matt. 7:7–8; James 1:5)? Is the only test of a religious truth whether it is found in the Bible? Is it absolutely impossible for God to speak through other channels or by other means or to reveal additional instructions and dispense additional inspiration beyond the purview of the Holy Bible? I believe these questions to be neither irreverent nor blasphemous. The Bible is what it is, and I am the first to admit that it is a spiritual standard, a moral masterpiece. If, however, God is, as Jesus instructed, the God of the living and not the God of the dead (Matt. 22:32), then surely there must be provision made for revelation and scriptural direction for current circumstances and customized challenges associated with this time in earth's history.

CONCLUSION
DISCERNING THE SPIRITS

What We Have Learned
Gerald McDermott

In an earlier chapter I wrote that I grew up with crucifixes. I used to see them at church every Sunday when I went to Mass, above my parents' bed, and all over my grandmother's house. But I never really understood what they meant, except to think every once in a while that Jesus had suffered. Even after having theology class four times a week for four years at a Jesuit high school in New York City, I didn't know what connection they had to me.

But then one night when I was eighteen years old, after having concluded in my freshman year at the University of Chicago that Christianity was an irrelevant escape for weak old women, I went to a prayer meeting. It was at the end of a long weekend at home during which I had argued with my mother about religion. She kept saying Jesus was real, and I kept insisting he was not, throwing out every argument I could muster. I remember thinking that I wasn't even sure of what I was saying, but I was afraid that if my mother was right about Jesus, I would have to change my lifestyle, which I didn't want to do.

Then, inexplicably, I was overwhelmed by a picture in my mind of Jesus hanging on the cross. I had the distinct impression that this Jesus was saying, with deep love and patience, "Gerry, I have been waiting for you for eighteen years, while you have been more or less indifferent to me. I will not club you over the head, nor will I force myself on you. But I will wait for you to come to me, because I love you."

I still did not understand what Jesus's dying on the cross had to do with me, but I did conclude that Jesus was real and that I had best reorganize my life around that reality. It wasn't until several months later that a young woman explained to me that Jesus died for my sins, taking upon himself the suffering and death and separation from God that I deserved.

That was more than thirty years ago. I have journeyed a considerable distance denominationally and theologically—from living in Christian communities for seven years, to being a Baptist pastor, to taking on a sacramental outlook and then being ordained as an Episcopal priest. Now I teach full time at a liberal arts college and serve part-time as a teaching pastor at a Lutheran church.

Early on in my evangelical life I was told that Mormonism is a cult with radically un-Christian beliefs. Chief among these, I was told, were the ideas that we are saved by our works and that Jesus is not God. Their focus, I thought, was on Joseph Smith rather than Jesus Christ.

Then, a number of years ago, I met Robert Millet and some of his colleagues at Brigham Young University. I learned from Bob's books and our conversations that Bob and others have been bringing a new emphasis on grace to the LDS community. I also discovered that there was more emphasis on grace in the Book of Mormon and other parts of the LDS canon than I had imagined and that Mormons worship Jesus as a God. I saw a concentration on Jesus that I had previously thought to be absent.

But there are still problems. As I have tried to show in this book, there still are considerable doctrinal differences not only between evangelicals and Mormons but also between Mormons and the general stream of orthodox Christianity. This raises the question of how orthodox Christians can discern the presence of the Spirit in any community or movement that claims to be Christian but is doctrinally or experientially different. In this chapter I will first make some suggestions about how we can discern truth from error. Then I will discuss the question of whether we can learn anything from communities we believe to be in error, and what, if anything, I have learned from my friend Bob and the LDS community. Finally, I will answer in rudimentary fashion three difficult questions—Can we work together? Can we pray together? Can we worship together?

How Do We Discern?

Once we have established that there are serious doctrinal differences (which is the case I have tried to make in the previous chapters), the real question then becomes whether we can discern the presence of the Spirit of Jesus in communities with which we disagree on some fundamental beliefs about Jesus. I don't think there are sure-fire answers here, but I do think we can agree on some general guidelines.

Jonathan Edwards provides some help here, especially because discernment of spirits was one of the chief burdens of his career. His *Distinguishing Marks of a Work of the Spirit of God* is particularly helpful. In his September 1741 commencement address at Yale College, Edwards reflected on the chief controversy of his day, the religious revival (later known as the Great Awakening) that had been sweeping through the American colonies since the fall of 1740. Christians debated whether this revival was of the Spirit or was inspired instead by human enthusiasm or even the devil. Edwards set out five earmarks of a work of God that is inspired by the Spirit.[1]

1. It raises esteem for Jesus and establishes the truth of the gospel.
2. In it the Spirit works against Satan's kingdom, which encourages sin and cherishes lust.
3. It inspires a greater regard for scripture.
4. It leads people to biblical truth, such as the ideas that there is a God, he is great, he hates sin, all will die and face judgment, we are unable to please this God by our own efforts because of our overwhelming sinfulness, and therefore we desperately need a savior.
5. It inspires both humility and love for God and neighbor.

It seems to me that Mormonism gets mixed marks on this scorecard. As Professor Millet presents the faith of Mormons, it does well on points 2, 4, and 5. Most of the world has noticed Mormon resolution against moral sin and lust (#2). There is a running theme in the Book of Mormon that we need the work of Christ to atone for our sins and get to God (#4), and Mormons I know demonstrate both humility and love for others (#5). Their manifest commitment suggests love for God. If some seem proud of their religious achievement and appear to behave more for their own advancement than for self-forgetting love for God—well, the same could be said of many of us in evangelical churches.

Bob and I would differ on points 1 and 3. I do not doubt that Mormons love Jesus, but orthodox Christians have a different view of Jesus and therefore a different esteem for him. For Mormons, Jesus is one of several Gods and was not always God. Hence, their view of the gospel, for which the identity of Jesus is central, is different. I have also argued in chapter 1 that the Mormon canon has a tendency to relativize the classical canon. As a result, it seems to me, classical scripture is set

1. Jonathan Edwards, *The Distinguishing Marks of a Work of the Spirit of God*, in *The Great Awakening*, vol. 4 in *The Works of Jonathan Edwards*, ed. C. C. Goen (New Haven, CT: Yale University Press, 1972), 213–88.

219

on a lower (if only slightly) plane than the "modern" scripture coming through Joseph Smith. That is why I think Mormon regard for ancient scripture is different from that of orthodox Christians.

Three More Criteria

Terrance Tiessen is an astute evangelical scholar who has published an important book in the emerging field of evangelical theology of world religions. In his *Who Can Be Saved? Reassessing Salvation in Christ and World Religions*, Tiessen suggests another way of assessing religious movements. He argues that we should evaluate a movement's orthodoxy, orthopraxis, and orthokardia. *Orthodoxy* means, literally, "correct belief." This involves, he argues, trust in the grace and mercy of a holy and trustworthy God. It acknowledges the Creator as God and gives him thanks (Rom. 1:18–32).[2]

Tiessen notes that Abraham did not know of the Trinity or the atonement by Jesus (of course, Mormons differ on the second point, as we have seen in chapter 4) but is said by Paul to have been justified by faith (Romans 4). He also observes that when evaluating religions, truth is more important than love, because truth gives shape to love. Love for, say, the relatively distant Allah of Muslims will be different from love for Jesus, who tells his disciples they can call him "brother" and "friend," which suggests a God far closer to the believer than Allah. Hence, the truth about God will determine the kind of love one has for God.

On this score, it is clear that the LDS Church is related to the family of Christian communities. It is quite different, obviously, from Judaism or Islam, which reject the gospel explicitly. Mormons reject the relativism of some postmodern religions and, unlike many other spin-offs from the orthodox tradition, robustly profess the full deity of Jesus Christ.

Orthopraxis means "correct action or behavior." Tiessen points out that Jesus put a premium on this criterion, telling his disciples that a tree that does not bear fruit (presumably referring to Christian practice) will be cut down, and that we will be judged in the end by how we have treated "the least of these" (Luke 13:6–9; Matt. 25:45). Mormons are known for their ministry to the whole person in their own communities, and more and more LDS members are being recognized for their benevolence in the wider community.

Orthokardia ("correct heart") calls to mind the Mosaic prophecy, "And the LORD thy God will circumcise thine heart, and the heart of thy seed,

2. Terrance L. Tiessen, *Who Can Be Saved? Reassessing Salvation in Christ and World Religions* (Downers Grove, IL: InterVarsity Press, 2004), ch. 17.

to love the LORD thy God with all thine heart, and with all thy soul, that thou mayest live" (Deut. 30:6). Tiessen reminds us that this was Jesus's first and greatest commandment (Matt. 22:38), and that on matters of the heart only God can judge. So individual Mormons may have defective theology but better hearts than some evangelicals.

This calls to mind two other important suggestions from Tiessen. The first is that evaluation of a religious system is different from evaluating an individual who holds to the system. As I sometimes put it, we aren't saved by our theology but by Jesus Christ. We will all find that our theologies were deficient when we see Jesus "face to face" (1 Cor. 13:12), and our heart relation *to* Jesus is finally more important than our theology *of* Jesus. The two are interrelated, of course, for if we think Jesus saves those who deserve it, we will surely be less grateful (and perhaps even fail to know the true God at all) than if we know Jesus saves helpless sinners. But in theory, a Mormon who believes Jesus was not always God but now is the supreme God for us, who saves us by his suffering, could possibly have more love for Jesus than the evangelical who has more orthodox theology but in spite of that theology is secretly proud of all he has done for Jesus.

This underscores Tiessen's second point, that "not all theological deficiencies are equally serious, and an individual can be seriously wrong about points of theology, and still be properly related to God."[3] Rejecting the Nicene definition of the Trinity but holding to the full deity of Jesus and salvific value of his cross and resurrection seems not as serious as denying the incarnation and atonement. Holding to salvation by grace through the merits of Christ but having a deficient view of matter is better than rejecting Christ's deity and teaching salvation by works, both of which views are held by Jehovah's Witnesses. Therefore, we have to say that Mormons are closer to orthodoxy than Witnesses.

Mormons and Samaritans

Another evangelical scholar of the religions, Ida Glaser, has compared religions outside the Christian family to the Samaritans.[4] It occurs to me that this comparison might be useful for our discussion of evangelical-Mormon differences. Not that the LDS Church is pagan, so I hope my

3. Ibid., 422.
4. Ida Glaser, *The Bible and Other Faiths: Christian Responsibility in a World of Religions* (Downers Grove, IL: InterVarsity Press, 2005), ch. 11. Since writing this chapter, I learned of a similar approach in Scott McKinney, "The Samaritan Paradigm," *Christian Institute for Mormon Studies, Proceedings and Papers,* vol. 1 (Salt Lake City: Utah Institute for Biblical Studies, 1992).

Mormon readers will not stop in horror at this point. Although Samaritan beliefs are far from Mormon ones, their relationship to mainstream Jewish beliefs is similar to that between Mormon and mainstream Christian beliefs. Let me explain.

There was intense, mutual hostility between first-century Jews and Samaritans. The result was complete separation between the two communities. As the Apostle John put it, "The Jews have no dealings with the Samaritans" (John 4:9). Jews despised Samaritans because of Samaritan departure from traditional Jewish belief and practice, and perhaps also because mainstream Jews considered Samaritan religion to be something of a rival. After all, Samaritans told would-be adherents that the only proper place for worship was Mt. Gerizim, effectively ruling out Jerusalem. (Notice the similarities to Mormon-evangelical relations: there is a long history of hostility and separation, based on each community's belief that the other has departed egregiously from early truths; each views the other as a rival, sometimes competing for the same potential converts.)

Yet Samaritan religion was closer to mainstream Judaism than most Jews wanted to acknowledge. Samaritans worshipped only Yahweh, opposed religious images, and kept the laws of Moses. They accepted only the Pentateuch, but so did the Sadducees. They changed some parts of the biblical text, but so did the Qumran community that produced the Dead Sea Scrolls.[5] (Notice, again, a similar pattern: Mormons worship the Father, Son, and Holy Spirit—just as evangelicals do—while rejecting the Trinity. They accept biblical law as normative. Like the Samaritans, Mormons changed the biblical text, first by adding to it and then by reading the classical canon through the lens of new texts.)

The biggest difference between mainstream Judaism and the Samaritan sect was that the Samaritans had their own temple, their own priesthood, and their own special biblical text. How intriguingly similar to our subject: Mormons share many beliefs with mainstream Christians and differ on some others concerning God's origin, relation to the creation, and Jesus's ministry after the ascension. But among the most striking differences are, like the Samaritans, separate temples, priesthoods, and biblical texts.

Glaser points out that Jesus did not always follow the Jewish custom of avoiding Samaria.[6] At one point, he told his disciples not to go there (Matt. 10:5–6), but John tells us that he himself deliberately traveled through Samaria, and in the process crossed "barriers of prejudice and tradition" by talking to the Samaritan woman.[7]

5. Jeffrey S. Rogers, "Samaritan Pentateuch," in *Eerdmans Dictionary of the Bible,* ed. David Noel Freedman (Grand Rapids: Eerdmans, 2000), 1159.

6. Glaser, *Bible and Other Faiths,* 164.

7. Ibid.

Perhaps it is instructive to us that when dealing with this religious community that was within the Jewish family but also clearly divergent, Jesus did not compromise truth. He did not say theological differences were insignificant or moot, or suggest that the Samaritan woman need not change her view. On the contrary, he told her forthrightly that "salvation is of the Jews" (John 4:22). But he also told her that mainstream Jews were wrong when their main point of contention with Samaritans was over the proper temple. The more important point, according to Jesus, was not *where* to worship but *how*: "They that worship [God] must worship him in spirit and in truth" (John 4:24).

How interesting, too, that Jesus held these theologically deficient worshippers up as examples in two of his more arresting stories. The first was his parable of the Good Samaritan, in which he famously suggested that this despised Samaritan kept the law "better than the best Jewish law-keepers."[8] The second was the story of the ten lepers, where the Samaritan was the only one to return to give thanks for his healing (Luke 17:11–19).[9]

Perhaps we can learn from this that while Mormons depart from the Christian tradition in terms of orthodoxy, some of them may be able to teach us things in terms of orthopraxis and orthokardia.

Learning from Those Outside Orthodoxy?

I was surprised some years ago to discover that Jesus often pointed to those with sub-orthodox or even pagan theology as examples of faith. On several occasions Jesus praised the faith of pagans and urged Jews to learn from these pagan examples. He commended two pagans on his visit to Nazareth, whose citizens rejected his claim to be the servant of the Lord spoken of in the later Isaiah passages (Luke 4:14–30; cf. Isa. 61:1–2; 58:6). "Is not this Joseph's son?" they asked skeptically (v. 22). They demanded that he do miracles as he had done in Capernaum (v. 23). Jesus replied, "Verily I say unto you, No prophet is accepted in his own country. But I tell you of a truth, many widows were in Israel in the days of Elias, when the heaven was shut up three years and six months, when great famine was throughout all the land; But unto none of them was Elias sent, save unto Zarephath, a city of Sidon, unto a woman that was a widow" (vv. 24–26).

Zarephath was on the Phoenician coast south of Sidon, in the heartland of the Baal cult (1 Kgs. 16:31). The woman had only a handful of meal,

8. Ibid., 166.
9. Ibid.

but when Elijah commanded her to make a cake out of it, she proceeded to bake, trusting Elijah's promise that God would miraculously multiply the meal (1 Kgs. 17:1–16). Of course, she was also desperate and had nothing to lose, since she and her son were doomed to die soon with or without the handful of meal. But Jesus commended her nonetheless because of her faith in Elijah's word, which was the word of the Lord. She had less evidence for faith than the residents of Nazareth had, but believed that God was speaking and could be trusted.

Then Jesus pointed to another pagan exemplar of faith, Naaman the Syrian general, who trusted Elisha's word from God that he would be cured of his leprosy if he would dip himself in the Jordan River (2 Kgs. 5:1–14). Jesus said, "Many lepers were in Israel in the time of Elisha the prophet; and none of them was cleansed, saving Naaman the Syrian" (v. 27). Jesus suggested that Naaman the pagan had more faith than his Jewish contemporaries and that his boyhood Jewish neighbors would do well to learn from this heathen. From the context it also appears that Jesus was contrasting Naaman's humility (doing what at first he considered ridiculous) with Nazareth's pride. Jesus's reference to the "bruised" and "blind" (v. 18) suggested that his hearers needed to acknowledge their sins and need for help. But in their rage they refused to humble themselves and instead drove Jesus out of town (vv. 28–29).

Most readers of the New Testament are also familiar with the story of the centurion who sought healing for his slave (Luke 7:1–10). When Jesus came near, the Roman soldier sent friends to tell Jesus not to bother coming any further because he was confident Jesus could heal his slave from a distance merely by uttering a word. Jesus "marveled" at this faith response, and told his hearers, "I say unto you, I have not found so great faith, no, not in Israel" (v. 9).

My point is not to suggest that Mormons are pagans. Far from it—Mormons have faith in Christ and say his work is what saves us. But I am impressed that if Jesus said we can learn something about faith from those who didn't believe in the Father of Jesus, perhaps we evangelicals could learn a thing or two from our Mormon friends—even while holding that their theology strays from orthodoxy in some significant respects.

What Evangelicals Can Learn

For example, I have learned from my friendship with Bob and the literature in his LDS tradition that the Mormon community can teach American mainstream Christians a number of things. As I have already indicated in the preceding chapters, evangelicals and other orthodox can learn that Jesus is in the Old Testament, not only as an object of prophecy but also as the central actor; that Jesus was actively involved in the creation of the world; that there are three distinct persons in the Trinity; that the Jesus of history is also the Christ of faith; that the Jesus of the Gospels is the authentic Jesus; that church is essential to the life of faith in a host of ways; that unity of doctrine is an important goal for the church; that church discipline is needed at times to effect that goal; that Christians must eschew cheap grace, which would separate faith from works and discipleship or justification from sanctification; and that faith is true faith only when it "worketh by love" (Gal. 5:6).

Of course, it is true that all of these things can be learned from the Bible and orthodox tradition without encountering Mormon communities. They are what could be called inherent truths in scripture that have been forgotten or until now rarely seen. For, as Ajith Fernando has put it, our cultural conditioning may prevent us from "learning some of the things clearly taught in the scriptures. Other cultures may not have these cultural hindrances."[10] Our inability as evangelicals to see these things is a result of both the peculiar ways in which the evangelical subculture has evolved in the twentieth century, and the influence of secular Western culture. This combination has led, for example, to many evangelicals thinking they can have Jesus as savior without having him as Lord.

For reasons too complex to unravel here, the Mormon subculture evolved differently in the past century and, while missing some doctrinal essentials, has also preserved some important elements of the biblical vision that many mainstream Christian subcultures have lost—such as recognizing the utter disconnect between someone confessing Christ and at the same time thinking she can live without costly self-denial.

Can We Work Together?

What about working together arm in arm for something related to the kingdom of God? Many evangelicals would never consider it. They think that by so doing they would be implicitly approving every point of Mormon doctrine.

Hendrik Kraemer (1888–1965) wouldn't think so. A Dutch Reformed missionary for twelve years in Indonesia, Kraemer was famous for his arguments against syncretism (mixing religions), insisting that Christian faith contains a unique message that is not shared by any other religion, surface similarities notwithstanding. Yet Kraemer encouraged cooperation with other religions "on a pragmatic basis and with a pragmatic goal

10. Ajith Fernando, *The Christian's Attitude Toward World Religions* (Wheaton, IL: Tyndale House, 1987), 111; quoted in Tiessen, *Who Can be Saved?* 433–34.

in mind, out of a common feeling of responsibility and concern for man and his needs," provided that "one does not seek first for a common religious basis which transcends or presumably unites the religions."[11]

In other words, working with other religious communities can enhance ecumenical social action—or what some call missions of mercy. As the new millennium begins, evangelicals and other orthodox Christians have discovered that they often have more in common religiously and ethically with other religionists than they do with liberal Christians. For example, at the 1995 United Nations Conference on Population and Development in Cairo, Muslims and Roman Catholics worked as allies to fight an abortion rights initiative led by a hard-edged U.S. delegation. Only by their united efforts was the notion of enshrining abortion-on-demand as an internationally recognized human right abandoned by its proponents. In 2004 and 2005 I spoke at two LDS-organized conferences on the family, both of which explored the secular and religious reasons why heterosexual marriage is better for children and society than all of its rivals. Mainstream Christians, Jews, and Mormons helped educate each other in efforts to strengthen society and their respective religious communities.

The chances of our winning similar battles in the future on other social and moral issues will be improved by our willingness to work with Mormons—or anyone else, for that matter—on issues such as stem cell research, euthanasia, infanticide, human cloning, and religious persecution. We should be willing to continue to work together to defend the biblical vision of marriage, the rights of the poor, the ecosystem, and social justice, without compromising our respective faith allegiances. Such efforts do not violate our biblical faith but appropriate common biblical understandings even while we differ on other biblical doctrines.

Can We Pray and Worship Together? Should We?

Now for the most difficult question—Can or should we pray together or worship together?

My first response is that there is a difference between prayer and worship. Informal, private prayer among friends can tolerate doctrinal differences as long as each person is allowed to pray in her particular tradition. But worship is usually public and typically involves human speech and actions by one or a few that are meant to represent the de-

---

11. Hendrik Kraemer, "The Role and Responsibility of the Christian Mission," in *Philosophy and the Coming World Civilization: Essays in Honor of William Ernest Hocking*, ed. Leroy Rouner (The Hague: Martinus Nijhoff, 1966), 249; cited in Tiessen, *Who Can Be Saved?* 464.

votion of the whole group. In that case, a Mormon can feel "forced" to be included in worship to a Trinity in which she does not believe. An evangelical could be "coerced" into adoration of a Father and Son who are considered two different Gods. Both situations are intolerable for the person who does not share the theology of the group. We do not want our presence to be gathered up, as it were, into the corporate worship of a God we consider false.

But if I am dining with a Mormon friend, I have no difficulty asking him to pray a blessing over our food. We both know that God hears the prayers of those with deficient theology—which means all of us. When I hear him pray, I imagine the triune God listening. When he hears me pray, I think he imagines Father, Son, and Spirit as three separate Gods inspiring and disposing the prayer. We agree implicitly that all prayer is to the Father by the Spirit in the name of the Son, but we disagree on the relations among the three. We are not joining in common worship but agreeing that we need to be thankful to the Father of Jesus Christ. We believe we are praying in one accord to that extent, and at the same time, we recognize that because of our different views of the Trinity, our accord is fragmentary and imperfect.

Both Mormons and evangelicals who think seriously about their faith would not be able to join a public, interreligious blended prayer that seeks to express a least-common-denominator religious feeling supposedly shared by the two faith communities. The prayer would fail to satisfy either community's serious believers who believe that true prayer is made to God in specific ways revealed in their distinctive scriptures.

This means that other kinds of prayer are also illicit. We should never pray together when the purpose of the prayer is simply social. "To propose interreligious prayer on simply subjective grounds, such as common friendship, trust and respect, is to devalue prayer."[12] The only purpose of prayer should be reverence for and relationship to the objective reality of God. So we can say Yes to multireligious prayer events where both evangelicals and Mormons pray in their own way to the God they think revealed in their scriptures. But we would have to say No to interreligious prayer events where one person is chosen to pray for all, eliminating or minimizing real differences. This shows respect to neither community and creates confusion for many—not to mention violating the consciences of many.

In sum, there are very limited ways in which we could pray together. Since corporate worship demands agreement on the object of worship, the two communities with different views of God therefore cannot wor-

12. Gavin D'Costa, *The Meeting of the Religions and the Trinity* (Maryknoll, NY: Orbis, 2000), 156.

ship together with integrity. One can observe the worship of the other community, but authentic participation in the other community's worship seems impossible.

We can still love and respect each other, however, even if we don't worship together. Considering the past history of Mormon-evangelical relations, that will be no mean accomplishment.

What We Have Learned
Robert Millet

I'm a slow learner. Some lessons in life, so obvious to most folks, sometimes come to me way down the road if at all. Let me share two quick illustrations. While I grew up as a member of a minority faith primarily among Baptists and Catholics, as I mentioned earlier, I was LDS through and through and pretty much oblivious to the feelings and inner commitments of my friends of other faiths. Oh, I knew they went to Mass or to church on Sunday and that they memorized their catechism and read their Bible; that they didn't eat meat on Friday and did not (for the most part) go to dances; and that their allegiance was to someone called the pope (who lived a long way from Louisiana), or that their parents took them to revivals or crusades and that they admired this fellow named Billy Graham. But I suppose I never knew anything about their faith that didn't show; I never knew what went on in their hearts or how they felt about what they believed.

When I was a little older, one of my Methodist friends invited me to church with him. My mom approved (she had grown up as a Methodist), so I thought it would be rather fascinating to see what really went on in other churches. We met that day in a beautiful cathedral, a place of worship like I had seen on TV or in the movies but had never visited personally. The worship service was, of course, very different from a Mormon sacrament meeting—the music, the sermon, and the communion. I was in a new world and found myself somewhat befuddled but also extremely curious. I observed with great interest the reverence and sense of surrender possessed by the congregants as well as their attitude of awe toward Deity. And then something unexpected happened: as we had begun to sing a hymn, I glanced over to my friend, only to see tears making their way down his cheeks. He was clearly moved very deeply by what he was experiencing. And I was moved by what I saw in him. You see, it had never occurred to me—as odd and parochial as this may sound—that people of other faiths had what we Latter-day Saints called a "testimony," a conviction, borne of the Spirit, as to the truthfulness and relevance of that in which they were engaged. My somewhat narrow world broadened a bit that day, and my feelings toward people different from me have never been the same.

During the 1970s the Church of Jesus Christ of Latter-day Saints chose to purchase space and place inserts within selected issues of *Reader's Digest*. The articles addressed a number of subjects, ranging from heaven to happiness, from morality to meaning in life. I remember very well going to the dentist one weekday morning (my all-time least-favorite exercise) and sitting in the waiting room to be called back to the torture chamber. I knew from experience that I had at least 15–20 minutes on my hands, so I reached over to one of the lamp tables and picked up a copy of *Reader's Digest*. I browsed the contents quickly and happened upon one of the LDS Church's inserts. This particular article dealt with communication within families, especially between parents and children. I read it carefully. It was well-organized, well-researched, and well-written.

I should have felt a sense of righteous pride in the fact that my church, once a somewhat obscure and isolated movement, had managed to contribute to a publication read all across the country, one that plumbers and priests, cabinet makers and college presidents frequented. But that wasn't what I felt. Instead, my thoughts went something like this: "What a waste! What possible good is that simplistic article going to do? There's not an ounce of doctrine here. Nobody is going to think twice about Mormonism. I'll bet we don't baptize a soul from these silly inserts!" This reaction gives you at least a glance into my worldview at the time—if what we do doesn't contribute directly to the conversion and baptism of people into the LDS faith, it has no value. I tossed the magazine back onto the table and sat quietly for a moment. Then I felt what can only be described as a kind of spiritual scolding, a realization that my values were warped, that I was suffering from a terrible case of tunnel vision. I found myself asking: Is the article really worthless? Does it serve no function? Is there no one out there who may be assisted by it? What if a grieving parent gains an insight or feels some inspiration in regard to approaching their prodigal child? What if a wandering teen reads the article, 'comes to himself,' and decides to go back to the place where he has always been loved and welcomed—to go back home?

In the years since this experience, and particularly during the last decade, I have encountered men and women of faith throughout the globe, persons who love God and have devoted themselves, heart and soul, to the worship and service of Jesus Christ. My associations with evangelical Christians have been sobering and sweet and satisfying. I have been driven to my knees and to my mental extremities. I have learned a ton about Christian history and traditional Christian doctrine, but in the process, and in a most unexpected manner, I have learned half a ton about Mormonism. One simply cannot engage persons of another faith in a sincere and serious way without coming to view one's own tradition with new eyes and a new heart. While my personal convictions as a Latter-day Saint have actually been strengthened, my outlook on life—especially my perception of my Christian brothers and sisters and the faith they espouse—has expanded dramatically. I have prayed that God would bless me with a greater portion of his love for my friends of other Christian denominations, and I am bold to testify that God answers prayers.

Gerry McDermott and I obviously see things differently on some issues raised in this book. I suppose there will always be differences, no matter how hard we may try to reason through and reconcile our respective positions; that's perhaps as it should be. This is not an ecumenical effort, to be sure. Outreach and interfaith dialogue need not and, I think we would both agree, should not result in costly compromise or concession. We must, however, be open to similarities where they exist, and we must not be afraid to identify and even embrace them. An acknowledgement that we agree on certain doctrinal matters is not cause for fear and trembling, nor should it be viewed as a crisis of conscience. Where there are similarities, we ought to rejoice. Where there are differences, we ought to keep talking, analyzing, and searching for deeper understanding into our neighbor's mind and heart.

In that spirit, I'd like to give my response to Jonathan Edwards's "distinguishing marks." I appreciate Gerry's acknowledgement that Mormonism scores well on points 2, 4, and 5. Let me address, one final time, item 1. I suppose all I can do is share my own impressions and my own conclusions when it comes to the LDS view of Jesus Christ. I definitely do not want to be perceived as boastful, nor do I mean to disparage any other person's faith convictions when I say this: I do not understand how I could love Jesus Christ, honor his name, accept and bow before his Godhood, and surrender myself to his majesty any more than I now do. I do not understand, nor can I conceive, how an acceptance of the doctrine of the Trinity or an admission of the fact that Jesus Christ has been God for all eternity (in the triune Godhead of Father, Son, and Holy Spirit) would change the certitude within my mind and the conviction within my heart that Jesus of Nazareth is the Lord God Almighty, the Holy One of Israel, my God, and my King. And I would add further that this vision of the Christ is not based principally on doctrinal understanding, but rather on personal experience with the Savior and his atoning mercies. I do not think that I have delivered a sermon or a lecture during the last thirty years in which I have not stated or implied that Jesus is indeed the foundation of my faith and that his atoning sacrifice brings life and light and substance to everything else.

Now to point 3. I fully understand Professor McDermott's suggestion that the LDS addition to the canon of scripture *could* weaken one's appreciation for the received scripture, namely, the Holy Bible. But again, my whole point is that for me and for millions of Latter-day Saints it does not do so. My love for the Book of Mormon, Doctrine & Covenants, and Pearl of Great Price do not in any way affect adversely my feelings for the Bible. At the time of this writing, I am finishing the book of Jeremiah, which I have devoured with great relish. In the coming two semesters I will teach a course on the Gospels and then on the second half of the New Testament, and I look forward to that more than I can say. I would have to agree that a typical LDS posture toward scriptural interpretation entails bringing all available scripture to bear in the understanding of a passage, but that's no different from using everything within the Old and New Testament to understand a difficult passage in Ezekiel or Revelation. When the risen Lord, while walking on the road to Emmaus with two disciples, taught the gospel, notice what he did: "And beginning at Moses and all the prophets, he expounded unto them in all the scriptures the things concerning himself" (Luke 24:27). That is, Jesus drew upon numerous selections from what we know as the Old Testament to demonstrate the unifying witness of all the prophets that he was indeed the Promised Messiah, for "to him give all the prophets witness" (Acts 10:43). In short, I do not love the Bible less because of the Book of Mormon any more than a good Baptist loves the writings of Isaiah any less when he begins a serious search and study of Paul's epistle to the Romans.

I especially appreciate Professor McDermott's reference to a matter that should always be a point of discernment in regard to one's Christian walk—namely, *orthokardia*, or a "correct heart." If it is anything at all, Christianity is all about relationships, particularly one's relationship with deity, much more than it is about precise theology. No one loves doctrine more than I do, and no one could possibly delight in unending doctrinal discussions more than I, but I am the first one to acknowledge that the true measure of my Christianity is and will forevermore be what kind of a person I am becoming and the extent to which I manifest in my daily life what Paul called the fruit of the Spirit (Gal. 5:22–25). People may disagree as to whether Jesus's birth was a virgin birth. They may disagree as to whether he performed miracles, even raising people from the dead. And they certainly may disagree as to whether he took upon him the effects of the sins of all humankind and also rose from the dead into glorious immortality. No one, however, who has the slightest awareness of the message of the New Testament will disagree on one matter—Jesus loved people. He was willing to be inconvenienced. In other words, it seems to me that it matters precious little whether a man or a woman can quote scriptures left and right if they dislike people and are in the business of insulting, attacking, and belittling, even when they say that what they are doing is actually "speaking the truth in love" (Eph. 4:15). True Christians ought to both talk the talk and walk the walk.

I was particularly touched by Professor McDermott's discussion of "Mormons and Samaritans." I think I know Gerry's heart well enough to know what he intended here, and it is appreciated. There's a simple principle that the Savior taught that we too readily forget: not only did he tell us that we should love one another, that is, those of the household of faith, our friends; he also charged us to love our enemies (Matt. 5:44). So if there are evangelical readers who for some reason feel as though Latter-day Saints are enemies to the cause of Christ (and I do sincerely hope that this book has done some good in correcting such a misperception), they still have the responsibility to love their Mormon neighbors. Likewise, Latter-day Saints who may be put off and offended by counter-cult groups who attack regularly with pamphlets, books, and videos, and who may thus feel that such rabid individuals are enemies to our effort to build the kingdom of God, are charged to love such folks. It's easy enough to say "I love you" or "I love you enough to want you to understand clearly that you are bound for hell and damnation." But love is more than a simple expression, a vague sentiment, a passing comment; we are expected to share the love of God with people in the way Jesus did. We will always, of course, fall short of that lofty ideal; we'll miss the mark when it comes to treating people with tenderness and respect. But this does not excuse us from being involved regularly in the "target practice" of daily life in the sense that we are trying to demonstrate love, God-like love that lifts, lightens burdens, and offers support. No, I'm not offended by being referred to as a Samaritan; the leaders of the Jews referred to our Master the same way (John 8:48).

Two evangelical friends of mine and Gerry's are Richard Mouw (president of Fuller Theological Seminary) and John Stackhouse (professor of religion and philosophy at Regent College). The following sentiments, expressed by Mouw and Stackhouse, reflect my own feelings as to how evangelicals and Latter-day Saints can and ought to interact with one another. First from Rich Mouw's book *Uncommon Decency: Christian Civility in an Uncivil World*:[13]

> As Martin Marty has observed, one of the real problems in modern life is that the people who are good at being civil often lack strong convictions and people who have strong convictions often lack civility. (12)

> Christians need to be careful about seeing civility as a mere strategy for evangelism. As an evangelical Christian I want to be careful not to be misunderstood as I make this point. I want people to accept the evangel, the good news of salvation through Jesus Christ. I place a high priority on the evangelistic task. But this does not mean that Christian civility is simply an evangelistic ploy—being nice to people merely because we want them to become Christians. (28)

13. Richard Mouw, *Uncommon Decency: Christian Civility in an Uncivil World* (Downers Grove, IL: InterVarsity, 1992).

The quest for empathy can be helped along by a good dose of *curiosity*. We ought to want to become familiar with the experiences of people who are different from us simply out of a desire to understand the length and breadth of what it means to be human. (63–64)

We cannot place artificial limits on how God may speak to us. This has relevance to our encounters in the public square. When we approach others in a civil manner, we must listen carefully to them. Even when we strongly disagree with their basic perspectives, we must be open to the possibility that they will help us discern the truth more clearly. Being a civil Christian means being open to God's surprises. (67)

[We need] to have such a total trust in Christ that we are not afraid to follow the truth wherever it leads us. He is "the true light, which enlightens everyone" (John 1:9). Jesus is *the* Truth. We do not have to be afraid, then, to enter into dialog with people from other religious traditions. If we find truth in what they say, we must step out in faith to reach for it—Jesus' arms will be there to catch us! (106)

I have a hunch about what is going on with some Christians who worry about being "compromised" by their involvement in non-Christian settings. I suspect they are being influenced in some *good* ways by their work, but they're nervous about how to interpret this experience. (112)

Now to quote a few observations from John Stackhouse's book *Humble Apologetics: Defending the Faith Today*:[14]

If I go no further than to think that it's okay for you to do your thing and I to do mine, then where is the incentive to seriously consider whether I should adopt your thing and abandon mine? (41)

[A]pologetics could easily become a form of intellectual browbeating. It [is] warfare waged on behalf of the neighbor's soul by mowing down his resistance and presenting the Gospel with irresistible argument in hopes that he would relent and believe. (72)

Instead, our objective as those called to love God and our neighbors—to seek their best interests—is to offer whatever assistance we can to our neighbors toward their full maturity; toward full health in themselves and in their relationships, and especially toward God. Our mission must be as broad as God's mission, and that mission is to bring *shalom* to the whole world. In short, when it comes to our neighbors, our goal is to help our neighbors to be fully converted into all God wants them to be. (72–73)

14. John Stackhouse, *Humble Apologetics: Defending the Faith Today* (Oxford: Oxford University Press, 2002).

It may be that we disagree religiously because one of us has a superior interpretation of the same reality we're all talking about. It may also be, however, that we disagree because we are talking about different parts of a complex reality. And it may conceivably be a matter of both problems. The skillful apologist tries to sort that all out with her neighbor as well as she can. (94–95)

If one is not sufficiently sympathetic, not sufficiently vulnerable to changing one's mind, not sufficiently willing to entertain the idea that these people might just be right—then it is most unlikely that one will enter into that religion far enough to understand its essence. (101–102)

God cares about people more than he cares about "truth" in the abstract. Jesus didn't die on the cross to make a point. He died on the cross to save people whom he loves. We, too, must represent our Lord with love to God and our neighbor always foremost in our concerns. (142)

We must undertake the sometimes laborious, but necessary, task of building bridges of understanding before we can encourage our neighbors to cross over. (178)

In particular, we should abandon apologetic presentations that, to borrow from such actual book titles, presume to put things *Beyond Reasonable Doubt*, that tell us to *Be Sure!* or that, perhaps most famously, provide us with *Evidence that Demands a Verdict*.

We should instead adopt the voice of a friend who thinks he has found something worth sharing but recognizes that not everyone will agree on its value. Indeed, we should adopt the voice of the friend who wants to stay friendly with our neighbors whether or not they see what we see and believe what we believe. To put it more sharply, we should sound like we really do respect the intelligence, and spiritual interest, and moral integrity of our neighbors. We should act as if we do see the very image of God in them. We should therefore avoid any attempt to manipulate them into religious decision. And we should continue to love them whatever their response to the gospel might be—as God does. (229)

Professor McDermott asks some very important questions relative to evangelicals and Mormons: Can we learn from one another? Can we work together? Can we pray and worship together? My colleague Stephen Robinson shared an experience with a group of us once that addresses to some extent the challenge we face in working together. He explained that he and a number of other Latter-day Saints attended a meeting in the local community convened for the purpose of finding ways to confront the rising tide of pornography. After the LDS folks had been there just a short time, Stephen was approached by one of the leaders of one of the Protestant churches in the area. The man said, essentially: "I'm sorry to have to say this, but there's quite a bit of concern among some of our people here that the Mormons have joined this meeting. If you choose to stay, a number of church groups will leave." Stephen indicated that he and the other Mormons left for the evening and had one clear observation to make about the experience: these people hated Mormons more than they hated pornography.

I recognize that this is an isolated instance and that very often varied groups work together on moral causes and family issues in society. More specifically, Latter-day Saints have worked arm in arm with both Roman Catholic and evangelical groups in standing up and speaking out against efforts to destroy the nuclear family, to redefine marriage, and to secularize our society. The point I would like to make here is that it is not only a nice thing for Mormons and evangelicals to work together on common causes in society; it is a necessary thing. To put it bluntly, if we cannot put aside or deal responsibly with theological differences long enough to allow us to act jointly as concerned citizens in a world of eroding values, then we will all lose in the end. Lucifer will have won a victory. Yes, I believe strongly that we need to learn to work together.

Well, should we pray or worship together? I was once in an interfaith dialogue at Fuller Seminary with my friend, Pastor Greg Johnson, when I heard Rich Mouw close the meeting and use words something to this effect: "We're grateful for what has taken place tonight and appreciate the good will and good ideas that have flowed from this exchange. Now let's lift our voices heavenward to the only God who truly hears and answers prayers." Rich then offered a beautiful prayer of thanks and petition and closed it "in the strong name of Jesus Christ." It never occurred to me that I should not be a part of that prayer experience or that I was having evangelical views forced upon me because I bowed my head, closed my eyes, and yielded my heart to the Person whom I believe to be the same Person to whom Professor Mouw was praying. I think most readers will discover that Latter-day Saints do not feel in any way uncomfortable either praying or listening to prayers offered by persons of other faiths, and especially Christian faiths. Mormons pray to the Father, in the name of the Son, by the power of the Holy Spirit.

I have attended a number of worship services held in more traditional Christian churches during the last decade and have enjoyed very much the exchange, the learning, the inspiration, and the expansion that I received. I have not been troubled or unsettled by either the prayers or the sermons. I have not felt unwelcome, nor has anyone been unfriendly in any way. The greatest point of tension in the area would obviously come in the performance of or participation in sacraments or ordinances, especially Communion or the sacrament of the Lord's Supper. I suppose

I could take Communion in another church, do so in remembrance of the broken flesh and spilt blood of our Redeemer, and not feel terribly uncomfortable. And yet it would certainly be the case that I do not acknowledge those performing the ordinances to have the necessary priesthood authority to do so. The same would be true in regard to the ordinance of baptism. While Mormons perform what might be called a Trinitarian baptism (we baptize in the name of the Father, the Son, and the Holy Spirit), we do not believe the authority to perform that ordinance resides either in the priestly hierarchy of Roman Catholicism, Orthodox Christianity, branches of Anglicanism, or the priesthood of all believers among Protestants in general. Thus, individuals would need to be baptized as Latter-day Saints before coming into our church, just as Latter-day Saints would be required to be baptized as a part of their union with a Catholic or Protestant group. Now while that posture may seem exclusionary, it is what makes me a Mormon: I believe there was a falling away following the deaths of Jesus and the apostles during which time divine authority and sacred truths were lost to the world. Again, I do not believe that the Christian church died or that the lights completely went out in AD 100, only to be illuminated once again in 1820, but I do believe that the Reformation, though God-ordained and God-orchestrated, needed to be supplemented by a Restoration through the call of modern apostles and prophets.

One question that Professor McDermott did not address that I feel to be important is the matter of interfaith marriage. While LDS Church leaders would never counsel one spouse to divorce the other because of religious differences (cf. 1 Cor. 7:14), persons of different faiths (such as Nicene Christians and LDS Christians) who are anticipating marriage would certainly be counseled concerning the potential problems and consistent challenges that such a union would result in. Successful and happy marriage is hard enough to accomplish when the couple has everything going for them, including their religious views. To add the roadblock of major theological distinctions between their respective worldviews would be to prevent the kind of emotional and spiritual intimacy that Christians are called upon to develop within the married state. For Latter-day Saints, marriage is first and foremost a religious ordinance and is only incidentally a civil rite. Therefore, for God to be the base of a triangle between two sincere truth-seekers within a marriage surely requires that they believe alike and attend church together. In short, while divorce is seldom the answer (unless more serious problems exist), couples should understand how difficult it will be to lead separated spiritual lives and still enjoy communion with God and the blessings of heaven.

As I indicated earlier, I have never been more committed to the doctrines and practices of the Church of Jesus Christ of Latter-day Saints than I am right now. At the same time, I think I've never been more liberal, in the proper use of that word (open, flexible, teachable), than I am right now. I believe in God and that he governs in the affairs of men and women. I also believe that he is working in mysterious ways among men and women throughout the earth. Our problem is one of a limited perspective, a restricted vision of things as they really are. As God begins to enlighten our understanding, he also begins to broaden our perspective and deepen our love for all of his sons and daughters. Once again, the prayer of each of us might be the same as that of Elisha on behalf of his young servant as the twosome found themselves surrounded by the Syrian armies. Elisha was in tune with the Infinite and recognized that the forces of heaven were far greater than the evil forces on earth, so he prayed: "'Lord, I pray thee open his eyes, that he may see.' And the Lord opened the eyes of the young man; and he saw: and, behold, the mountain was full of horses and chariots of fire round about Elisha" (2 Kgs. 6:15–17). May God grant that each of us may, in our own distinctive way, come to see.